LIFEARTS

It should be clearly understood that no work of this kind can take the place of a doctor's authority or prescriptions. The effects of medications and recipes contained herein may vary with the individual, and the publisher and authors can accept no responsibility for them.

LIFEARTS

A Practical Guide to Total Being—New Medicine and Ancient Wisdom

by Evelyn de Smedt et al.

Translated by Lowell Bair

Illustrations by Valerie-Catherine Richez

ST. MARTIN'S PRESS, INC.

NEW YORK

Manufactured in the United States of America
Library of Congress Catalog Card Number: 76-50060

Library of Congress Cataloging in Publication Data

Smedt, Evelyn de.
Lifearts.

Translation of Techniques du bien-etre.
1.   **Conduct of life.   I.   Bardet, Vincent, joint author.**
II.   Title.
BJ1582.S5513   1977   613.7   76-50060
ISBN:0-312-48570-7

CONTENTS

nourishing yourself

healing yourself   65

A DAY, A LIFETIME

The frantic pace of civilization subjects us to constant stress. Disoriented by ceaseless scientific advance, frightened by the fragility of his physical existence, which seems governed only by a continual tendency toward standardization, the human being tries to control his wild race through time. We may well speak of "Fragmented Man": While society makes it possible to live and work in the world at large, the individual often finds he has thereby lost his personal identity, unable to reintegrate and rediscover himself, without first allowing himself the time to examine his own needs, to recognize his own face in a crowd.

Enslavement of consciousness, the dissolution of a unified body-mind-spirit, the essential balance that must be recovered in the self—all are involved here. Yet history shows that the individual has extraordinary powers of adaptation, enabling him to overcome some of the harmful effects of his own actions. There is every reason to believe that we are on the brink of a radical mutation of the human race; whether for better or worse will depend on us.

Rational investigation of the past, the accumulated knowledge at our disposal, and the essential need for a synthesis of the different currents of mankind have resulted in the demystification of history and religion. In his constant struggle for life, man has also struggled to gain a harmonious relationship between himself, his environment, and the universe itself. Through many thousands of years, he has developed practices enabling the development of greater resistance to stress. They open the way to a more conscious adaptation to the world and ourselves, a "total being" that can be characterized not so much by a luxurious (and dangerous) physical comfort, as by a voluntary desire for balance.

Now we can begin to understand the curious and unknown mechanisms of our being, we can try to live the adventure of the mind; each of us is beginning to realize that the world is more than what we have reduced it to. From now on, as Artaud has written, we must "turn our backs on culture that has never coincided with life."

Theory is not enough. It is necessary to be truly practical, to make known the methods by which we can be reunited with our bodies. The main paths to that rediscovery of life are the practices of daily living: knowing yourself, nourishing yourself, staying healthy, and finally, being fully in the world. To relearn the art of living, conscious of your body and reintegrated in your being.

This book, the fruit of several people's experience, does not claim to speak of all the ways of action bequeathed to us by the recent or remote traditions of our planet. It is a personal journey, an open structure that leads from the outside to the inside. An everyday experience.

To change the world, to change life . . . does not the first step consist of ridding ourselves of accumulated rubbish, in rediscovering ourselves? The world is the world by my particular vision. And meditation must coexist with action.

Marc de Smedt

knowing yourself

YOGA

"Yoga" is a word as misunderstood as it is debased. Everyone talks about yoga. Newspapers refer to it often, show some of its poses, and give advice on how to "stay young" by means of it. Most people know it comes from India and, with the help of certain articles in the press, they imagine bearded, emaciated yogis twisted into bizarre positions, with their eyes turned upward and their bodies covered with ashes. That has been yoga's popular image.

In India, one often encounters sadhus or sannyasis (disciples of Shiva and wandering monks) moving in groups or sitting under a sacred tree, smoking a *shilum** or doing yoga exercises. Appearances, however, are as usual deceiving. Yoga goes back to at least the third millennium B.C., and it is a true science providing methods of awakening which enable the individual to open many doors within himself. Our intention here is not to appeal to occult references or plunge into complexities of a system that is infinitely beyond our understanding, but to give a few clear ideas and describe some techniques that can be applied by anyone willing to take the trouble.

Yoga (from *yug:* "bond") is not merely an elaborate form of gymnastics; it is also an inner search. The yogi wants to attain a particular "state of being." There are as many types of yoga as there are means of reaching those new states of being, different for each person, since individuals are multiple and diverse.

The *Bhagavadgita* gives eighteen uses of the word "yoga," one per chapter. There is yoga of confusion (Vishuda Yoga), of love (Bhakta Yoga), of renunciation (Sannyasa Yoga), and so on. In fact, any method of progress can advance us along our inner path toward self-enlightenment, and our progress is itself already liberation. The yogi's procedure corresponds to a need to harmonize himself with the universe by connecting himself to cosmic laws and his own internal laws, which are cosmic laws in microcosm. He must transcend himself endlessly.

Five Basic Yogas

In India, for the sake of clarity and simplicity, five specific yogas (like the fingers of the hand) have been categorized.

Hatha Yoga, widespread in the West, is first of all a yoga of discovery of the body. The practice of Hatha Yoga relaxes the body, makes the mind aware of its physical being, and enables balanced development in the midst of the outside world. Yet this yoga, the only one

_____

*A clay or stone pipe for smoking *ganja* (Indian marijuana).

taught in our society, has always been regarded by gurus as a single phase, and never as ultimate fulfillment.

Bhakta Yoga takes the path of worship, of universal love. Everyone says, "Love God," says Vivekananda, but people do not know what it means to love; love exists where there is no bargaining, fear, or self-interest, where there is only love for love's sake. The goal is to enter into the deep intimacy of each person and thing, and find their primal truth. We thereby reach our own fundamental truth.

The danger in practicing Bhakta Yoga is blind devoutness.

Jnana Yoga, the way of knowledge by reason, is a method for critically investigating the basic conditions of knowledge: time, space, causality. The goal: reaching the center from which the directions of all planes of existence take their departure. The powers of the mind are scattered rays of light, says Vivekananda; to form a torch, they must be concentrated in a single beam.

The risk: becoming lost in intellect and cold logic, in wordy argumentation which cuts one off from reality.

Karma Yoga, the yoga of action, induces the adept to acquire perfect self-mastery in the world. It is the way which "starts from the inside and leads to the outside," and makes it possible to discover the secret of the laws underlying all action.

Finally there is *Raja Yoga*, the royal yoga, the yoga of synthesis and mastery of energy which can bring serenity, "that foundation of all effective action, the foundation of happiness," as Nietzsche said. It is a quest for one's unknown self, a return to the origin.

We will deal here exclusively with Hatha Yoga, a technique which "takes care" of the body and is at the same time a sacred discipline.

Each civilization carries with it its share of harm and progress. Today, while humanity has taken giant steps in its development, people have cut themselves off from their bodies by placing too much trust in technological comfort. Man has formed habits that impede his body. He eats, breathes, and sleeps badly, he takes little exercise (or falsely believes he exercises). Tobacco, coffee, meat, and little pills stimulate his body, while television, alcohol, overeating, and other little pills are supposed to relax it. A bent back, a flabby belly, lazy intestines, pimples and sores, almost chronic colds, fatigue, deterioration of the body, and overstimulation of the mind are his daily lot.

The picture becomes darker still; look about you and listen to conversations: People seldom if ever feel "glad to be alive," not to mention neuroses of all sorts, the sickly anxiety, and the latent aggressiveness that afflict our contemporaries. There can be no doubt that our form of civilization is at fault in all this, but, from the viewpoint of the yoga adept, it is madness to try to influence the outer world and change society if one is not determined above all to change oneself. Our action, whatever it may be, will then take on more force and truth. To achieve this, we must first alter our habits and become more aware of the mechanisms of our body and their interaction with the elements of our environment.

Today, at least in our cities, increased tension is the result of our constant pursuit of money and happiness. This tension affects the body, impeding the digestive, breathing, and mental processes. Thus "knots" are formed in the body which prevent full enjoyment of life. It is not necessary to withdraw from the world in order to find a balanced life: It is enough simply to question certain ways of acting and begin listening to our body and its needs.

Relaxation is a basic need. Yoga can lead us to it and introduce a new dimension into our life. If we understand the mechanics of our movement, if we know how to relax our muscular and nervous systems, stop thinking, and find energy in ourselves, we act more effectively and widen the fields of our consciousness, intuition, and vision. Yoga is a reintegration of our own body. As Sri Aurobindo says, for the knowing person the body is a sacred stage on which an indescribably profound play is performed, which is why knowledge or, better, conscious experience of the body is fundamentally important to the yogi.

And André van Lysebeth, reminding us that man is no longer adapted to nature and would be totally helpless if a cataclysm forced his return to life in a wild state, concludes:

"The preservation and development of human biological capital may depend on the correct practice of Hatha Yoga."[*]

But, as Sivananda says, an ounce of practice is worth more than tons of theory, so let us be more specific.

Relaxation

The first requirement is to set aside a period of calm and solitude during the day. Take off your shoes, loosen your belt, open any buttons that constrict you. Lie on the floor (on a rug or mat), on your back. Place your arms straight along your body and let your feet point away from each other, slightly and naturally. Let your head lie comfortably, with your neck relaxed. A firm cushion under your neck or lower back may help you to relax, but it is preferable to lie with nothing under you, like a corpse; and that, moreover, is the name of this posture: *savasan*, the "corpse pose."

Let yourself go. Be inert. Stop the swirl of thoughts and images in your mind and concentrate on your body. Stretch. Move your fingers, spread your arms and legs, bend and unbend them, roll from one side to the other. Then do nothing. Leave your body motionless and focus your attention on the tips of your toes. Think, "I'm relaxing my toes, one after another; I'm relaxing the soles and insteps of my feet." Drive away each contraction by thought. Try it, it is very effective. Go up along your whole body in this way, stopping at each point, up to your cheeks, your eyelids, your forehead.

Remain inert. Breathe calmly, taking a long time to exhale. Let yourself float with your eyes half closed. Abandon your muscles and limbs to gravity, to the earthly "magnet." Feel warmth slowly spreading through your body, float. . . .

Before standing up, stretch unhurriedly, and slowly come back to reality.

You will have a feeling of lightness and greater well-being. You will now be ready for action or leisure, with renewed vigor.

Practice this form of relaxation at the beginning, middle, or end of every day, and whenever you feel excessive tension—which greatly reduces the effectiveness of your activity. You must learn how to disconnect certain overloaded internal systems and "let the machine cool off." This is the best way of keeping your mind serene, not making a mountain out of the slightest complication, and avoiding depressions and other breakdowns. Fear, anger, and chronic aggressiveness can also be overcome, for nothing actually has the importance we attach to it.

Those moments of calm and relaxation taken during the day enable you to keep your distance from everything. Events take place outside of you and you intervene at the right times, whereas constant excessive tension brings on degeneration of the whole body and loss of control of its faculties.

The Dynamics of Breathing

Breathing plays a fundamental part in yoga. Before discussing it more specifically, we must understand the Indian notion of *prana*. Long before science discovered electric and magnetic fields, yogis had already detected the subtle energy contained in the atmosphere and the elements. It has now been proved that the bodies of mammals carry on constant biochemical exchanges with the environment. Assimilation of negative ions is essential to life. The number of those available ions is much smaller in the polluted air of cities.

Fatigue, nervousness, and a disorderly life, cut off from natural rhythms, cause a considerable loss of ions and therefore of energy. We must enhance our electric metabolism by increasing our reception of prana, which can be done through the dynamics of breathing in *pranayama* (expansion and control of prana).

---

[*]André van Lysebeth: *Je perfectionne mon yoga (Perfecting My Yoga)*; Flammarion.

For yogis, the skin, tongue, lungs, and nose are the main centers for absorbing prana. But our bodies are covered with clothes (which, if they are made of synthetic materials, repel the negative ions in the air and thus increase fatigue), our noses are often stopped up or badly used, and our lungs are fouled by bad breathing (from the top of the chest), tobacco, and harmful vapors (fuel oil and various gases). Furthermore, we are not *aware* of our breathing, even though our lives are based on it.

Yogis advocate bodily hygiene before everything else. The skin should be cleaned often and exposed to fresh air and sunlight as much as possible. We should run barefoot on the ground and rejoice in nature.

When you get up in the morning, look at your tongue: It may be covered with a thin, whitish coating. The worse your physical condition, the more your tongue will be coated in this way. Clean it every morning with a wooden spoon or spatula: Open your mouth, stick out your tongue as far as you can and scrape its surface. It will take on a pleasant pink color and, since your salivary glands will function better, your sense of taste will become more acute. Even if it is a little unpleasant at first, after a certain time you will do it spontaneously.

To clean the nose, yogis have discovered the nasal douche, known as *neti*. Salt water is used (one teaspoon of sea salt per pint), either warm or cold, depending on whether you want to remove mucus or produce an invigorating effect. The container can be either a bowl or an old teapot, whose spout will make the operation easier. With a teapot, insert the spout in your right nostril, tilt your head to the left and let half of the water flow slowly into your nose, keeping your mouth open. Then do the same with your left nostril. With a bowl, hold it horizontal and put both nostrils into the water. Do not inhale, but "pump" with your glottis, making a swallowing motion. Let the water come into your throat until you taste it, then let it flow out. Repeat three or four times and then finish up by blowing your nose vigorously to drive out the remaining water. The resulting sensation may be strange at first, but if you continue you will soon have a very pleasant feeling of freshness, and this practice is one of the best ways of avoiding colds.

Brush your teeth after both procedures, using a toothpaste with a base of plants or seaweed. Try it and see how your head clears up!

Breathing

Let us now consider breathing itself. Breathing techniques are found in all traditions. Breathing is the essential vital act, and the inward and outward movement of air is related to the universal rhythms of expansion and contraction. In each organism, billions of cells need the oxygen carried by the blood, and they expel carbon dioxide as a kind of gaseous "ash."

Breathing is living, yet most people no longer know how to breathe. During their first few months of life, the ebb and flow of their breathing was full, deep, and easy, but it becomes more and more tense with age. As the individual acquires bad physical habits and wears constricting clothes, his body falls prey to chronic tension, and he forgets the importance of breathing. Even if he practices gymnastics he is taught to breathe by inflating his lungs, whereas balanced breathing is naturally abdominal.

For yogis, exhalation is the important act: Inhalation takes place afterward, automatically. The deeper exhalation is, the more powerful inhalation will be. Exhalation should take at least twice as long as inhalation. If exhalation is carried to its extreme, if the spongy tissue of the lungs is thoroughly compressed and vitiated air is expelled, inhalation will enable the air sacs to be filled with fresh air.

It is good to practice long exhalation during relaxation exercises and yoga poses, or even in the street, at work, in bed, morning and evening. Take a moment of calm, a pause, and stop thinking about all the movement around you. Withdraw into yourself. Breathe slowly, emptying your lungs as much as possible. During that period of immobility you will be "recharged," physically and psychically. You will feel the circulation of your blood, oxygen, and energy.

As Dr. Peschier has stated, voluntary breathing is the most important means at our disposal for increasing organic resistance. This form of breathing is inseparable from the spirit and exercises of yoga. Yogis recommend breathing as if each person had been given a certain number of breaths at birth, and his life would last until he used them all up. This image seems strikingly appropriate when we think of the quick, irregular, shallow breathing of most people, who are hypertense, have contracted abdomens and disorderly minds, move stiffly, and lead hectic lives.

Yogis also advise holding air in the lungs briefly (one to three seconds) after inhaling: the moment of silence between two musical notes.

The Power of Sound

A yoga once frequently practiced is Mantra Yoga. Bound up with breathing, it is also related to the chanting of sacred texts and the repetition of certain sounds that are found in all traditions. Arthur Avalon defines a mantra as power in the form of a sound. Sound is a vibration. We now know how greatly some sounds can disturb biological balance: Beyond a certain number of decibels, sound causes organic lesions and may give rise to very serious disorders.

Western science has only begun to explore the field of sound: the practical applications of ultrasounds, for example. But while sonic vibration can have harmful effects, it can also have beneficial ones. And yogis long ago discovered the amazing effects of sound on the body and the mind.

In the West, the scientist Leser-Lasario was one of those who rediscovered that force and used it to cure others, often after using it to cure themselves. When he was eighteen, doctors judged him to be incurably ill. One day, some neighbors asked his parents to mind their baby a while. The baby lay on its back, babbling. Leser-Lasario was fascinated by the complementary, natural relations between its breathing and its sounds. It was unconsciously breathing like a yogi: Its deep breath started from the abdomen and it "chanted" until exhalation was complete. The vibratory effect of sound on that small, barely formed body was quite pronounced and, depending on the nature of the sound (la, la, la; po, po, po), the effect started from different regions of the body.

Acting on brilliant intuition, Leser-Lasario began imitating the baby. Day after day, trusting in nature, he made those monotonous vocal sounds for hours at a time. Within a few weeks his condition began to improve. "It invariably produced quite specific effects," he said. "I became convinced that something was happening in me. All my organic functions seemed to be taking place more harmoniously, and certain vowels produced sharply localized effects. The sound 'ee,' for example, cleared considerable quantities of mucus from my throat and bronchia, until the tissues regained their normal condition. How did it happen? Was my circulation regularized by that method which combined breathing, vibration, and the alteration of inner feeling? Perhaps each vowel acted on a specific part of my body and would eventually cure it completely. If so, I had found a way to control my circulation and the reactions of my sympathetic nervous system, and to send at will an afflux of nourishing blood to the thirsty tissues that required it." Then came thirty years of experiments and countless cures.

At this point let us describe some keys to this technique, which you can put into practice anywhere. You need only a few minutes of calm during which you can vocalize a vowel sound and concentrate on it while you exhale. The relaxing effect will be immediately perceptible, but only daily repetition produces a lasting effect, by a kind of inner vibratory massage.

Ee acts on the head, the nose, and the larynx, by vibrating upward. It dispels headaches and restores good humor. Vocalize it for a long time, with a smile on your lips, and concentrate on the special feeling it arouses: It is a bright, gay sound.

Ah acts on the brain and the upper part of the lungs. It is a more serene sound.

Eh invigorates and regularizes the throat, neck, vocal cords, and thyroid gland.

Oo acts on all the abdominal organs, including the liver, regularizes the intestines, and may relieve constipation.

O is a deep, weighty sound that seems to evoke meditation, a sound of wonder and fulfillment. It makes all the chest bones vibrate, stimulates the lungs and the diaphragm, and increases vitality and concentration. Its effect also extends to the intestines and the genital glands. Its vocalization slows down the flow of exhaled air.

The basic mantra of traditional yogis was *OM*, the cosmic sound. *Mmm* makes the cranial nerves vibrate and awakens energy. When *OM* is pronounced in two stages during a long exhalation, in a continuous sound, it helps the gradual relaxation of the muscles, and if you concentrate intently on that magic sound it will empty your mind of its uncontrolled images, because it completely occupies the field of consciousness. It brings calm and peace.

The preceding pages give enough details to begin several beneficial practices. But the importance of becoming aware of one's body and its reactions must be stressed. Yoga is not a mechanical form of gymnastics, but a prodigious way of working on oneself. When you relax, you should feel the slightest tactile sensations of your body on the floor and the gradual slackening of your muscles. First explore your body by contracting its parts as much as possible and moving your muscles. Also move your jaws, your eyes, your tongue; smile; draw your forehead into a frown, then release it. Next, focus your attention on breathing and on sound if you want to vocalize a few vowels. When you hold your breath, notice your heartbeat and the presence of your internal organs.

In the West, because of our Judaeo-Christian civilization, we have to some extent forgotten the body. Yet it underlies all our reactions and is the basis of our balance or imbalance. It is a wonderful tool which asks only to function at its highest potential. We are our bodies, so let us liberate them and feel ourselves living.

A person feels agitated, depressed, or inert because he has only superficial reasons for living. He has lost contact with the deep self; he is no longer able to turn inward and become aware of his universal nature as a living being.

I am life. . . .

All the exercises described above lead the individual to meditation on himself and the world. There is no use thinking; we think much too much and too fast. Ramana Maharishi says, "If, instead of a host of ideas, there is only one which occupies the whole field of attention, it becomes a power in itself and can exercise great influence." We must therefore *concentrate*: on an act, an object, a person, a gesture, a sound. We must always concentrate, instant by instant. It is a long journey, and it may begin during those moments of calm withdrawal into yourself which you take in the midst of each day's agitation. Your life will gradually be changed.

A Few Postures

In speaking of methods of relaxation, we have scarcely begun to open the door of yoga. Let us now consider a few postures, or *asanas*, which can be quickly learned by anyone.

The best conditions for a session of postures are as follows: in the morning, *before eating*, after a pause for relaxation, in a well-ventilated place. The ideal setting is, of course, outdoors in nature, but indoor yoga is possible if the air is not stale. You should be lightly dressed: only in loincloth in warm weather, or loose clothes without underwear if it is cold. A slight stiffness and soreness of the muscles is quite common at first—how many years has it been since they stopped working?

André van Lysebeth gives an important ten-point code for practicing the asanas effectively:

1. The asanas are not exercises of strength. They act by themselves, not by violence.

2. Slowness of each movement is essential to the effectiveness of yoga.

3. Maintain each asana for the prescribed time.

4. Contract only those muscles necessary for maintaining the asana, and relax all others.

5. Focus your attention on the area of the body for which the asana is intended.

6. Returning to the starting position must also be done very slowly.

7. Between two asanas, rest a few seconds by relaxing as many muscles as possible, including those of the face.

8. If you are short of time, reduce the number of asanas, but never speed them up.

9. Always perform the asanas in the same order.

10. Always end your session with the savasan, the "corpse pose," for relaxation (minimum time: one minute).

Asanas

SHOULDER STAND

Sarvangasan

Lying flat on your back, slowly raise your legs straight up, remembering that in yoga you must never make abrupt movements. If necessary, bend your knees a little while you *slowly* raise your legs, but do not contract your calf muscles by pointing your toes upward. Bracing your arms against the floor, with your abdominal muscles taut and your feet and knees joined, raise yourself to a vertical position and take the final pose by supporting yourself with your hands on your lower back. The back of your neck and shoulders should be pressed down firmly but easily against the floor, and your chin should be held against your breastbone. Hold the pose for one minute, breathe, and relax as many muscles as possible.

This asana is excellent for stimulating blood circulation, decongesting the organs, and correcting defects of the spine.

Lower yourself without letting your body fall heavily: Your spine should "unroll" on the floor. Do not get up abruptly; first, take the balancing "counterpose": the Fish.

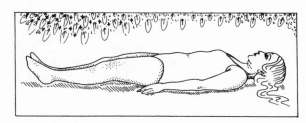

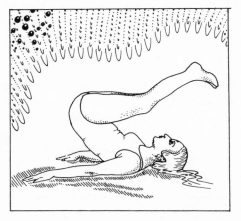

FISH POSE

Matsayasan

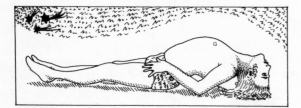

Sit on the floor with your legs extended, then lean back and support yourself on your elbows. Tilt your head back as far as possible, arching your back. Let your head slowly go down as you move your elbows forward. Leave your posterior pushed against the floor, with your back still arched; you should gradually be able to put your hands on your thighs. Take ten slow, deep breaths. This asana balances the shoulder stand. It is good for the back muscles; it expands the chest and strengthens the abdomen.

Lie flat on the floor by releasing the tension of your back muscles and letting your head slide. Relax for a minute or two.

HEAD-KNEE POSE

Paschimothan Asana

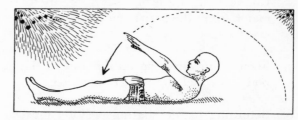

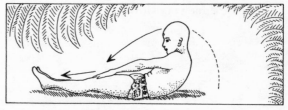

Lying on the floor with your arms extended behind your head and your body stretched out and relaxed, lift your arms and bring them down on your thighs, moving your head and torso in the same arc. Here again, the back should "unroll." Watch your hands as they slowly move from your thighs to your shins. Bend your body double until your chest touches your legs and, if possible, your forehead touches your knees. Then slowly make the same movements in reverse until you are again lying on the floor with your arms extended behind your head.

Repeat the entire sequence three times. The last time, grasp your big toes, keep your elbows pressed against your body, and take five or six deep breaths.

This asana invigorates the nervous system and stimulates all the abdominal organs by internal massage.

COBRA POSE

Bhujangasan

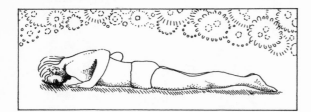

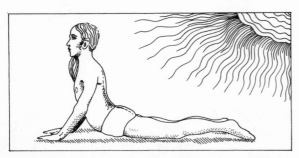

Lying face down on the floor, lift your head and trunk as much as possible, stretching your neck and all your back muscles. Do not use your arms to lift yourself; they should only serve as a support. Slowly lower yourself to the floor and repeat the movement three times. Then begin again, this time using your arms to lift yourself so that your spine is curved backward. Keep your head erect and breathe through your nose, deeply and continuously. Your navel should remain near the floor. The nervous system and the whole spine are benefited by this asana.

SPINAL TWIST

Instead of bending the spine in one direction or another, this asana twists it. It is a simple pose: You have only to follow the drawings, bending your right leg to make your body twist to the right, then bending your left leg to make it twist to the left. These twists stimulate the nervous system and the kidneys.

HEADSTAND

Sirshasan

This vertical posture and the lotus are the most representative of yoga. The headstand is excellent because of the blood drainage it causes in all parts of the body. It also favors the intellectual functions and the whole psychic balance through the irrigation of the brain that it produces. It is good for the eyes, hearing, the skin of the face, and the scalp. If the head rests solidly on the floor, at the peak of the triangle formed by the forearms, this pose presents no special difficulties. You should take it little by little, however, gradually find your balance upside down, and work against a wall at first, if necessary. Breathe normally through your nose without stopping, stressing exhalation.

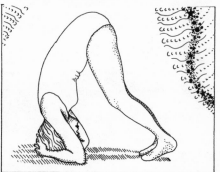

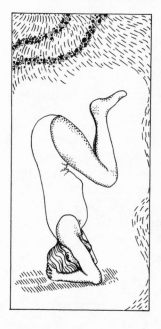

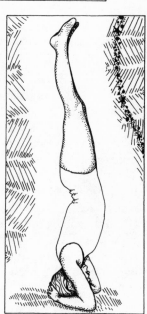

THE HALF LOTUS

This is the perfect posture, the posture of meditation. It soothes the mind, regularizes all the organic functions, and stabilizes the body. Sitting on a firm cushion with your knees apart, bend your left leg and put it under your right thigh. Then bend your right leg and place it on your left thigh, with the soles of your feet turned upward; you will gradually find the most comfortable position of this foot on your thigh. Keep your back erect and arched at the level of the fifth lumbar vertebra. Your neck should be straight,with your head balanced on top of your spine. Place the weight of your body on your knees. Gradually relax all your muscles, exhale slowly, inhale naturally with your belly; you can thus remain motionless, calm, and collected, in the half-lotus position. Alternate the positions of your legs often.

AND THE LOTUS

The full lotus is taken little by little. It consists in having each foot on the opposite thigh, sole upward. Its effects become more pronounced as the angle formed by the thighs diminishes, which improves the balance of the body and the massaging of the internal organs.

ZAZEN

THE MOUNTAIN

Connect yourself, harmonize yourself, let go.

That, in substance, is what the Buddha Sakyamuni said to his disciples. One day in Benares, by way of a sermon, he took a flower and turned it between his fingers. Only Mahakashyapa understood, and smiled. Buddha gave him the flower and Zen. Connect yourself to the cosmos, bring yourself into harmony with others, let go of the ego: that is the Buddha's message. To achieve it, there is a direct method, the steep way: *zazen.*

The son of the ruler of a small mountain kingdom, Gautama Siddhartha (Sakyamuni) was born at Kapilavastu in the sixth century B.C. One day, with his faithful servant, he rode away in secret on a white horse. He left behind a palace, wives, children, and wealth. When he reached the edge of the woods he sent his servant back with the horse and plunged into the primal forest, determined to resolve the problem of birth and death. He studied under the best teachers of Vedanta and yoga. In those days, yoga was not something to be taken lightly: The course of study included (and still includes in traditional India) such practices as being buried underground, fasting for forty days, and meditating on a corpse.

After six years of study, research, and self-mortification, he suddenly asked himself, "What am I doing here?" and decided to finish once and for all with the problem of birth and death, which he still had not solved. He went away, alone. As he was wandering half-dead on the road, he was sheltered by a young woman named Sujyata. She gave him milk and fruit and tenderly took care of him. He then set about achieving his purpose.

Sujyata made a grass cushion for him; he sat down under the Bo tree, a fig tree, and stayed there seven weeks. He discovered zazen. One night, shortly before dawn, he awoke in the light of Venus. "In the last watch of the night, I attained ultimate knowledge. . . . The shadows were driven away and light appeared." He had discovered a diamond; was he to keep it hidden? He had found the key; was he to give it to others? When he decided to devote his whole earthly life to transmitting the secret, Sakyamuni became Buddha.

Buddha's life has been condensed into a quatrain:

Buddha was born at Kapilavastu.
He achieved the Way in the province of Makada.
He preached at Benares.
He entered into nirvana (that is, he died, at the age of eighty) at Kuchira.

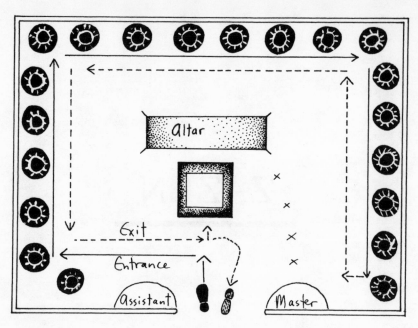

The dojo

Having been planted in Indian soil, the seed of Zen (in Sanskrit, *Dhyana*: "meditation," "concentration") sprouted in China with Ch'an, the Chinese Dhyana, full of vitality and cosmic force. After five centuries of development (seventh to twelfth centuries), the plant of Zen blossomed in Japan: after traveling to China, Master Dogen (twelfth century) brought the secret to his native land. Zen is zazen.

Transmission of Zen can take place only under certain conditions. It perpetuates the original climate: Buddha takes a flower in his hand, someone smiles. Beyond good and evil, beyond knowledge and nonknowledge, a basic energy is involved: Man must become God or Buddha. Transmission is carried out by a master; directly, outside of writing, "from my soul to your soul."

Roshi (meaning Zen master) Taisen Deshimaru, a disciple of Kodo Sawaki (died in 1965), restorer of the Soto Zen founded by Master Dogen, brought to the West the seed formed in Japan: the essence of Zen.

Transmission occurs in a *dojo* (a place where meditation is practiced).

The dojo is the place where one sits in zazen with the Master. Master Dogen writes in the *Shobogenzo* ("Treasure of the True Law"), "Those who are not sincere must not enter here." The dojo is like a sandalwood forest. No tree of bad quality can grow there, for sandalwood trees are thick and leafy. *Shikantaza* ("to simply sit"), *mushotoku* ("without purpose or a wish to gain benefits")—that is the spirit of Zen.

HOW TO SIT

The process of humanization, from the anthropoid to Homo sapiens, is the story of achieving an upright posture that made possible the development of the brain. The practice of zazen presupposes the guidance of a master who has been traditionally initiated and is linked to the Buddha by the lineage of the Zen patriarchs.

Zen sitting can be broken down into three elements:

Posture of the body.
Breathing.
Attitude of the mind.

POSTURE

Seated on a *zafu* ("cushion"), with your legs crossed in the lotus or half-lotus position, you push against the earth with your knees and against the sky with your head. Your spine is straight, your pelvis is tilted forward at the level of the fifth lumbar vertebra, your belly is relaxed from top to bottom, and your chin is drawn in. You are like a bow whose arrow is the mind. Seated in this way, without purpose or a wish to gain benefits, keep your eyes open, directed downward about three feet in front of you, looking at nothing. Your left hand rests in your right, palms up, thumbs joined like the horizon, "neither mountain nor valley." Your shoulders droop naturally. The tip of your tongue is on your palate.

That is the seated posture which is taken for about twenty minutes at a time.

Next you take another Zen posture, the *kin-hin* (*kin:* "woof of a loom"; *hin:* "to walk"), and walk in the dojo for five to ten minutes, which provides a welcome change of position. You begin by standing up. Close your left hand, palm down, thumb inside, with the root of the thumb touching your solar plexus. Place your right hand flat over your left hand. Hold your forearm horizontal. Direct your eyes downward about ten feet in front of you. Begin walking with your right foot, while breathing deeply and putting pressure on the base of your big toe, and on the solar plexus with your left thumb. This way of walking assures that your body will be well balanced on its center of gravity.

BREATHING

Breathing is of fundamental importance. In the beginning is the breath. In the act of breathing, energy is transmitted to all the cells of the human body. The first goal of Zen breathing is to

Master Kodo Sawaki in the zazen posture

maintain a slow, powerful, natural rhythm. When you deliberately exhale as long as possible and keep your attention focused on your posture, inhaling comes naturally. During exhalation, air is slowly and silently expelled, and the thrust of this expulsion should go down powerfully into the belly. You "push on your intestines." Masters compare Zen breathing to the lowing of a cow or the exhalation of a baby that cries as soon as it is born.

ATTITUDE OF THE MIND

In zazen, *you must not think* with your head. The unconscious ideas and images that well up

Neither mountain nor valley

Master Deshimaru in the kin-hin posture

must be neither stopped nor maintained. "Pass, pass, pass. . . ." Master Deshimaru says often. Master Dogen said, "If you have your hand open, you can grasp all things; if you abandon, you can have all things. If a bottle is full of water, you cannot fill it with wine, but if it is empty, you can." The empty bottle is cosmic consciousness; the open hand abandons the ego. Sitting in the zazen posture, you let thoughts and mental images pass like clouds in the sky while you concentrate on the posture. Think with your body. Think without thinking, with all contradictions transcended. This is the state of consciousness/nonconsciousness of nothing, the fullness of the One, *Hishiryo.*

After a session of zazen, the master often makes *sampai*—prostrates himself three times with his forehead against the floor—in front of a wooden statue of the Buddha. He is not merely paying homage to the wooden statue. His gesture is addressed to his disciples and to all buddhas.

THE SPIRIT OF ZEN

Master Dogen always stressed, on the one hand, the fact that *satori* ("awakening to reality") is zazen; and on the other, the clear but hidden fact that Zen consists in being concentrated here and now, in everyday life. All our acts, and all the elements of our universe and of the Universe, become the spirit of Zen. Anyone entering a dojo, however, cannot fail to notice certain objects and signs: first, a stick (the *kyosaku*) and a collective chant (the *hannya shingyo*); and second, a symbolic garment (the *kesa*).

THE KYOSAKU

If, during a zazen session, you feel uncomfortable in your posture or if too many thoughts are passing through your mind, or if you are threatened by sleepiness, you can ask for the stick.

You make *gassho* (you bow with hands joined), and the master or his assistant raises his stick and gives you, "from my soul to your soul," a blow on the shoulder muscles which instantly clears up all blockages of the autonomic nervous system. Then the master and the pupil bow together, in gassho, silently. The one who holds the kyosaku walks in kin-hin, without a sound. Deeply concentrating, he intuitively understands everyone's posture. The atmosphere of the dojo depends on his concentration.

The kyosaku (from *kyo:* "attention," and *saku:* "stick"), the stick that awakens attention, is also the spirit of Zen. It is an instrument of the right act, the receptacle of a prehistoric wisdom (and humor). Its blows are effective at all levels of being. They are always given and received with great respect for the other and for others.

THE HANNYA SHINGYO

Each zazen session ends with the collective chanting of a sutra (sacred text), the sutra of great wisdom.

The hannya shingyo is chanted in the zazen posture, while exhaling deeply, to the rhythm of clappers or a wooden gong. It is the central text of Mahayana Buddhism.* This mantra of some two hundred words is a condensation of six hundred books, and it in turn can be summed up in a single word: *ku,* "vacuity." "Vacuity is not empty," says Taisen Deshimaru. "It is the universal, it is the All."

TRANSLATION OF THE HANNYA SHINGYO

The future Buddha, in true freedom,
walked, full of compassion,
in the deep and perfect way
of wisdom.
Full of mercy,
he leaned down
and saw only
five moving structures
of the advancing mind.
He saw
that in their essence
they were empty.
And the Master said:

O Sariputra, beloved disciple,
here,
form is emptiness,
emptiness is form.
Form is nothing other
than emptiness,
emptiness is nothing other
than form.
Although there is form,
there is emptiness;
although there is emptiness,
there is form.
It is the same
with sensations,
and perceptions,
and the preformed structures
of consciousness.
O Sariputra, dear disciple,
here,

all qualities
have the character
of emptiness.
They have neither birth
nor decline;
they are neither
defiled nor pure,
neither incomplete nor complete.

Therefore,
dear disciple,
where there is emptiness
there is
neither form,
nor sensation,
nor perception,
nor preformed structures,
nor consciousness.

Neither eye nor ear,
nor nose, nor tongue,
nor body, nor thought.

Neither form, nor sound,
nor smell, nor taste,
nor touch,
nor object of thought,

---

*The "open" branch of Buddhism, or the Great Vehicle, according to which all beings are called upon to become Buddha, that is, to harmonize themselves with the order of the universe, here and now.

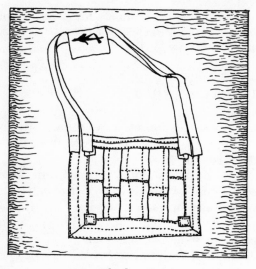

The kesa

nor field of vision,
nor even an object
of consciousness.
Neither knowledge,
nor ignorance,
nor even
decline and death,
nor disappearance
of decline and death.
Neither suffering,
nor creation,
nor end,
nor way,
nor knowledge,
nor gift,
nor the refusal of a gift,
nor obtaining,
nor nonobtaining.

Therefore,
O Sariputra,
because of his detachment,
because of his confidence
in perfect Wisdom,
the future Buddha
does not know
anxious thoughts.
He does not tremble.
Consoled by what
is not nirvana,
he has overcome
what might have
threatened him with death.
All those who appear
as Buddhas
in the three periods
of time,
trusting
in perfect Wisdom,

awaken,
clearheaded,
to the supreme, just, and perfect
light.
Perfect Wisdom
must therefore be known.
This is the great mantra of knowledge,
the incomparable mantra,
the unmatched mantra,
the consoler of all suffering,
the mantra of truth,
without error.

This unsurpassable mantra
is the incantation of Great Wisdom
which is said thus:
"Go, go, go beyond,
go all together,
beyond the beyond
where lies the way of Satori,
which is the wisdom of Buddha."*

THE KESA

When he had stood up from under his fig tree, the Buddha went to a place on the bank of the Ganges where the dead were burned. He took pieces of shrouds, washed them in the water of the river, sewed them together, and dyed them with ocher. The word *kesa* comes from the Sanskrit *kasaya,* which means "color of ocher, brown."** Shortly before his death, Buddha gave his garment, the kesa, to Mahakashyapa.

Transmission of the kesa is transmission of the spirit of Zen. When Master Dogen traveled in China, his greatest emotion came when he heard the monks of Master Nyojo's monastery chanting the following sutra as they put their kesas over their heads, after their dawn zazen:

> *Universal garment, boundless and beatific,*
> *Now I have the satori of the Buddha,*
> *To help all beings,*
> *O wondrous emancipation!*†

---

*"Gya-tei, ha-ra gya-tei hara-so gya-tei, bo-ji, bo-ji so-waka." Intellectual understanding of this text is less important than its sonic vibrations and the breathing exercises it provides. Individual vibrations and breathing are mingled, and during the chant they secrete harmony in the place of wisdom.

**In *La nature humaine, le paradigme perdu,* Edgar Morin sees the use of ocher (along with the stick, fire, and flint) as a sign of the appearance of Homo sapiens.

†*Daisai gedappuku* *hibi nyorai kyo*
 muso fukuden e *kodo sho shu jo.*

When Dogen heard that sutra, he wept.

The kesa is made of lengthwise rectangular strips of cloth. Because of this, it is called *fukuden e* ("rice paddy") in Japanese.

In our time, disciples (*bodhisattva*) receive a mini-kesa called a *rakusu*. And Master Yoka (seventh century in China) wrote in the *Shodoka* (chant of the satori immediate), "Winter and autumn mists, dew, clouds, and springtime mist are the true kesa that clothes our body."

Being Born Again

Master Dogen always said that one zazen, or a fraction of a second of a zazen, is attainment of the state of Buddha. It is good to do zazen often and regularly; each day, for example, at sunrise and/or sunset. It is even better to take part in a *sesshin*. A sesshin is a period of more intensive training lasting one to four days, with four to seven hours of zazen each day. The pupil gets up at six o'clock and goes to bed at ten. His schedule includes discussions, *mondo* ("questions and answers") with the master, *samu* ("manual labor"), meals taken in silence, and concentration.

Beneficial effects on the body and the brain can be felt even more strongly in the course of a sesshin than after an isolated session of zazen. Life in the dojo is an apprenticeship for real life; right thoughts, words, and acts are produced by a person in harmony with himself, others, and the cosmos.

EFFECTS ON THE BODY

Western man often conceives of himself as a subject separated from objects, as a body detached from the cosmos; zazen dispels that illusion of reason. Body and mind are one. They are different frequencies of the same vibration, different forms of the same energy. Zazen amends the physical constitution by acting on the root of everything; the spine is straightened, the nervous system is strengthened, the functioning of the cerebral cortex is regularized, and the activity of the subcortical structures (or inner brain) is increased. The body, supple and alert, finds its balance. Intuition is unconsciously developed.

In 1967 a study of zazen, nervous physiology, and health was carried out in a laboratory at the University of Tokyo. Taisen Deshimaru was one of the people studied. The observations that were made show the following:

1. Circulation of the blood is improved. The pituitary, thyroid, and adrenal glands release larger quantities of hormones. The activity of the cells is increased.
2. The number of calories needed is reduced.
3. If internal organs—lungs, stomach, intestines, liver, kidneys, spleen—are in poor condition, they gradually return to normal. The spine, so often deformed in the West, is straightened.

A zazen master's electroencephalogram shows an extension of alpha waves throughout the brain, particularly in the occipital and parietal regions. These waves indicate the calm and peace experienced by the subject, and the complete absence of mental work, thoughts, and sensations.

When Zen masters say that intuition is developed and wisdom appears in an *unconscious* way, and that we must "think without thinking," the notion of the unconscious on which they base their statements comes from the oldest Indian and Buddhist traditions.

During zazen, the unconscious rises toward consciousness. And, as Erich Fromm says, zazen plunges into the source of creation and draws on all the life that is in it.

Seekers like Aldous Huxley and Timothy Leary, and scientists like Heisenberg and Einstein, help us to understand the concept of the void (*ku*).

R. L. Vallée, an atomic physicist at the research center in Saclay, France, recently made an extremely important discovery: the universe is formed from energy, and the void is a form of energy (neutrinos). Matter, in its primary

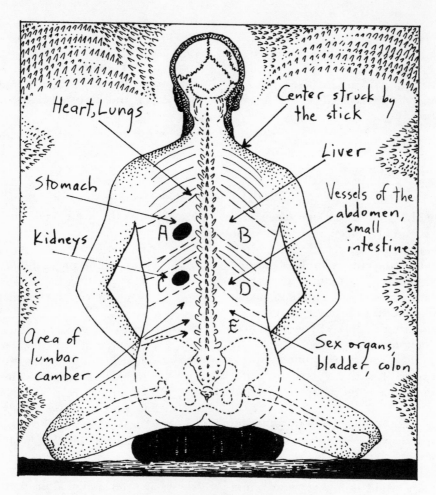

Zazen, a "barometer of health"
A, B, C, D, E: painful areas during the zazen posture in persons
whose corresponding organs are sick to some extent.

form as particles, may be described as concentrated energy, something like a "coil" of vibratory waves. Each element of the cosmos is in interaction with the others: "All phenomena of nature capable of being apprehended experientially in the universe are coherent, which means that they all depend on each other more or less closely and through more or less complex reactions, and that each of them is manifested as the local resultant of universal dynamics. Thus they can never, in space and time, be in contradiction with the state of the universe as it must be at that place and at that moment."

The cells of the wood in the table I am touching are composed of atoms, and the constituent elements of those atoms are pure vibrations. The void is omnipresent, in perpetual

fluctuation. The void contains the potentiality for everything.

REAL LIFE

In the West, the goal of life is considered to be fulfillment of the personality. When the sutra speaks of "achieving the Way," it refers to an experience that goes far beyond the boundaries of the ego.* Anticipating the most recent discoveries of science, Oriental thought, particularly Buddhism, formulates a concept of the world that is an experience: We live in a universe of relativity where everything is inter-

---

*That is, the personal, egocentric self which produces illusions.

dependence, cause-and-effect relations, and where everything is energy.

Such an experience explodes the little ego; thus it is never lived consciously, and yet it is recognizable. It is "here and now," harmony with oneself, with others, and with the cosmos.

In Zen, knowing and studying oneself has nothing to do with introspection. We are in the world. There is nothing to fear, there is no reason for anxiety, real life is here and now. The mental finds its right place in that life. You need not seek anything. There is nothing that need be sought. Real light is everywhere. Satori consists in consciously/unconsciously living and being the true intuition of primal existence, from the top of our head to the soles of our feet, in every cell of our body. Zazen is the native land. Zen is the light of the origin.

Thinking with the body is the Way to be in harmony with oneself.

After six weeks of zazen under the Bo tree, Sakyamuni awoke in the light of Venus.

Zen masters have often compared awakening to the spark produced by the impact of one piece of flint on another. The Japanese word for "awakening" is *satori*.

A woodcutter was working in the forest. He had heard of a prodigious animal, the satori animal, and strongly desired to possess it. One day the satori animal came to visit him. He ran after it and was amazed to hear a voice saying, "You won't have me because you want to have me." The woodcutter went back to his woodcutting. He completely forgot about the animal and no longer thought of anything but his work. The satori animal came to him and was crushed by the tree he had just felled.

Right action

The methods we have just discussed enable "fragmented man" to reassemble himself. Before trying to change the world, the apparent source of all your ills, you should first change yourself. There, at least, you can act in a direct, effective way and make slow progress from day to day. As you pursue your practices, you will soon see that each act of daily life is affected by your new state of mind. You will regain an energy that you thought you had lost since childhood, and discover a concentration in action that you had thought impossible. If you regularly practice a discipline of concentration, you will feel clearheaded. Your mind no longer will be cluttered with chaotic thoughts, and your attention will be focused on one thing at a time, fully.

It would be a mistake, however, to believe that universal remedies or miraculous techniques have been revealed to you: Making a few movements, practicing correct breathing, and sitting in silence are not actions that will instantly give you power and enlightenment, or prevent you from having difficult moments. But in that slow discovery of yourself you will find keys to your own action: how to use your body and mind correctly, how to behave in the midst of vibrations that are conflicting or simply different. If you feel overwhelmed by events, find a few moments of calm, exhale slowly, let your thoughts pass, and relaxation will come. Your whole organic system will be recharged automatically.

It has been proven that sleep is favorable to the synthesis of proteins, which are essential to our intellectual and nervous development. By the sustained practice of meditation you cause your brain to be flooded with the same alpha waves that are found in deep sleep. Putting yourself into such a state of relaxation while practicing the technique of prolonged exhalation enables your body to eliminate nervous tension and give your brain a rest. The neurons stop transmitting too many electric impulses, a process of classification and synthesis takes place on the unconscious level, proteins change their configuration, and the "unloaded" cortex is ready to receive and see only what is essential. As soon as you return to action, connections are made without "short circuits" and the current (information) flows. The whole cerebral system is strengthened and improved, because each experience then brings consciously lived information. Ordinarily, very few acts in a day are perceived with full awareness. The more you concentrate on the act of the moment, the more clearheaded you are.

We have no word to translate the Japanese *ki,* which expresses a concept found all over the Far East. Ki is our vital force, the attentive energy that we put (or fail to put) into an act, our nonthought, intuitive, deep awareness. Itsuo Tsuda points out the following Japanese expressions:

"*Ki ga chiisai,*" "His ki is small," i.e., "He worries too much over nothing."

"*Ki ga ōkii,*" His ki is large," i.e., "He doesn't worry about trivial things."

"*Ki ni naru,*" "It attracts my ki," i.e., "I can't get that idea out of my mind, something about it holds my attention in spite of myself.*

Ki is both vital energy and attention. The Japanese masters situate a center three fingers below the navel: the *hara,* or "ocean of ki" (*ki-kai*). It is also our center of gravity. Deep breathing enables us to make it firmer. In the past, dishonored samurai committed hara-kiri by thrusting their sword into that point.

If we strengthen our ki by means of concentration techniques, we succeed in destroying anxiety, finding inner calm and detachment, gradually making each action right, and discovering in our life an unknown balance that will enable us to be spontaneously attentive and unconsciously direct our energy where it ought to be placed. From then on, we are no longer devoured by the world's chaotic agitation.

We are all so different, yet so similar in our structures. We are all guided by the same natural laws and cosmic rhythms. The main difference lies in each person's awareness of them, and in his way of using energies. It is no longer possible to enclose man in his little mechanical shell: He is a prodigious living electronic system. We bear as much resemblance to the computer, radar, and radio as we do to the automobile engine and its way of transforming the energy of petroleum to produce motion. The human being is a receiver-transmitter whose possibilities are sadly underdeveloped. Too often, he dreams his life and works frenziedly for possessions that he acquires but never enjoys. Sometimes he comes to realize that no one has liberated him, that he has benefited from nothing, that he has remained a slave to his needs, and that he has been passive in the face of events. He will die unsatisfied and bitter.

Each of us can free himself from that infernal cycle, each of us can actively overcome *all* difficulties. It is not a matter of will, because the will governs only relations between the cortex and the muscles; it is a matter of vital energy, of ki.

"Ki has no bounds. It transcends space and time. It is each person's viewpoint that limits it," says Itsuo Tsuda, master of *katsu-gen-kai,* a technique of regenerating movement. The Japanese martial arts (judo, aikido, karate) are other examples of the perfect use of ki: By concentration, one uses the adversary's flow of energy to turn it back against him and defeat him.

> *The heavy is the root of the light . . .*
> *The Tao eternally practices non-action, and yet there is nothing it does not do.*
>
> Tao Te Ching

---

*Itsuo Tsuda: *Le Non-Faire (Inaction),* Le Courrier du Livre.

nourishing yourself

Eating is one of the actions that bind us to the world, for in eating we incorporate external substances into ourselves. "To know the taste of a pear," writes Mao, "you must transform it by eating it." Guy Peltier, a chef, goes so far as to say that in this process "we digest the world physically." The essential phenomenon of digestion is still misunderstood: In its passage through the intestinal wall, swallowed food reaches an absolutely immaterial stage of existence; by his organs and the force of his personality, man causes within himself a rebirth of the realms of nature contained in that mass of food undergoing transformation. Just as the cosmos makes a visible plant appear from the point of contact represented by a seed, man creates his substance at the level of the point of contact represented by his organs.

From and by means of food, we thus create new human substances. It is essential to recognize the importance of what we eat, the necessity of high quality in our foods, and the need for a nutritional balance that must be found for each individual. Our present civilization, with all its problems and benefits, has enabled everyone, at least in the West, to feed his hunger. But the variety and quantity of foods have been increased at the cost of quality. Everyone knows this; it has become a fashionable topic in conversation and the press. But what is really being done to remedy the poor quality of what we put on our plates? Not much: People are pressed for time, canned and frozen foods are so convenient, and bad habits have become solidly rooted. Hippocrates' words are still pertinent: "When someone has fallen ill, he should change his way of living. It is clear that his way of life is bad, wholly or to a large extent, or in some way."

KNOWING FOODS

Most consumers still have an irrational attitude toward food. Their only basis of judgment is "I like it or I don't." An instinctive attraction to certain foods is still essential to the satisfaction of human needs, but in spite of the wise old saying "You should eat to live, and not live to eat," many illnesses are caused by undernourishment and overeating.

The body is a reflection of what it contains and assimilates: "Tell me what you eat and I'll tell you who you are." Man survives by eating food; everyone knows that, yet no one really knows it. We no longer know what to eat, or how, or how much. That act has lost all value. It has become nothing but a habit, a vague pleasure. Often, after eating "a good meal," we do not feel well. We are tired, poisoned by food that is too rich, and our words no longer give evidence of a clear mind.

Modern Errors

Older civilizations always attached great importance to the act of eating and considered food with respect. "He who eats without giving thanks, eats stolen food." In our time, traditions are disappearing, garbage cans are full of bread and other food, and human beings regard plants and animals as nothing but machines for satisfying their gluttony.

But all disobedience to the laws of life exacts its price. All that food eaten hastily while we think of an afternoon appointment, or casually while we discuss a business deal, completely forgetting the nutritive act itself, does more harm than good, because it is important to relax during a meal, chew properly, be calm, concentrate on the food, and avoid talking too much.

If eating became a conscious act at every meal, many stomach disorders would be eliminated. Being at table means breaking bread. A shared meal eaten in a spirit of friendship is a celebration of life in joy and mutual love. The meticulous Chinese eat with chopsticks, which are a symbol of peace, since they replace all cutting and stabbing instruments, and a symbol of the affectionate care with which the meal has been prepared, since the food is cut into small pieces beforehand and its inedible parts are removed.

Under those conditions, the act of eating

takes on a new dimension, a human dimension: It becomes a technique of relaxation, an exercise in concentration, and the satisfaction of a vital need. Through that art of living, everything regains meaning and we return to the important notions of balance and harmony. The glutton who used to stuff himself greedily and eat anything that came to hand is transformed into a calm, collected person with a clear view of his own development.

The overloaded body often suffers from excessive eating. Total or partial abstention from food benefits it by giving it a chance to cleanse itself thoroughly.*

Everyone should personally determine the amounts of protein, fat, carbohydrates, vitamins, minerals, and calories that are necessary to fulfill his physical needs, because no two people have the same bodily makeup or the same nature, or live under the same conditions. We should constantly be aware of all our thoughts, all our acts, everything. . . . "Man is not a separate entity in a universe created to serve him," writes George Ohsawa,** "born of the mud of the earth, he is the latest link in a series of beings with which he remains in symbiosis."

Yet how wasteful we are! We throw away food not because it is no longer good, but because we have too much of it or have stopped wanting it; we no longer know how to make use of leftovers. The industrialization of agriculture is responsible for the drop in the quality of food: Production is increased by larger and larger doses of fertilizer, chemical treatments, intensive irrigation, and selection of high-yield varieties. These techniques give the consumer food that looks attractive, but no longer has the taste or nutritive value of home-grown fruit and vegetables.

ARTIFICIAL SOIL

The media often speak of polluted vegetables, fruit, and meat: "Our foods are full of poisonous chemicals."

The soil itself is treated with pesticides, chemical fertilizers, and weed killers. The ani-

---

*See "Fasting" in the chapter on "How to Eat."
**See "Macrobiotics" in the chapter on "How to Eat."

mals that supply our meat are no longer fed naturally, but are given a diet that includes antibiotics, arsenic derivatives, estrogens and other hormones, enzymes, and even tranquilizers. Those who raise calves for veal on a production-line basis admit that they use chloramphenicol to lighten the color of the meat. Dosage: an injection of fifteen grams ten days before slaughtering, or three grams every other day till slaughtering.

We must also condemn the intensive use of antibiotics, which are found in varying degrees in all meats, especially beef, veal, and pork. Penicillin, aureomycin, and tetracycline, to mention only the best known, are used in massive quantities by stockbreeders.

Fish is not spared, since there are significant traces of antibiotics in the ice used for preserving it during transportation, as well as in canned and frozen fish. If to that we add the mercury, cadmium, and arsenic introduced into marine animals by the increasing pollution of the sea, not to mention the DDT that finds its way into shellfish, the growing number of poisonings is not surprising. All those substances may be invisible, but they are still present in our foods. When they are taken into the body day after day, the cumulative effect may have serious and often unforeseeable consequences. Many allergies have their origin here.

Not only animals are affected: Every year millions of tons of chemical fertilizers pollute plant life. One report lists twenty-seven pesticides that we eat every day with our vegetables, such things as parathion, heptachlor, and dichlorophenoxyacetic acid. The very names are frightening. Washing fruits and vegetables removes only part of those substances, half at most. And let us not forget those heavily used fertilizers, the nitrates: When they are transformed in the digestive system they give rise to nitrosamines, which are carcinogenic.

It is impossible to estimate the amount of those products consumed daily by a human being, and no one knows the level beyond which the body is harmed: various disorders, growth retardation, sterility, mutation of genes.

Additives are another affliction in our food: Artificial flavors and colorings are legion. In France, for example, there are eight red colorings, six yellow, three green, three blue, three black, and two orange, not counting the various shades in between. (In America the notorious Red Dye No. 2 was in use for many years until recently.) They are found everywhere, in pastry, butter, cooking oil, fruit juice, candy, canned food. . . . And our metabolism has to use all that to regenerate, or rather degenerate, our bodies!

The false need for "quick foods" is largely responsible for this state of affairs.

Take canned foods, for instance. They are convenient and easy to use, but canned vegetables and fruits have only slight nutritional value and merely give the illusion of filling the stomach. "A good canned food could be made only if it were possible to suspend the development of life for a certain period without destroying it, then let it resume its course when the food was consumed."*

The human desire to preserve food is contrary to the very principle of nature, in which everything is transformed. Not even alcohol keeps food intact. It "preserves" because it protects all foods placed in it, but it reduces them to a dead state. In both industrial and home canning, chemicals are usually employed: salicylic acid (in tomato juice, vegetables, jam), which is antagonistic to several vitamins; boric acid; sulfur dioxide, which destroys vitamin B_1.

Antioxidants are also used as preserving agents, either to prevent the darkening of fruit, fruit juice, and vegetables, or to prevent fats and oils from turning rancid. Although copper salts are not very toxic in the amounts used, they catalyze the destruction of vitamin C by oxidation. Colorings (saltpeter, cochineal, etc.) are used in preparing some sausages and canned meats, and alumina acetate is used for preserving some sausages.

Vacuum-packed foods are the most wholesome kind of preserved food. When a housewife opens a little packet of "dried soup," does she know that its main ingredient may be salt? Furthermore it is not sea salt, but sodium chloride combined with various additives (magnesium carbonate, sodium ferrocyanide, potassium ferrocyanide).

DECEPTIVE WHITENESS

Modern man is attracted by what is white, clean, and supposedly pure. He likes white bread, sugar, rice, and salt.

White bread loses most of its diastases through the removal of bran. It is therefore badly assimilated by the body and hard to digest. "Flour should contain a proportion of bran so that all the diastases (or enzymes) required for proper conversion into bread will be present. The conversion should take place slowly, with leaven. Baking should be done under conditions of perfect hygiene, at a moderate temperature which, unlike the high temperature at which white bread is baked, will not destroy vitamins and diastases."*

When chickens are fed on rice that has had its seed coats removed, they begin wasting away within a few days. If this diet is discontinued and they are fed on rice that still has its seed coats, they quickly regain their health. The seed coat obviously contains certain substances essential to life. Several Japanese scientists (Yoshida in particular) have discovered that the development of liver cancer in rats is favored when they are fed on rice with its seed coat removed, or on white flour, which no longer contains the B vitamins found in wheat. Scurvy and rickets often appear in undernourished children who eat mainly rice or corn without seed coats.

Each of us should take stock of his tastes, his real tastes, not those created by the latest advertising slogans, warped by habit, or even physiologically falsified by overindulgence in alcohol and tobacco.

We should think about our food every day. How will the human body react to all this in the long run if each of us does not become aware of the virtues of "natural eating"?

To produce food that will be a source of health, perhaps we must first respect the vitality of plants and animals. Organic farming answers this need, but it is not yet highly developed, and at present its products are bought chiefly by the affluent classes of rich countries.

We must rationally build our future. Our physical and mental health, and thus our

---

*Dr. Guierre: *Alimentation et diététique* (Le Courrier du Livre).

*Geoffroy, a French dietitian and founder of the *Vie Claire* movement.

whole development, depend on it. We must learn to select, prepare, and balance foods in accordance with each individual's needs.

Too few people realize that it is possible to be malnourished with a full stomach.

Components of Foods

Under favorable conditions, the body functions without requiring any special care. Under present conditions, to establish a new biological balance, we must learn how to nourish ourselves.

Man can draw on various sources of energy in food: glucides, protides, lipides, minerals, vitamins, trace elements. But alimentary science, which has isolated the nutritive elements, has forgotten that the human body also needs, for example, aromas, associations of tastes, and colors. It must be an organism receptive to what it eats, capable of becoming the elements themselves.

The way we eat is usually governed by habit, whereas we should require our food to be a source of energy that promotes the restoration of worn-out cells. Food should assure the body of protection, reconstruction, and activity; it should enable man to bring out the energy that is in him, rather than burdening him by giving him extra work. The notion of quality is more important than that of quantity.

We should eat only good, real foods which, by means of their infinitely complex organic combinations, give us the substances necessary for life. The makeup of those foods varies. The nourishment that a human being needs does not consist entirely of a certain ration of glucides, lipides, and protides: it also includes water, a large number of minerals and trace elements, plant cellulose, and vitamins.

A healthy human body is 58 per cent to 66 per cent water. All living tissues contain a large proportion of water. Human life requires a steady inner environment composed of what have been called vital humors: blood, lymph, interstitial fluid. The properties of these humors depend first of all on those of water.

WATER

Along with air, water is one of the elements from which the human body cannot be separat-

ed for very long. Much of the food we eat contains large amounts of water. Sweet fruits, raw salads, and fresh vegetables are about 90 per cent water, potatoes about 75 per cent. We also get water from foods that have been prepared with it, such as bread and boiled rice. On the average, the human body takes in about two quarts of water a day in food and drink. Oxidation of the hydrogen in food also produces what is known as metabolic water: about ten fluid ounces daily. About a pint is eliminated by the lungs and the skin, about three fluid ounces in excrement, and about three pints in urine. But these quantities are highly variable. In dry, warm air, pulmonary evaporation increases. Diarrhea and vomiting cause significant losses of water.

Water is necessary for our survival. If you live in the country, drink water from a spring or a well (after making sure it is not polluted by seepage). In cities and towns, tap water, even if it is not harmful, has an unpleasant taste. Use it, boiled, to make tea or herbal infusions. Or drink mineral water, preferably between meals.

MINERALS

The human body is made up not only of elements belonging to organic chemistry, but also of minerals, including metals and metalloids, acids and bases, positive and negative electrons.

Calcium is the mineral found most abundantly in the human body. It contributes to the coagulation of the blood, the permeability of the cells, and the strength of bones and teeth. In a crystallized form, it combines with phosphorus in bone and tooth cells. The daily need is about 0.8 gram. It is absorbed in the form of CaH ions through the presence of vitamin D and the action of the sex and parathyroid hormones. But bone and tooth calcium is in constant movement. Every day it is rejected by osteolysis and absorbed by osteogenesis.

Calcium contributes to certain processes that regulate the nerves and all the muscles, including the heart. To be assimilated, it requires the presence of *phosphorus.* Otherwise only a very small amount of it enters the bones. A diet rich in dairy foods (containing both calcium and phosphorus) and fruit (vitamin D) eliminates the risk of decalcification.

Sodium chloride (common salt) is the basic element in extracellular fluid. Intracellular fluid is rich in *potassium.* The good condition of the cells depends on a balance between sodium and potassium. If that balance is disrupted, the cellular membranes cannot maintain the metabolic processes normally; certain substances no longer succeed in penetrating the cells, while others escape from them. Sodium and potassium are not only found in the body in the state of a liquid solution: their proportion in bone is 44 per cent; in cartilage, 11 percent. They also enter into the composition of the endocrine and digestive glands.

Interaction between sodium and potassium underlies the excitability of nerves. Potassium ions leave the inside of a neuron while sodium ions enter it; then the original state is restored until the next excitation. The sodium-potassium relation also plays an important part in the mechanical activity of the heart.

Except where there are abnormal losses of salt, as in hemorrhaging or diarrhea, the amount of it contained in food is sufficient. Normally, any lowering of the amount of salt in the blood is limited automatically, because the interstitial fluid acts as a reserve. It is not necessary to add more salt to your food than is needed to satisfy your taste.

Iron is the main, irreplaceable substance which enables hemoglobin to pick up oxygen in the lungs and carry it to all parts of the body. It also enters into the composition of bone marrow, the liver, and the spleen. It participates in bioelectrical and biochemical phenomena. To be utilized by the body it must encounter trace elements: copper, manganese, cobalt.

When the amount of iron is inadequate, the blood is affected first and general anemia results. Then all tissues are insufficiently oxygenated. A slow poisoning begins. The appearance of cancer has been linked to a deficiency of iron in tissues.

Sulfur, a metalloid, enters into the composition of many organic chemicals essential to a number of important functions. For example, sulfur is present in the glutamic acid required by the nervous and cerebral system, and in glycine, an amino acid that plays a part in muscular activity. It contributes to the formation of bones, teeth, and tendons by aiding the assimilation of calcium. A depurative, an antiseptic, and a powerful disinfectant, it combats intestinal infections, diseases of the skin and bronchia, and hardening of tissue, the main cause of arteriosclerosis.

Magnesium is present in the cells of bone and such tissues as skin, muscle, viscera, and the cerebral system. It participates in the metabolism of other vital minerals such as phosphorus and calcium. A key element in the general metabolism of minerals, magnesium is necessary to reactions of muscular contraction and makes possible the action of the white corpuscles. Regular absorption of it enables the body to avoid many disorders.

In preparing daily menus, we should be concerned not so much with the amounts of various substances to be absorbed every day as with seeing to it that all seven of the "basic minerals" are present.

Good foods contain:

Potassium: fresh fruit and vegetables.
Calcium: wheat germ, chocolate, cabbage, citrus fruits, apples, dates, milk, cheese, certain mineral waters, red wine.
Phosphorus: giblets, meat, fish, eggs, milk and other dairy foods, wheat germ, dried fruit.
Magnesium: almonds, hazelnuts, dates, dried apricots, prunes, wheat germ, whole-wheat bread, beets, spinach, lettuce, bananas, raspberries, figs, milk, cheese, honey.
Sodium: salt, spinach, celery, leeks, carrots, parsley.
Sulfur: meat, milk, mustard, garlic, lentils, beans, parsley, watercress, spinach, cocoa, carrots, cabbage, rice, apples.
Iron: wheat, watercress, spinach, carrots, hazelnuts, almonds, onions, leeks, cabbage, lentils, corn, wholewheat bread.

To restore general harmony, it is good to take mineral salts over a period of several days from time to time. The body needs to receive mineral substances simultaneously. Science is barely beginning to explore the complex relations that unite minerals at the molecular level within the human body. There is a real synergism among minerals; that is, one does not act without another.

Some metals and metalloids are present in the body in minute quantities and are thus known as trace elements. They are catalysts necessary for proper functioning of the body. Without them, cellular metabolism is disturbed and certain tissues cannot be formed or carry out their functions. Their presence is essential to growth and life.

Among the trace elements, we can mention *iodine,* a metalloid required for the functioning of the thyroid gland. It decongests the lymph glands and augments cellular metabolism. An antiscorbutic and decongestant, it combats bronchitis, rickets, obesity, and skin diseases. It is contained chiefly in fish, marine plants, seaweed, unrefined salt, watercress, garlic, green beans, onions, spinach, asparagus, cabbage, honey, and egg yolk.

Copper plays a certain part in anemia; *bromine* is said to affect the pituitary gland; *nickel* helps to balance the liver and the pancreas; *fluorine,* a veritable mineral vitamin, aids in the fixation of phosphorus and sulfur; *cobalt* activates enzymes; *manganese* is found in enzymatic systems whose deficiency would prevent growth and cause debility and sterility.

To procure the trace elements, it is necessary to eat foods that contain them (fruit, vegetables, dairy foods, eggs, and others). Honey contains silicon, manganese, chromium, aluminum, nickel, lead, tin, titanium, and zinc.

Sea water contains ninety-two elements and a great wealth of living iodine. Its magnesium plays a part in calcium metabolism; its potassium is a constituent factor of hemoglobin, which is essential to the activity of the heart. If you live near the sea it is good to drink half a glass of sea water with a little lemon juice each morning for a three-week period every three months.

FERMENTS

Digestion requires the presence of ferments to carry out its successive conversions. Some of them, the diastases, dissolve food; others serve as catalysts; and enzymes complete the conversion of food, direct it to the right places, and fix it there. Some of these ferments are secreted by the body, others come from foods, but each has a specific property.

Ferments and enzymes are found in all fresh, raw foods—plant foods (fruit and vegetables), animal foods (eggs and dairy products), mixed foods (honey)—that are still in their initial state, without having undergone any changes other than natural fermentation, as in cheese, yogurt, and sauerkraut. But all methods of preservation alter ferments, partly destroying them by heat or neutralizing them by cold. To be assimilated, a sterilized or even pasteurized food requires the body to use its own reserve of ferments. A food preserved by freezing no longer has its original bacteria and the activity of its ferments is arrested. When it is thawed and returns to its normal temperature, excessive fermentation takes place, quickly followed by putrefaction. Dessication (powdered milk, dehydrated vegetables) causes food to lose many of its useful properties.

Assimilation of food may be facilitated by the presence of aromatics. These are plants that give off a strong smell which comes from essential oils: garlic, chives, fennel, chervil, parsley, sage, savory, tarragon, scallions, ginger. They stimulate the endocrine and salivary glands, aid in maintaining intestinal bacteria, and promote proper functioning of the liver. They are powerful disinfectants. They stimulate the taste buds and olfactory nerves, aiding good salivary and gastric secretion. Aromatics accelerate the secretion of the endocrine glands. But the essential oils they contain have some very volatile ingredients. In cooked foods, use them at the end of the cooking process. Use them often in preparing salads and other raw foods.

ACID-BASE BALANCE OF THE BLOOD

In the human body, the blood's pH, or coefficient of the power of releasing hydrogen ions, is a factor on which vitality and resistance to disease depend. To assure its proper functioning, the right balance between acids and bases must be maintained. Excess acidity of the blood weakens the body and favors infection. The blood should be richer in alkalis than in acids. A diet rich in sweet fruits, green vegetables, grain, and dairy foods, without an excess of animal protides, permits a perfect balance.

A number of illnesses are caused by the introduction into the body of too many foods that are strong acidifiers and weak alkalizers. The diet should always be rich in bases. To heal the intestines, eliminate acid foods and sugar, which burn intestinal bacteria and paralyze the parasympathetic nervous system.

Among plant foods rich in bases are fruits (except nuts and peanuts), vegetables (except leguminous plants such as peas and beans), potatoes, and whole cereals. Some acidifying foods are leguminous plants, tomatoes, nuts, peanuts, incomplete cereals, coffee, tea, cocoa, oils, meat, fats, cheese, egg white, and sugar.

VITAMINS

Minute amounts of these organic substances are essential to life. A deficiency of vitamins can cause various disorders and lesions. To live in good health it is not enough to take many vitamins in well-balanced doses; a little pill can never replace a meal or make up for lack of vitamins, since they can act in small doses only in combination with foods that promote their assimilation.

All vitamins come from plants: vegetables, fruit, grain, fodder. They are found in certain meats (brains and liver) and in milk and eggs, but they were already present in the plants eaten by the animals. Solar energy is the basis of earthly energy and the mainspring of all life. Plants receive it, accumulate it, and pass it on to the human beings and animals whose lives depend on it.

Certain substances used in preparing foods hinder the action of vitamins. Egg white (in excessive amounts) and paraffin prevent carotene from being transformed into vitamin A.

Vitamins are probably produced by microbes in the soil before being assimilated by plants and then by animals and man, who stores them in his heart, liver, kidneys, and glands.

The action of vitamins is specific. An excess of vitamin C cannot compensate for a deficiency of a B vitamin. Except for vitamin C, vitamins resist heat; they are not destroyed by cooking or the sterilization of food in the canning process. Complete and rapid freezing also preserves them. The body should get all the vitamins it needs from food and the environment. It is useless to take large quantities of synthetically produced vitamins. They came into the blood too suddenly and can no longer act as catalysts.

Each vitamin has its own particular function.

Vitamin A exerts a certain influence on the acid-base balance of the blood, helps to protect the eyes and maintain their functioning, balances the sex hormones, and wards off certain diseases. It contributes to the nourishment of bone, cartilage, blood vessels, the resistant parts of the digestive organs, and the skin. It also helps to retard the aging process by keeping the skin and mucous membranes in good condition.

Provitamin A (carotene) prevents miscarriage and hardening of the cornea of the eye. It combats infection, soothes menstrual pain, and prevents dry skin and mucous membranes, brittle fingernails, and dull hair.

Vitamin B$_1$ combats neuritis and beriberi and regulates the balance of the nervous system. It aids enzymes and ferments in enabling cells to absorb oxygen. Its presence is necessary in the oxidation of carbohydrates. The richer a person's diet is in sugar and starch, the more vitamin B$_1$ he needs. It is essential for diabetics. It also favors growth in young children and stimulates external and internal glandular secretions.

Vitamin B$_2$ participates in the respiration of tissues. It is necessary to the life of certain cells of the nervous system, the respiratory system, and the retina. It plays an important part in the conversion and assimilation of sugars.

Vitamin B$_5$ stimulates and protects the skin, fingernails, body hair, mucous membranes, and liver cells.

Vitamin B6 regularizes the metabolism of tissues, the liver, the nervous system, and the skin. It contributes to the formation of hemoglobin and enables the body to assimilate sulfur.

Vitamin B12 combats anemia and invigorates the heart.

Vitamin C combats scurvy and infections. It favors the development of bone, teeth, hair, and the crystalline lens of the eye. Its presence permits the cohesion of cells in organic tissues, stimulates the functioning of the adrenal glands, and increases the body's resistance.

Vitamin D is the antirickets vitamin. It increases the amount of calcium and phosphorus in the blood and combats bone deficiencies, dental caries, and growth disorders.

Vitamin E, the fertility vitamin, acts primarily on the genital organs and the nervous and muscular functions. A deficiency or absence of it causes sterility in men and women, impotence, certain kinds of eczema, and varicose ulcers with sclerosis.

Vitamin H combats seborrhea and neutralizes the toxic effects of food.

Vitamin K makes possible the balance and coagulation of the blood. (Certain bacterial fermentations in the colon maintain a source of vitamin K in human beings.) Newborn babies are lacking in it; the formula given to a bottle-fed baby should therefore include a little orange, tomato, or green vegetable juice. Vitamin K acts in the presence of bile in the alimentary canal.

Vitamin PP plays an important part in cell respiration and stomach secretion. It accelerates growth, promotes good functioning of the nervous system, assures vascular permeability, invigorates the blood vessels, and makes them supple.

Vitamin M is necessary for the formation of white corpuscles and bone marrow.

Vitamin V protects the digestive mucous membranes.

Vitamins are not foods in themselves, but they are necessary as catalysts. Each has its own chemical formula. Small amounts of them regulate the various metabolisms. A deficiency of them is easier to discern than their specific action. The amount of vitamins in a plant depends on the way it is grown and its degree of maturity at the time of harvest.

Here are the main sources that provide you with those essential substances:

VITAMIN A
Green vegetables, carrots, tomatoes, potatoes, butter, cheese, egg yolk, summer milk, honey, oleaginous fruits, vegetable oils, garlic, onions, grain, lentils, wild mushrooms, lemons, oranges, apricots, turnips, dried fruits.
Daily requirement: 0.5 mg. (All daily requirements given are approximate.)

VITAMIN B1
Husk and germ of grains, nuts, dried vegetables, summer milk, honey, eggs.
Daily requirement: 1.5 mg.

VITAMIN B2
Germ of grains, leaves of vegetables, summer milk, honey, eggs.
Daily requirement: 0.7 to 1.8 mg.

VITAMIN B5
Soybeans, bran, cabbage.

VITAMIN B6
Butter, liver, beef, milk, eggs, germ of grains, leguminous plants.
Daily requirement: 2 mg.

VITAMIN B12
Wheat germ, whole rice, germinated barley, fresh plant foods, yeast, liver.
Daily requirement: 0.001 mg.

VITAMIN C
Tomatoes, spinach, lettuce, red cabbage, oranges, lemons, aromatics (parsley, chervil, tarragon, etc.), watercress, potatoes, onions, radishes, summer milk, honey.
It disappears from stale vegetables.
Daily requirement: 75 mg for adults, 90 mg for adolescents.

VITAMIN D
Olive oil, green vegetables, sunlight, fish oils, herring.
Daily requirement: 0.25 mg.

VITAMIN E
Wheat germ, whole flour, lettuce, watercress, vegetable oils, eggs, honey, onions. It can also be obtained by synthesis.
Daily requirement: 1 mg; 2 to 5 for a pregnant woman.

VITAMIN F
Olive oil.

VITAMIN K
Tomatoes, oranges, green vegetables, cauliflower, carrots, grain, liver, honey.
Daily requirement: 0.1 to 1 mg.

VITAMIN M
Wheat germ, brewer's yeast, liver.
Daily requirement: 1 to 4 mg.

VITAMIN PP
Pimentoes, buckwheat, oranges, eggs.

VITAMIN V
Certain raw plant foods: cabbage, celery, lettuce, tomatoes, carrots, bananas. It is destroyed by heat.

Glucides

Glucides are carbohydrates or certain substances containing carbohydrates. Chemically, they are a combination of carbon and water: $Cm(H_2O)n$. They include -oses, whose molecules are of the glucose type, and -osides, each of whose molecules combines several -oses, with elimination of water. In food, there are the directly assimilable simple sugars: glucose (contained in grapes), fructose (in fruit and honey), galactose (in certain plants), mannose (in certain roots); and the compound sugars: sucrose (in sugar cane and sugar beets), lactose (in milk), maltose (in converted starch). These compound sugars must be converted into sucrase, lactase, and maltase before being utilized.

The main sources of glucides are sugars and fruits, grains, leguminous plants and dried legumes, tubers, vegetables, and mushrooms.

Digestion of starch begins with the amylase in saliva (which means we must chew our food well) and continues with the amylases of the pancreatic juice and the jejunal epithelium. Glucides are absorbed by the intestine almost solely in the form of -oses. Absorption begins in the duodenum and ends in the first three feet of the jejunum. Glucose and lactose are totally absorbed there. Since starch is hard to digest raw, it needs to go through a phase of predigestion, either by cooking or the addition of malt, almond paste, or almond milk. Sucrose, mal-tose, and glucose tend to slow intestinal transit a little, whereas lactose and fructose accelerate it.

The final stage of digestion of sugars and starch yields glucose, which passes through the intestinal wall by osmosis. It is then incorporated into the blood and conveyed to the liver through the portal vein. Its presence in the blood is always maintained at the same concentration. A surplus of it can be used for building up reserves of glycogen in the liver, or of fat in fatty tissue. This may cause obesity if the successive reactions have not taken place normally, because of a shortage of vitamin B_1, for example.

Without ferments, digestion is not possible. When they are fresh and raw, all plant and animal foods (fruit, eggs, vegetables, dairy foods, honey, etc.) have ferments and enzymes provided they are in their original state or have undergone only conversion by natural fermentation (certain cheeses, yogurt, sauerkraut).

It is not enough to supply the body with nutrients: protides, lipides, glucides; the body must also be capable of metabolizing them (converting them organically). And it should also be pointed out that when all the functions of digestion and assimilation are properly performed, lipides can be converted into glucides and even into protides.

All the energy used by living beings comes from the energy that the earth receives from the sun. In the body, transfer of energy in the course of conversion of glucides gives rise to a release of ionized hydrogen which combines with other elements, for each of the billions of cells in the body must breathe and constantly carry out those conversions in order to live. All this metabolism is the work of microscopic bodies: the mitochondria.

SUGARS AND FRUITS

Sugars are carbohydrates. But the sugar that the blood contains and transports from the liver to the muscles, the sugar that supplies the body with energy, is not the sucrose found in commercial sugar, which requires a conversion yielding a mixture of glucose and fructose that exists in a pure state in fruits and honey.

A large number of plants contain sucrose in a natural state. The sucrose sold to the consumer comes from sugar beets or sugar cane. Beet sugar contains many impurities, but cane sugar can be consumed in the form of molasses without even being refined.

Commercial sugar undergoes an operation known as clarifying, in which the crystals are rinsed by a spray of hot water. The law even allows sugar to be treated with bluing, to make it look whiter. Should we prefer brown or white sugar, cane or beet sugar? Cane sugar is more natural and brown sugar is superior to white, from a biological viewpoint.

Although it is warming and invigorating, sugar is an incomplete food which must be combined with other substances. Excessive intake of it may lead to many diseases. Commercial sugar is only a moderately utilizable seasoning. It should be used mainly in cooking and in small amounts. Traditionally, sweetened preparations have combined sugar with nitrogenous, fatty, or farinaceous substances. In cakes, for example, sugar is mixed with flour, eggs, butter, and such foods as almonds.

Commercial sugar should be avoided as much as possible, since it contains neither protective elements nor any of the ferments necessary for its utilization by the body. It is better to eat natural sugars such as honey, or the sugar contained in fruit.

Fruit is developed after the blossom is formed. It is rich in nutritive substances. Because of the seeds it contains, it has been compared to the egg of the world, the symbol of origin. In traditions all over the world—the fruit of the tree of the knowledge of good and evil in Genesis, the fig tree under which Buddha sat, the one that cooled Jesus with its shade—fruit or the fruit tree has taken on a rich symbolic meaning, representing such things as pleasure, a yearning for longevity, prosperity, and wisdom.

There are several kinds of fruits: amyloid, with a starch base (chestnuts, bananas); oleaginous, with varying amounts of fat (almonds, cacao, avocados, pine nuts, walnuts); aqueous and sweet (apricots, pineapples, figs).

Eaten raw or even cooked, fruits contain a great deal of vitamin C, varying amounts of the B vitamins (oleaginous), and vitamin A and carotene (apricots, peaches). Their phosphorus-calcium balance is excellent, especially when they are raw, but the acidity of some of them eliminates their contribution of calcium. All fruits are rich in iron, especially oleaginous and dried fruits. Cooking destroys some acidity, but certain fruits, such as plums and apricots, are much more acid when they are cooked. Adding sugar to them masks their acid taste but does not destroy their acidity.

Because of their richness in cellulose, all fruits are excellent stimulants of intestinal circulation. But since sending ripe fruit to market involves a risk of losses, the fruit in grocery stores has been picked green and contains less sugar than if it had ripened naturally.

We ordinarily eat fruit at the end of a meal, but it is digested better when it is eaten alone. It requires more gastric juice than cooked or already converted food, so chew your fruit properly. Do not mix sweet and acid fruits in the same meal.

Fresh fruit is both a food and a remedy.* It is excellent for human beings because of its trace elements, minerals, sugars, vitamins, and water. One cannot do without it very long without risking a slow but sure degeneration of the body.

---

*See "Fruits that Heal" in the chapter on "Healing by Plants."

GRAINS

Glucides are also contained in grains. The history of mankind is closely bound up with that of grains. They have always been used for coming to the aid of populations suffering from famine. Archaeologists have found remains of cakes made from millet and other seeds of wild plants dating from the Paleolithic period. Twenty-five hundred years before Christ, the Egyptians knew how to make wheat bread. Man takes 30 per cent to 50 per cent of his calories from grains. They are more than 50 per cent starch and contain a rather large proportion of protein.

You should eat some of those rich, economical foods every day to prevent deficiencies and make sure your body is properly balanced. Each grain has its own particular properties, but priority must go to wheat in all its forms: leavened whole-wheat bread, whole flour, whole-wheat pasta, pilpil (crushed wheat), couscous, cakes of various kinds.

Wheat seems to be the best balanced and harmonized grain for people in temperate zones. All the minerals existing in the human body have been found in wheat.

Wheat should be used as nearly whole as possible. Experiments have shown that bran contains an agent which neutralizes the cancer-causing action of certain products. It also contains substances that give protection against many disorders, whereas white flour probably favors the action of typhus. By eliminating bran, we deprive ourselves of an important source of silica, which enters into the composition of lung tissue and wards off tuberculosis.

Wheat also contains some particularly important trace elements—zinc, iodine, manganese, arsenic, copper—which assure the success of essential operations of conversion, assimilation, fixation, and utilization. Furthermore, wheat contains vitamins B_1, B_2, B_{12}, K, E, D, PP, and traces of carotene (provitamin A).

In order for wheat to retain all its original elements, it must be grown organically, in soil enriched only with humus and compost, without the use of chemicals.

Aside from bread, whole wheat can be used crushed (pilpil), cooked (boiled or in flat cakes), or raw and finely ground (muesli, pastry, gnocchi). The grain of wheat is even more nutritious when it has sprouted. Its calcium increases from 45 to 72 mg, its phosphorus from 423 to 1050 mg, its magnesium from 133 to 343 mg. Sprouting also gives rise to the formation of vitamin C and activates certain diastases that were already present in a potential state. Because of this predigestion effect, sprouted wheat is a fortifying food that can be readily digested even by a delicate stomach.

To make wheat sprout, place it in a container with just enough water to cover it and leave it for about a day. The next day, rinse it and put it in a dish without adding water. On the third day, begin the operation again. When the sprouts appear, the wheat is ready for use, but it will not keep for more than a day. Sprouted wheat is the source of wheat germ oil, a veritable superfood that contains all the fat-soluble vitamins and the vitamin complexes of cerebral and sexual activity.

Take one to three spoonfuls of sprouted wheat in other foods such as salad or soup, or between meals, every day for a period of three weeks every two or three months.

Bread

Wheat and rye have long been eaten chiefly in the form of bread, yet bread consumption has tended to decline steadily since 1914, however. White bread, made with degerminated wheat, has lost the appetizing appearance and delicious taste it once had. Today, wheat is selected for its yield per acre rather than its quality. The yeast used by bakers is no longer natural leaven, which causes fermentation in which proteins are broken down and produce valuable amino acids. About 70 per cent of the flour used in white bread is sifted. Too much sifting deprives the grain of the husk that contains nearly all its vitamin B. And the proportion of gluten increases toward the outside of the grain, the richest part being that next to the bran.

Whole wheat bread is now coming back into favor. It is bread made with the product of grinding the whole wheat kernel (bran, endosperm, germ). Unfortunately the consumer is often not adequately informed and must be satisfied with a few vague indications when he buys. Whole wheat bread should be made with leaven and whole grain that has been stone ground (not passed through rapidly rotating metal cylinders, which heat it), and baked in an oven heated by wood, steam, or electricity. If it is made properly, it will keep for about a week.

Such bread has great biological virtues: It is a complete, natural, vitalizing food with important amounts of vitamins B_1, B_2 and E. The presence of bran makes it stimulating to the intestine. But it should be chewed well and eaten in the right quantities. For someone who has been in the habit of eating half a pound of white bread a day, changing abruptly to half a pound of whole wheat bread is madness! The desirable amount of bread varies with individual needs and tolerances and the time when it is eaten.

You can also make your own bread from time to time.

The "daily bread" of ancient times is made with a tablespoonful of olive oil, a teaspoonful of honey, two inches of salt, and two cups of water. Mix these ingredients, beat vigorously, and add whole flour until the dough no longer sticks to your fingers. Shape it into small, flat cakes. Put them on an oiled metal sheet, leave them for an hour, then bake them in a very hot oven for ten minutes.

To make light pastry and good bread, use leaven rather than yeast. Make a ball of dough, following the recipe above. Leave it in a basin, covered with a cloth, for three days in a place where the temperature is about 60° to 65°. The dough will become soft and swollen with gas, with a winy smell. Knead it with two tablespoonfuls of whole flour. Let it rest two days. It will then be ready for use as leaven. Always keep a bowlful of it for making more. At 50° or less, leaven will keep for five days; at 60°, only three days. If a trace of mildew appears, it must be carefully removed.

To make your own whole wheat bread, put the leaven and a tablespoonful of sea salt in a large basin containing a pint and a half of nonchlorinated water. Stir to dissolve part of the leaven and the salt. Add two pounds of flour, stirring with a wooden spoon, then one pound, kneading with your fingers. When all the flour has been worked into the dough, knead it for another five minutes. Dust the outside of the ball with flour. Let it work and swell for eighteen hours at a temperature of about 60°. Just before baking, knead it again with a handful of flour. Separate the dough into several pieces and put them into floured molds. Bake them in a hot oven for about twenty minutes. Take the loaves out of the molds and put them on a metal grating after wrapping them in cloth to keep them from cooling too fast, which makes the crust too hard. Part of the wheat flour can be replaced with rye flour (up to two thirds) or barley, oat, or buckwheat flour (up to one third). Baking time will be increased by five minutes. The crust should turn dark brown.

Rice

Rice is the main element in the diet of about half the people on earth. It grows in a warm, moist climate. Before rice reaches the consumer, the hulls are removed from the untreated grains, known as rough rice or paddy; next, the seed coats are removed, then the grains are polished until they are smooth, and finally they are coated with starch or glucose and talc. This process changes rice into an incomplete food. As with wheat, the proportion of protides, vitamins, and minerals is higher in the bran. Brown (unpolished) rice is therefore a more complete food than white (polished and coated) rice. In fact, polishing causes rice to lose all its B vitamins.

Rich in starch (80 percent), white rice is about 7 per cent protides, but even in rough rice the protides are poor in certain essential amino acids (cystine and lysine), minerals, and B vitamins. This explains the frequency of beriberi among people whose diet consists largely of polished rice. Although brown rice contains less sulfur and iron than wheat, it has all the same minerals except copper. It also contains carotene and vitamins B_1, B_{12}, and PP. Rich in carbohydrates, it is energizing and very digestible. It can be eaten alone or with dried fruit (raisins, dates, figs) before strenuous work, without producing a feeling of sluggishness. Less rich in minerals than wheat, it can be eaten in large quantities without risk of fouling the body. It is excellent for people with arteriosclerosis. It also tends to lower blood pressure and is a natural laxative.

Brown rice requires careful preparation to keep its cooked grains from sticking together, and to make it a dish that is pleasing to the eye and the palate. First rinse it in cold water, then place it in twice its volume of water, with a pinch of salt. When the water boils, let it simmer on low heat, with a lid on the pot, for about an hour, until the water has evaporated. Take off the lid and briefly turn up the heat. When little puffs of vapor rise from the surface and the rice gives off a slight burning smell, it is ready to eat. If, at the bottom of the pot, there is rice that has turned yellow, do not throw it away. It is rich in minerals and both nourishing and tasty.

Corn

Corn originated in America, where it was the basic food of many Indian tribes before the European conquest. It is now grown all over the world. It regulates the thyroid gland and slows metabolism and oxidation. It occupies an important place in the diet of people who live in regions with a warm climate. The corn grown in those regions has large and sweet kernels.

A ripe corn kernel is about 7 per cent protides, 3 per cent fat, and 70 per cent starch. Its protein lacks certain essential amino acids, but it is rich in carbohydrates and contains many nitrogenous, fatty, and sugared substances, as well as potash and phosphoric acid. It is a good energizer.

Corn flour does not contain the seed coat, the proteinic layer, or usually the germ. It must be used fresh, since it spoils quickly. Corn favors the formation of fat. It should not be used as a basic food in the diet because it lacks two important substances: tryptophan (an essential amino acid) and vitamin PP.

Rye

In our time, when arteriosclerosis is so common, rye bread should be eaten more often. But since rye flour lacks cohesiveness and elasticity, wheat flour is usually mixed with it in the amount of 25 per cent to 30 per cent. Good rye bread has a distinctive aroma and a strong, rather bitter, and slightly acid taste. It is composed of 6 per cent to 8 per cent protides, 42 per cent to 47 per cent sugar, and vitamins equal to those of wheat, except for vitamin PP. People who lead sedentary lives or show signs of arteriosclerosis should alternate wheat bread with rye bread, which favors circulation, helps to keep the blood vessels supple, and combats fouling of the body.

Rye is a cooling food. It provides energy and helps to build body tissue because of its carbohydrates and nitrogenous substances. It can be eaten boiled or used in making gingerbread. The best gingerbread is made with rye and honey.

Buckwheat

This nutritious grain grows well in poor soil, yet it contains more calcium than wheat does, and it also has magnesium, phosphorus, and fluorine. The most valuable amino acids have been identified in its protein. Because of its vitamin PP, it strengthens the blood vessels and improves their permeability.

Buckwheat flour is 60 per cent starch, 10 per cent albumin, and 8 per cent fat, and has all the mineral wealth of the seed. Buckwheat is a complete, nutritious food which balances the nervous system.

Millet

Millet is often neglected in Western countries, yet it is rich in phosphorus, magnesium, iron, silica, fluorine, manganese, and vitamins A and B. It is an excellent food for people suffering from weakness, nervous depression, or mental fatigue. Well supplied with vitamin A, it has a reputation for preventing miscarriages, correcting deficiencies in pregnant women, and strengthening the body's natural defenses.

Oats

With a composition similar to that of wheat, oats have important nutritive properties. They contain many minerals (sodium, iron, calcium, magnesium, phosphorus), vitamins B_1, B_2, and PP, carotene, and traces of vitamin D. They also have a stimulating substance which is said to contain a growth hormone.

Oats seem to act as an accelerator of the thyroid functions. They stimulate and accelerate metabolism (which is valuable in winter) and contain a hormone similar to folliculin that is said to combat sterility and impotence. They are excellent for diabetics. They are used in the form of groats (in which the kernels are broken but not ground fine) and oatmeal (which is 66 per cent glucides, 16 per cent protides, 6 per cent lipides, and contains a number of minerals). It would be advantageous to replace your morning coffee with oat flakes (oatmeal or muesli).

Barley

Besides its nutritive value, barley has significant cooling powers. It contains all the minerals found in wheat. Its vitamins B_1, B_2, and PP permit better utilization of food, and its carotene favors rejuvenation of tissue. Its phosphorus makes it a valuable food, particularly for the nerve cells. It also assures good use of calcium by the bones.

It is sometimes used in the form of flakes and flour. Its sprouted kernels form the malt that converts starch into maltose. Malt flour, which invigorates the stomach, contains vitamin B_{12}. If you have difficulty digesting starch, add malt flour to starchy foods a few minutes before serving and leave them on very low heat. Use one heaping spoonful per portion.

Roasted sprouted barley is used as a coffee substitute. Barley soup has good properties. Eat it to alleviate inflammatory diseases of the digestive system or urinary passages, or to drain the bile ducts.

LEGUMINOUS PLANTS AND DRIED LEGUMES

These include such foods as dried beans, lentils, chick-peas, soybeans, broad beans, and sesame seeds. They grow easily, without exhausting the soil; in fact, they enrich it. But they should be eaten young and fresh. They are poor in fat (except for soybeans and sesame seeds) and rich in protides, phosphorus, and magnesium; broad beans and lentils contain a great deal of iron.

Dried legumes are very nourishing for strong stomachs and intestines, but they are hard to digest. They produce purine and uric acid abundantly. Soak them in water several hours before cooking, cook them for about two hours, and chew them carefully. Even when they are digested well, they seem to disrupt the body, and if they are eaten in overly large amounts they may cause outbreaks of rheumatism, skin diseases, or liver congestion. They should not be eaten by people suffering from rheumatism, liver ailments, arthritis, or colitis.

When peas are picked in early spring, their composition is similar to that of green vegetables. In summer they become farinaceous. Fresh, small peas are naturally sweet and are tolerated by everyone.

We should be careful about the amount of dried legumes we eat. Lentils are the least fermentable and most digestible. Broad beans, either raw with salt or cooked, are a pleasant dish; chick-peas, well cooked and chewed, are easy to digest; soybeans (the basic food, along with rice and fish, in northern Asia) are very nutritious. Combined with rice, soybeans are an almost complete food (12 per cent to 24 per cent fat, 35 per cent protein, 12 per cent to 32 per cent glucides); they contain sugar and two kinds of protein.

Split peas are dried peas with their outer coverings removed. They produce large volumes of intestinal gases and are highly indigestible. In general, it is better not to eat them.

Sesame is widely grown in India. It favors endocrine balance and is a symbol of longevity and strength. Rich in proteins and amino acids, it also contains vitamin B_{12}. Its seeds are rich in fat.

TUBERS

Potatoes, Jerusalem artichokes, and manioc are 17 per cent to 23 per cent sugar. The edible part is a swelling of the root in which the plant accumulates provisions.

The potato is a mass of starch in water, rich in ascorbic acid and potash. An energizing food poor in protein, it is better for health when it is boiled or baked without being peeled (it then keeps its salts and ascorbic acid). It is 77 per cent water and 2 per cent protides, but the biological value of its main protein, tuberin, is equal to that of animal proteins. It has a good phosphorus-calcium balance, and contains a great deal of potassium (0.45 per cent) and vitamins C, B, and PP. The potato is a valuable food whose discovery has contributed toward eliminating famines in regions with a poor soil and rainy climate. It is easy to digest if not combined with indigestible fats. By weight, it contains fifteen times as much vitamin C as meat, half as much as lemon juice, and as much as tomato juice.

The composition of the Jerusalem artichoke is similar to that of the potato. It contains less sugar, but both have about the same calorific value. Rich in insulin, the Jerusalem artichoke can be eaten by diabetics. Its taste recalls that of the artichoke. If Jerusalem artichokes are combined with dried legumes, the deficiencies of the former are corrected by the concentrations of the latter.

Potatoes and Jerusalem artichokes, both farinaceous, can never replace grain. Remember that in energy and nutrition, four ounces of grain are equal to a pound of potatoes.

VEGETABLES

These foods are relatively poor in glucides and proteins, but rich in various minerals, water-soluble vitamins, and provitamin A. Containing cellulose that cannot be attacked by the digestive enzymes in the human body, they stimulate intestinal movement. Depending on the specific vegetable, different parts of the plant are used: root, stem, flower, or fruit.*

As a general rule, white vegetables are less nourishing than green, yellow, brown, or red ones. Colors marks the presence of chlorophyll or the pigments by which the plant absorbs the solar energy that enables it to fix carbon dioxide from the air. From carbon dioxide and water vapor, chlorophyll synthesizes sugars and starches. The chlorophyll in raw cabbage, for example, in association with iron, makes production of hemoglobin possible. Raw cabbage is thus a good remedy for anemia.

Two important sources of energy, among others, govern the body: the energy that results from the conversion of various foods and the solar energy stored by chlorophyll. This stored solar energy is released as soon as the food makes contact with the taste buds. Green vegetables are able to transmit their energy to us even before digestion. All green plants possess that valuable property. Fruits also pass through the chlorophyll stage in which they receive the solar energy they accumulate until they are ripe.

But that energy should be recovered from fresh, raw plants, because the heat of cooking dislodges chlorophyll as it does enzymes. Chlorophyll is necessary to life. Even plants without chlorophyll, such as mushrooms, can live only if they attach themselves to the roots of plants with green leaves or use humus that comes from decayed leaves.

MUSHROOMS

They are up to 80 per cent water. Their nutritional value comes from the presence of nitrogen (4 per cent), sugar (10 per cent), and cellulose. They are nourishing and digestible if they are not accompanied by too much fat or aromatics.

If you pick mushrooms yourself, be sure to examine them carefully, Throw away those that look old and in bad condition, because the putrefaction of mushrooms causes toxic substances to appear. You must also know that each edible species has a corresponding poisonous species with essentially the same appearance. It is wise to dig up a mushroom to make sure it has no volva or bulb at the base of its stalk.

Eat mushrooms the day they are picked, or the next day, cooked in a little fresh oil. You can also dry them in sunlight and open air, or preserve them in jars.

Remember that the symptoms of mushrooms poisoning do not appear until about twenty hours after eating, and that by then it is futile to wash out the stomach.

Picking mushrooms will acquaint you with the charm of autumn woods veiled in mist and dripping with rainwater. There is a dimension to be discovered in mushrooms. A subtle relation has always existed between them and mankind. What are they? A storm brings rain, and lightning places the seed of the sky in the open earth. The next morning, a magic population of bright domes rises from the moss. Behind the magic of forms there is another magic, subtle and marvelous, but that is another story.

*See "Vegetables that Heal" in the chapter on "Healing by Plants."

Lipides

Each organ contains a constant amount of fat, and the body always maintains reserves of fat which vary with diet, climate, and the individual's activity. These fats, whether of plant or animal origin, are known as lipides. They are combinations of glycerol and fatty acids (organic acids), greasy substances, insoluble in water, which are found in the cells of the body and in the form of reserve and protective tissues.

The lipides are the vehicle of the fat-soluble vitamins A, D, E, K, and F.* Digestion of lipides takes place by means of bile which emulsifies fat. The body requires a certain amount of bile to maintain a basic medium in which secretions of the stomach, pancreas, and intestine can break down fats.

Digestion of lipides is very slow. Excess lipides feed reserves of fatty tissues, in which they are converted into glucides.

Lipides have a high energy value. They are the body's main reserve of calorific energy. They come from fats in food, or those resulting from the conversion of glucides, or the ternary components of protides.

The main sources of lipides are oils, fats, and dairy foods.

Oils, Fats, Dairy Foods

Oil which can be consumed without any processing, except for clarification by decanting, is obtained by a first cold pressing of oleaginous fruits such as walnuts, hazelnuts, almonds, and olives. When they are pressed a second time, they yield oil of inferior quality. The residue is used for making soap.

Industrial oils, such as peanut oil, for example, are obtained by either pressing or extraction. High pressure is used, and the fruit is heated to about 95°. The combined action of heat, air, and metal affects some of the most fragile components of the oil. In extraction, the fruit is ground in a liquid that dissolves the oil, then the oil is separated from the solvent; foreign substances are often dissolved along with the oil.

It is therefore dangerous to use those oils. They contain too many impurities and are the result of refining operations that remove substances which play an important part in the assimilation of fat. Those operations produce the clear, odorless, tasteless oil chosen by the uninformed consumer. Avoid peanut and corn oil; instead, use unrefined oils and those made from walnuts, olives, sesame seeds, or sunflower seeds. At present there are virtually only two fatty foods that sometimes can be obtained in their natural state, made by traditional methods: olive oil and butter.

It is inadvisable to consume animal fats from the bodies of slaughtered animals, especially for people with bad digestion.

When made without chemical additives for preserving or coloring it, butter is a wholesome food, containing many fat-soluble vitamins. But cooking makes it indigestible. (Lipides consist largely of fatty acids whose physical composition is destroyed by heat.) And if too much of it is eaten, it may lead to the depositing of cholesterol in tissues. Choose perfectly prepared butter, carefully washed and containing neither lactose nor casein, and keep it protected from air and light in a wooden or earthenware container. If it turns rancid on the surface, it can simply be washed again.

Vegetable fats, indigestible, acidifying, and devitalizing, are residues of plants. Coconut fat has a high melting point and favors the depositing of cholesterol. Palm oil resembles lard in composition and is scarcely any better.

Animal and vegetable fats are necessary for proper functioning of the organs. But do not overload your body with them, and be on your guard against cheap fatty substitutes. Above all, a food should be natural or biologically wholesome. Respect your stomach by avoiding the by-products of the food industry.

Protides

These play a part in all the essential vital processes and are found in all cells in various forms: peptides, proteids, albumins, globulins, glutelins. Proteins are not reutilized in their original state. They first must be broken down, then reconstituted. When they have been digested in the stomach, their conversion contin-

*See "Vitamins" in the chapter on "Components of Foods."

ues in the intestines. Their breakdown requires a great expenditure of organic energy and their nitrogenous residues are then converted by the liver into urea, which is eliminated by the kidneys. The operation yields peptides and amino acids.

Amino acids are often thought of as being found primarily in meat, but the better part of them is contained in soybeans, eggs, grain, cheese, and legumes. They are used in tissue-building and all the vital functions.

Proteins in the body are rapidly disintegrated and reconstituted. There are continuous exchanges of amino acids or groups of amino acids, a veritable chemical whirlpool.

A law formulated by Rubner states that the biological value of a protein is determined by the amino acid it contains in the smallest amount, and that the absence of an essential amino acid in a protein makes it totally inadequate. Amino acids that come from plants, dairy foods, eggs, and honey are far superior to those of meat. However, in cooking, foods poor in amino acids can be combined with foods whose proteins are richer.

With the aid of gastric enzymes, protides are digested during the entire movement of a mass of chewed food. They are absorbed by the blood soon after a meal. In some people, they enter the bloodstream intact. They then behave as foreign bodies or poisons and give rise to allergies in such forms as hives, rheumatism, and asthma.

Protides are necessary to all life. Their molecules are about 11 per cent nitrogen. Human beings lose nitrogen in urine, feces, sperm, menstrual fluid, hemorrhaging, and bleeding from injuries. The human body has a daily need of a little less than half a gram of protides per pound of weight.

Animal flesh is rich in amino acids. But animals receive those protides from plants that have carried out the first synthesis of amino acids. It is therefore possible to synthesize amino acids directly from protide-bearing substances in plants. Many of these substances are found in good whole wheat bread, since the fermentation of yeast favors the breakdown of wheat proteins. They are also present in legumes (beans, soybeans), oleaginous fruits (almonds, walnuts, hazelnuts), grain, and mushrooms. But even though a prolonged vegetarian diet (excluding all foods of animal origin) may provide an overall amount of protides that far exceeds the individual's need, it may still not contain the quantity of essential amino acids required to assure the body's growth and maintenance.

PROTIDES OF ANIMAL ORIGIN

The large amount of amino acids in foods of animal origin is enough to compensate for their poverty in certain protides of plant origin. Milk, cheese, and eggs are quite capable of supplying everything the body needs for its building, repair, and maintenance.

Milk and cheese

Milk is the food of young mammals before they are able to chew. Each species requires milk with a composition adapted to the needs of its young. Human milk is a perfect food for human babies; it meets all their requirements for growth and maintenance. Animal milk—from cows, for example—can be assimilated and digested only by vigorous children. Although it contains protides, lipides, vitamins, and mineral salts, it is deficient in iron and copper and poor in glucides. Furthermore, a milk diet causes constipation because of its lack of cellulose waste products.

Milk slows digestion, tends to make the body sluggish, and may even give rise to a kind of poisoning in adults who swallow it without setting off salivary secretion. Fresh raw milk is appreciably more digestible and vitalizing than cooked milk. Milk is a culture medium very favorable to microbes and viruses; pasteurization rids it of pathogenic microorganisms without impairing its nutritional qualities or destroying its vitamins. But it is better to take it as an ingredient in other drinks, or in sauces. The addition of sugar to condensed milk makes it considerably less toxic to fragile bodies, but milk is not a food for adults.

The drawbacks of milk disappear if it is transformed by developing the diastasic elements it contains. Yogurt is milk curdled by means of a bacillus. It is easy to make raw milk curdle by keeping it warm and covered with a cloth. It can then be eaten for breakfast or at the end of a meal. Milk curdles when the casein it contains in a colloidal state congeals, keeping a large part of the fatty substances within it. Whey contains part of the sugar of the soluble protides, mineral salts, and milk.

Despite its deficiency in sugars, cheese eaten with whole wheat bread and fruit becomes an ideal food. It is 18 per cent to 30 per cent predigested protides, with all the essential amino acids. When neither dried nor creamed, it is 20 per cent to 30 per cent fatty substances, by weight. Its caloric value is three times that of meat. An important source of valuable vitamins (B_2, B_{12}, A, D) and mineral salts, it also provides the body with a number of beneficial digestive enzymes.

Goat's-milk cheese is easy to digest and very nutritious. Roquefort made from ewe's milk is the richest in albumin, butter, and mineral salts. But be leery of blue (moldy) cheeses; they can cause fetid stools and affect ailments such as arteriosclerosis. Reject dead, "processed" cheeses of the "crème de gruyère" type which come from melted cheese unfit for human consumption.

Eggs

Certain components of eggs help the body, and especially the blood, to mobilize fats. An egg contains about six grams of fat. Rich in protides, lipides, vitamins, and minerals, eggs can be recommended as a valid substitute for meat, though it must be remembered that they are not tolerated well by bodies in weak condition. But when they are combined with flour in cakes, they are good for everyone. They may become indigestible when combined with bad-quality fats.

Eggs are the best food of animal origin. Avoid duck eggs, however, since they are more toxic and more easily infected. Whenever possible, choose eggs that come from a farm where the hens eat a natural diet. The shell should be intact, the white, translucent, the yolk, homogenous.

MEAT PROTEIN

Man kills other animals for food. He is the only animal that cuts up meat and cooks it. The proportion of meat in an individual's diet should vary with the amount of his activity. Meat often becomes harmful when it is mixed with other foods which retard complete digestion of it or, through fermentation, make it putrefy before its waste products have been eliminated from the intestines. Nevertheless, man can get a large part of his protide ration from meat. It is, on the average, 16 per cent protides and 60 per cent water and fats. Cooking destroys 20 per cent of the vitamins in meat and 95 per cent of those in fish.

Meat contains rather significant amounts of uric acid and purine. Since it is poor in calcium, it does not have the recalcifying value of dairy foods, eggs, and grain. Its proportion of iron is equal to that of eggs. It contains only about a fourth as much phosphorus as cheese, but much more potassium.

Extremely fresh meat is tough. It should be allowed to undergo an inner transformation that will make it more tender. The meat of a freshly killed animal seldom contains pathogenic microbes or parasites, but it soon becomes an excellent culture medium for most germs. It can also be infected because of incorrect methods of preparation. Bad meat is more likely to be consumed in such products as salami and bologna. Avoid eating raw meat unless you know exactly where it came from. If you kill a chicken or rabbit yourself, take out its entrails quickly and carefully. Wash meat to remove the products of beginning putrefaction that soon appear on its surface.

Cooking destroys the molecular balance of meat. When it is boiled it becomes less toxic but also less tasty; prepared with fatty substances, it takes longer to digest. Roasting and broiling are the best ways of cooking it.

The leanest meat is the most wholesome and digestible. The quality of meat depends mainly on the life the animal led before being killed. When possible, choose a grain-fed chicken, and beef from a steer that grazed in a pasture. Avoiding eating those anemic, white-fleshed calves raised in livestock "factories" with massive doses of antibiotics, and those mass-produced chickens that never see daylight, whose meat separates so easily from their bones after cooking. Beef from cattle that are stuffed with grain, deprived of sunlight, and treated with various chemicals is another kind of meat to be avoided as much as possible.

It is said that eating meat gives increased energy. This is true if the meat is wholesome and comes from an animal raised under natural conditions, but false if the animal was raised artificially. And it is wrong to assume that if some is good, more is better: One meat meal a day is enough for even an active worker. A plateful of beans or lentils has more nutritional value than a steak.

HOW TO EAT

The body expends energy, and therefore heat that keeps its temperature constant. Man has energy needs that he can satisfy in various ways: eating, movement, rest, breathing, meditation.

This need varies with each individual's nature and activity.

Caloric Value of Foods

Each food can be regarded as a fuel with a specific value. A gram of glucide will produce about four and a half calories, a gram of lipide eight or nine. Someone who does a great deal of heavy physical labor needs about five thousand calories a day, but half that amount is enough for someone who gets little exercise; mental work causes only a minimal expenditure of calories. A meat meal containing the same number of calories as a vegetarian meal does not have the same effects on the body. Foods can, of course, be classified according to their calories, but no food should be allowed to heat the body at the cost of deteriorating it.

Calories belong to the realm of physics. Their application to food disregards minerals, vitamins, and individual variations in the powers of organic conversion and assimilation. It leads to feeding the weak like the strong and the sick like the well, since it considers only a person's body weight in calculating his daily ration. "Our grandparents ate a little of everything, but moderately," says the French dietitian Carton, "and without calculating the caloric value of their food; they did not, of course, have to worry about the 'doctoring' of food that now makes it as dangerous as certain clumsy treatments."

Choosing the kinds and amounts of food on the basis of a calorie guide cannot keep a person in good health. It is true that in winter the body needs to burn more calories, but that is no reason to increase the amount of meat in your diet. Although meat is pleasant to eat from time to time, animal fats and proteins come with a heavy proportion of waste products. Your body can get all the calories it needs from dried fruit, peas, lentils, whole-grain flour and pasta, and eggs.

Macrobiotics

Many health-food stores display a bewildering number of books and pamphlets extolling the virtues of vegetarianism, grain diets, diets of fruit and milk, and so on. The variety seems endless, and the neophyte is at a loss to decide how he should eat in order to be healthy and obey the rules of nature. In our opinion, none of these diets should be followed exclusively. They are all interesting because of the properties they discover in various foods, but they are all guilty of fanaticism to some extent. There is no ideal diet for the whole human race; each person must find the dietary balance that suits him best, taking his activities and environment into account.

Let us take macrobiotics as an example. This diet has created an interesting synthesis that can have good effects on the body if it is used correctly (which is rare). But if it is misunderstood, macrobiotics can lead to serious states of weakness; here again, moderation and intuition are essential.

Man is an omnivorous animal; in the course of his history he has adapted to all climates and changes. His capacity for assimilation is great. But that body which enables him to adapt to any environment is a fragile mechanism that must be used properly. It may withstand abuse for years; a person can get used to being a hundred pounds overweight or, without even realizing it, being undernourished because he is artificially nourished, but his body gradually deteriorates and loses all its potentialities, then begins literally disintegrating, part by part.

"Eating is a serious act on which many events, good or bad, depend," George Ohsawa tells us. "It is therefore important to realize that each person either builds his health or opens the door to illness by his judicious or faulty choice of the foods that make up his daily diet."

Macrobiotics, which comes to us from the Far East, is intended to be both a rule of life and a guide to wisdom, and it reflects the rhythms that underlie the order of the universe.

"If man ardently wants to live in good health and happiness, he must live close to nature." That is the teaching that Ohsawa, a philosopher and scientist, presented in a number of books, including *Macrobiotics: an Invitation to Health and Happiness, You Are All Sanpaku,* and *The Unique Principle: the Philosophy of Macrobiotics.*

Ohsawa tried to explain and apply the single principle of Far Eastern philosophy and science, "whose physiological application," he said, "guarantees infinite freedom, eternal happiness, absolute justice, and peace for the world, and cures all acute, chronic, or incurable diseases." And he stated, "I do not want to influence anyone; I give the means of solving everything, but everyone must find the truth himself."

Ohsawa was born on October 18, 1893, in Kyoto, Japan. In his childhood he was separated from his parents, brothers, and sisters. At that time, his country was undergoing a crisis; life was difficult and often miserable. At sixteen, he was afflicted with tuberculosis of the lungs and intestines. Judged incurable by Western medicine, he studied Indian, Chinese, and Japanese medicine, and at twenty he regained his health by means of macrobiotics. He later traveled with his wife through Africa without ever being vaccinated, and he cured the tropical sores they developed.

Beginning in 1956 he tirelessly imparted his teachings in France, Belgium, Switzerland, Germany, Sweden, Italy, Great Britain, and the United States, through lectures, practical courses, and cures. Toward the end of his life, in Tokyo, so many sick people came to his little apartment that he could not receive them all. "Time is too precious," he said; "I have too little of it left." On April 24, 1966, his heart stopped. Macrobiotic restaurants and food stores are still being created on the basis of his doctrine, and his practical teachings are propagated fervently and effectively.

The first step toward understanding and feeling what Ohsawa taught is learning to distinguish the yin and yang of all things in the universe, and thereby knowing their force of polarity.

YIN AND YANG

About six thousand years ago the philosopher-emperor Fu Hsi, leader of a primitive nomadic people, discovered the ultimate, unifying cause of visible and invisible phenomena. He used the terms "yin" and "yang" to designate the polarization of the universe into two antagonistic and complementary forces, centrifugal force and centripetal force.

It can be said that the yang force produces sound, heat, and light, while the yin force is the source of silence, calm, cold, and darkness.

YANG	YIN
Center	Periphery
Hard	Soft
Solidity	Fragility
Masculine	Feminine
Dry	Wet
Seeds	Fruit
That which concentrates	That which dilates
Activity	Passivity
Dynamic	Static
Order	Disorder
Summer	Winter
Sun	Moon
Day	Night

Application of this principle is found in the science of macrobiotics, or "technique of longevity" (from the Greek makros, "long, large," and bios, "life").

"Man, like all animals, is a transformation of food," says Ohsawa. The quality of our blood depends on the quality of our food. It is important to know that we renew a tenth of our blood every day, and all our cells every three months. "Our physiological life is a process that makes red blood from chlorophyllous products." It is therefore a process of developing yang from yin matter. By culinary preparation we can facilitate that physical and chemical transformation of plants by means of yang factors such as salt, fire, pressure, and dehydration. This process also takes place naturally in our digestive organs.

Furthermore, our nervous system—composed of the sympathetic system which assures the development and movement of all the tissues and organs of our body, and the parasympathetic system, an element of slowing and compensation—rests on the same principle. Yang energy is conveyed by the sympathetic system, yin energy by the parasympathetic sys-

tem.* Our body is thus under the influence of two basic, antagonistic forces. As Ohsawa says, "Health is a good balance between two antagonistic systems. Sickness is therefore a temporary or chronic imbalance between those two opposing forces. . . . An excess of yin foods makes the sympathetic system dominant, while with an excess of yang foods the parasympathetic system is dominant."

AN ESSENTIALLY VEGETARIAN DIET

Plants absorb inorganic elements and transform them into organic foods that nourish animals and human beings. Ohsawa: "We depend on plant products. . . . All plant foods are virgin matter for maintaining and building our bodies. Meat and all animal products are not virgin matter for us."

If we are obliged to eat animal foods, we should take them only in very small amounts. The macrobiotic diet consists chiefly of grain (brown rice, wheat, buckwheat, millet, barley, rye, oats). One may also add vegetables grown in the region where they are consumed and seaweed. The sodium-potassium ratio of grain corresponds to that of our seven to eight million cells. If we eat complete foods, our body is able to make its own vitamins and enzymes.

As condiments, macrobiotic cooking uses unrefined sea salt, miso (soybean paste), tamari (nonchemical soy sauce), bouillons such as dried fish bouillon, and pure oil made from olives, sesame seeds, or sunflower seeds.

"Fish, fowl, shellfish, eggs, and fruit may be used from time to time," writes Ohsawa, "but allowances must be made for individual cases and the yin-yang balance of prepared foods."

In warm weather, vinegar, wine, lemon juice, ginger, or spices may be added to "yinify" certain foods that are too yang.

In applying the yin-yang principle we discover a new and more aware method of cooking and choosing foods, and we find that its effect on taste is far from displeasing.

---

*See "Acupuncture" in the chapter on "The Body and the Cosmos."

YANG	YIN
GRAINS	
Wheat	Germs of grains
Rice	Corn
Buckwheat	Oats
Millet	
VEGETABLES	
Dandelion	Eggplant
Endives	Tomatoes
Leeks	Lettuce
Chick-peas	Sweet potatoes
Radishes	Pimentos
Onions	Beans
Parsley	Cucumbers
Carrots	Asparagus
Salsify	Spinach
Watercress	Artichokes
Roasted pumpkin seeds	Bamboo sprouts
Dandelion roots	Pumpkin
Garlic	Mushrooms
Lentils	Peas
	Beets
	Celery
MEATS	
Pigeon	Snails
Partridge	Frogs
Duck	Pork
Turkey	Veal
Chicken and duck	Beef
must be grain-fed.	Chicken and mutton are very slightly yin.
DAIRY FOODS	
Roquefort	Yogurt
Goat's-milk cheese	Cream
	Butter
	Milk
BEVERAGES	
Camomile tea	Coffee
Bancha tea (Japanese green tea)	Coca-Cola
	Champagne
Yannoh (Ohsawa coffee)	Wine
Lotus tea	Beer
	Black tea

YANG	YIN
CONDIMENTS	
Cinnamon	Ginger
Fennel	Curry
Chervil	Pepper
Thyme	Lemon juice
Onions	Vinegar
Parsley	Mustard
Unrefined sea salt	Cloves

These foods must always be eaten in their natural state, never as prepared products of the food industry. The yin-yang balance varies with the seasons and the places where the plants grow.

It is absolutely necessary to chew as thoroughly as possible. Today, how many people are still aware that a meal is an essential, precious, sacred act? How many regard it merely as a pleasure and swallow their food gluttonously, scarcely tasting what they eat?

Yet the kitchen is "the workshop of life." Hence the need to balance negative energy and positive energy, yin force and yang force. Modern life, hectic, noisy, and disruptive, carries us along at an accelerated pace. To help the body withstand stress and the constant fatigue we impose on it, we need more yang energy so that we can concentrate better. The body thus regenerates itself more and the mind is clearer and more alert. We should try to regain that harmony.

According to Ohsawa, grains are the primary foods and must be distinguished from such secondary foods as vegetables, soups, and chick peas. Grains should compose 60 per cent of our diet. Foods rich in plant proteins—particularly millet, sunflower seeds, and sesame seeds—make it possible to balance exclusively vegetarian meals. Sunflower seeds should be eaten ground (mixed into sauces or used to make bread) or roasted. Sesame seeds should be lightly roasted and crushed with 15 per cent to 20 per cent sea salt to form what is known as gomashio.

Here are a few suggestions for macrobiotic cooking. First of all, replace white bread with whole wheat or rye bread. Use vegetable oil instead of butter for cooking.

Brown Rice. See "Rice" in the chapter on "The Components of Food."

Vegetable Nitsukes. Cut the vegetables lengthwise, sauté them in a little oil, and add gomashio.

Millet. For each cup of millet browned in oil, add two cups of water. Simmer on low heat until tender.

Croquettes fried in vegetable oil can be made with all cooked grains.

A bowlful of cold brown rice each morning, with olive oil, gomashio, and a few drops of tamari (soy sauce aged and prepared traditionally), drives parasites out of your intestines and regularizes digestions. With tea and fruit or fruit juice, it is a complete breakfast.

Vegetable Pie. Sauté carrots, onions, cauliflower, etc. in oil and cook with a little water. Line a pan or baking dish with dough made with whole-wheat flour, water, and salt. Put in the vegetables, stir some roasted flour into the juice left over from their cooking, and pour this sauce over them. Bake in a medium oven until the mixture is bubbling and the crust browned.

Chapati. Make dough with flour, salt, and water. Shape it into little balls, then flatten them and either bake them or cook on a griddle like pancakes. Serve with nitsukes or honey.

Fruit and Vegetable Salad. Cut apples, carrots, and cabbage into small pieces and place them briefly in boiling water. When they have cooled, mix them with a sauce composed of four spoonfuls of oil, one spoonful of tamari, and an egg.

Stuffed Cabbage. Separate the cabbage leaves and wash them carefully. Cook buckwheat grains or groats in twice their volume of water. Beat two eggs. Put some oil in a cast-iron casserole and make thin, alternating layers of buckwheat, egg, and cabbage leaves. Cover and bake for an hour. Serve with tamari.

Raw Sea Bream. Use the fish in the form of fillets. Sprinkle salt on them and let them drain in a strainer for about twenty minutes, then slowly run cold water on them till they become firm. Lay them on grated carrots and chopped radishes. Serve with a sauce composed of lemon juice, tamari, and grated ginger.

Buckwheat. Sauté two cups of buckwheat grains or groats in a spoonful of oil, then boil slowly in two cups of water, with a little salt, until the water is absorbed. Serve with soy paste and nitsukes of green vegetables.

Baked Apples. Wash the apples. Make a hollow in each of them, fill with sesame butter, sprinkle on a little cinnamon, and bake in a casserole with a little water, at a moderate heat, until done.

Ohsawa Coffee (Yannoh). Three spoonfuls of brown rice, two of wheat, two of azuki beans (Japanese red beans), one of chick peas, one of chicory. Roast the ingredients separately, shaking in a pan over an open flame, then mix, cook in a little oil, let cool, and grind fine. Use one tablespoonful of this powder per pint of water and boil for ten minutes. Recommended for constipation and chronic headaches.

Ohsawa also advises fasting, which enables the body to rid itself of the bad or excessive substances it has accumulated. "Tradition requires it, wisdom recommends it, and reason demands it: we must know how to fast."

KNOWING HOW TO EAT

Although some people have ridiculed Ohsawa's philosophy, the facts show that he was able to bring health to sick people whose condition was judged hopeless by Western medicine. And, above all, macrobiotics can help to restore a destroyed balance by treating a patient with good food, rather than overloading his body with medicines that tire it.

Macrobiotics does not mean eating brown rice every day; it means balancing the energy of what we eat and what we do, of what we receive and what we give. As Ohsawa writes, it also teaches us to take "responsibility for our own acts and the choice of our daily foods, and to know the consequences of the former and the effects of the latter." We learn not to be automatons with mechanized acts and thoughts, but to remain clearheaded, knowing how to choose and regulate our lives in accordance with our own individual rhythms.

"Happiness and unhappiness, sickness and health, freedom and slavery depend only on our attitude in life and in our activities. The latter are determined by our understanding of the world and the universe."

Ohsawa had great difficulty in making Westerners really understand his principles. They misapplied his teachings; after having overeaten in the past, they adopted a rigorous, useless asceticism. The reason is that those who followed his advice went from a high-calorie diet to a low-calorie one, which naturally made them lose weight. This can relieve the symptoms of many illnesses: kidney and cardiovascular disorders, sometimes diabetes, various kinds of discomfort, and feelings of weakness, high blood pressure, colds, influenza, chronic bronchitis. The former sufferer may then be so impressed by his "miraculous" recovery that he makes an absolute law of the diet responsible for it; he believes that a dish of rice, four carrots, and a little gomashio or tamari are enough to assure him of freedom and health.

That is where error sets in. As a dietitian points out, strictly following a diet takes less effort than learning what nutrition is, that is, knowing how to balance all the components of food (lipides, vitamins, protides, etc.) in relation to oneself and one's own activity. It is good not to be overweight. Statistics compiled by insurance companies show that, on the average, someone 10 per cent below his ideal weight will live considerably longer than someone 10 per cent above it. But once a person has lost weight and perhaps recovered his health, he must know how to rebalance his food intake, without staying on a hypocaloric diet or going back to a hypercaloric one.

By his yin and yang theory (traditional in the Orient), Ohsawa simply wanted to provide a means of achieving greater subtlety in the search for balances among foods. His theory went beyond the categories he had to use. Thus he classified foods as yin or yang according to the amounts of sodium (yang) and potassium (yin) they contain, but for him this was only one way of approaching the matter.

And he always declined to answer the question of whether someone should stay on a vegetarian diet or not; he simply said, "You

will decide later." The body needs a certain number of amino acids in order to live. Getting a proper dosage of them is what matters most, but to do that we must know where they are found. Meat is only 12 per cent essential amino acids, the rest being waste products that are useless in themselves. That amount can be obtained from the seeds of leguminous plants: from a purely rational viewpoint, a bean sandwich has as much value as a meat sandwich. (Beans have been called "the poor man's meat.") But all this does not mean that we should not eat good meat from time to time (though we should avoid veal and pork). Like meat, lentils, almonds, and walnuts also contain amino acids.

Moreover, too much grain is hard to digest and creates acidity. Here again, knowing the proper amounts is important. Because of their starch, grains are our best fuel: The cells are continuously nourished by them, whereas substances whose sugars are directly assimilable (such as meat and white sugar) give energy that is immediate but short-lived because it is quickly burned up, which leads to the harmful urge to overeat or take snacks all the time. Whole grains also help the intestines work, which is particularly beneficial if they have grown lazy from digesting too much food that has been impoverished and partially predigested by preservation and chemicals.

Brown rice, wheat, pilpil or bulgur (crushed parched wheat or rice), whole flour, corn, and millet can be an important culinary discovery: They are as tasty as they are healthful.

Do not buy food too far in advance, especially hulled grains and whole flour, because they deteriorate rapidly when they are not loaded with preservatives. Millet turns bitter if it is stored too long. Avoid mixing plant and animal proteins: grain and meat, dairy foods and soybeans. Always balance the phosphorus in grain with the calcium in cheese; the balance between phosphorus and calcium is as important in nutrition as that between sodium and potassium. Drink milk moderately. Eggs should always be fresh (those bought in a store are sometimes three weeks old). And always eat a great deal of vegetables in season,* steam-

---

*See "Vegetables that Heal" in the chapter on "Healing by Plants."

cooked, boiled (in soups put through a blender after cooking), or fried in the form of nitsukes.

To yangify a food, sauté it in a little oil without covering it, to release the most yin of its volatile elements and make its acids evaporate.

Do not peel vegetables; brush them, wash them quickly, and chop them. Vegetables lose fewer vitamins when they are fried than when they are boiled.

In your soups, use certain plant parts wrongly considered inedible (leek roots, carrot tops, which are rich in vitamins and minerals).

Avoid preserved fruit. Eat fruit fresh and mixed into salads; cut into pieces, with a dressing made of yogurt, a spoonful of fresh cream and some honey; add dried fruit. With meals containing grain, avoid eating fresh fruit, which creates gastric acidity. Instead, eat cooked fruit, dried fruit (raisins, figs), or almonds.

Choose your wine carefully. It is better to drink good wine, even if you must drink it less often. Red wines are preferable, since white and rose wines more often contain additives. Replace coffee with tea. Drink herb teas,* with their great variety and diverse properties.

Varied cooking is the best means of maintaining health and appetite.

Dietitians always try to set up a diet that provides daily rations of all kinds of food necessary to human life. Avoid that overly strict rule and heed your body's demands instead. Eat calmly, do not drink during meals, chew as well as possible, and concentrate on your food.

During a meal, you can freely forget everything, except what you are eating. The more attentive you are to that, the easier digestion takes place and the better energy flows.

*See "Useful Herbs" in the chapter on "Healing by Plants."

FASTING

When we open our morning newspaper we sometimes see reports of hunger strikes: A few demonstrators, defending a cause that means a great deal to them, have decided to make a public protest by going without food as long as possible. They fast. Fasting is seen as a last resort, the ultimate means of making oneself heard and understood. To many people it is almost frightening because they regard it as an approach to death, a kind of slow suicide or, at best, a dangerous game. Yet everyone knows that fasting has always been recommended in religion, and although strict observance of Lent is rare in our time, many still feel that it must be based on something valid.

Fasting is widely misunderstood; the reason for it is no longer apparent, its meaning has been lost. It is by no means a masochistic act. Human beings, as well as animals, have always fasted—that is, voluntarily abstained from food—and drawn great physical, psychic, and spiritual benefits from that form of asceticism.

WHAT IS FASTING?

We can define fasting as complete or partial abstention from food and drink, or food only, for periods of varying length.

Most animals instinctively know when to stop eating. It is well known that certain animals fast during the mating season. Many fishes, such as the male salmon, do not eat during that period, and neither do auks and ganders.

With human beings also, despite preconceived ideas to the contrary, there are times when resting the body is more important than nourishing it. Children know this: They sometimes refuse to eat or they fall asleep at the table, unconsciously preferring sleep to food. The overtaxed body often suffers from excessive intake of food, and not eating gives it a beneficial physiological rest.

Throughout history, sages, philosophers, and members of religious orders have fasted as a way not only of detoxifying the body but also, by the same process, purifying the mind and making it dominate matter.

Religious fasting has been practiced in all times and all over the world.

Socrates and Plato regularly fasted for ten days at a time. Pythagoras would not accept pupils until they had fasted for forty days.

Moses fasted for forty days on Mount Sinai when he received the Tables of the Law. At each important time in his mission, Jesus went off into the desert or the mountains and fasted. The practice of fasting took root in the early Christian church when penitents and anchorites "withdrew to the wilderness."

Fasting is, in one sense, expiating sins committed against the body and purifying the mind by strengthening it with the aid of a discipline. Purification is spiritual as well as physical. Modern man has forgotten this and it is hard for him to enter into the spirit of fasting, since it requires him to free himself from the needs and desires multiplied and exacerbated by his consumer-oriented society.

Researchers have observed the changes that fasting produces in the subject's body. None of the body's vital tissues can be damaged so long as its reserves are not exhausted. When it is not occupied with the long and difficult work of digestion, it carries out a "general cleaning," beginning by eliminating pathological and harmful tissues. The process deserves to be better known, considering the polluted environment in which we live. The symptoms which occur show that the body is revitalizing itself, although one must still act with caution, discernment, and knowledge. Fasting does not mean starving to death, as in a famine. It means undertaking a course of treatment.

WHAT HAPPENS
IN A FASTING BODY?

During a fast, the body burns off excess calories acquired from overly rich food. The skin takes on a fine texture and a pinkish color. It relaxes and wrinkles disappear. Circulation is improved. Bones, teeth, nerve, and the brain do not deteriorate; they are maintained, even to the detriment of less important tissues. Except in very long fasts, there is no decrease in the number of muscle cells, only an elimination of useless matter stored by the body under the skin, between muscles, or in the blood vessels, joints, intestines, or muscles (in the form of fat). The body also lives on the reserves of vitamins accumulated in its glands. Saliva diminishes considerably. It may even become thick and sticky.

Fasting gives a complete rest to the stomach, small intestine, and colon, which thus become free to repair their damaged structures and remedy certain deficiencies. Bacteria are eliminated from the digestive system. All germs may disappear from the stomach after a week of fasting. It is a rapid means of combating bacterial decomposition.

The effects of fasting on the sexual functions vary with individuals. Desire usually diminishes, but potency is strenthened after the fast has ended. The sterility of some women has been cured in this way, and so have cases of impotence that had lasted for years.

All through a fast, the rate of heartbeat varies greatly, increasing or decreasing in accordance with the body's needs. Starting at about eighty beats a minute, it goes down to below sixty at first, then is stabilized there. Fasting stops constant stimulation of the heart, thus lifting a heavy burden from it and allowing it to rest. The blood is purified and the heart strenthened. Metabolism functions at three quarters of its capacity and stays at a uniform level until hunger returns. The senses of sight, touch, hearing, and smell become keener. The eyes become clear and bright.

Fasting does not cause deficiencies. The body controls the utilization of its reserves: It uses up some of them rapidly and conserves others in order to redistribute them. Chemical balance is restored, and therefore the whole balance of the human being. Fasting is a physiological rest. It is to the organs of the body what a good night's sleep is to a tired worker. Our latent energy is uncovered, bursts forth, and develops. The brain, irrigated by purer blood, functions clearly. Dr. Shelton writes that all the essentially mental powers—reasoning ability, memory, attention, association—are improved during a fast, and that the spiritual forces of intuition, sympathy, and love are more fully developed.

Fasting returns the body to its normal condition. It is certainly a fine remedy for sickness. But even more than a miraculous remedy, it is a very powerful weapon which remains effective, no matter what disorders may afflict the patient.

FASTING, A WEAPON AGAINST ILLNESS

Before trying to heal ourselves, we should first fast, a practice often overlooked by modern medicine. Animals instinctively stop eating when they are sick. Warmth, rest, fasting, and water to satisfy thirst: Those are a sick person's real needs. Fasting has been practiced continuously for ten thousand years to relieve human suffering. "Rather than resorting to medicine, fast for a day," said Plutarch. Since many illnesses result from bad or excessively rich food, we should let the body cleanse itself naturally before trying to cure it with medicines, which often load it with toxins that it must eliminate.

The body absorbs its useless flesh and tissue by autolysis, a process which can resorb tumors and other growths.

Absence of desire for food, caused by illness, sorrow, anger, agitation, or fatigue, is a means used by nature to indicate that the digestive organs are incapable of performing their functions. In cases of acute illness, the whole body is engaged in the work of eliminating toxins and not in that of assimilating food. There is no danger of starvation; the body has ample reserves. Contrary to general opinion, eating is not a prime requirement for regaining strength during an illness.

Fasting can cure many cases of vomiting, diarrhea, obesity, and insomnia. It does not act on illness directly. By stopping certain activities of the body, it enables tissues to repair themselves and restores chemical balance. In this way, the patient acquires more vigor and regains his health.

Fasting purifies and strengthens the body and makes the mind capable of returning to its normal condition. But it should be done only in certain ways and at certain times. It is important to know how to fast.

HOW TO FAST

There is no single best time for fasting: We should fast whenever the need for it is felt. The season is unimportant. It has been said that summer is more propitious, but the essential factor is the conditions under which fasting takes place. It is a delusion to think that you can work outside your home or carry on sustained activities while you are fasting. A fast should be undertaken in a certain spirit of calm and return into the self, which requires good physical conditions. There is no need for luxury, but you should be warm because of the feeling of chilliness experienced at first, and surrounded by a friendly, sympathetic atmosphere.

It is, of course, preferable to fast in a group because, aside from emulation, a shared experience is always more fruitful. Why not to withdraw for a few days with several other people,

in the country if possible, and fast together? But it is not hard to fast by yourself, even if you live with others, provided they at least understand and share the spirit in which you do it.

Before undertaking a fast you should always achieve a certain tranquility and mental balance, and be in a place with adequate ventilation and a comfortable temperature. In our society it is hard to fast outside of vacations, although most people can manage to take a weekend now and then to break their eating habits and thus clean out their bodies. Ideally, you should fast without a time limit, to avoid anxiety over going back to work and worrying about your strength, vitality, or weight.

A real fast should last at least six days. The benefits derived from it will then reach their true dimensions. Fasting does not necessarily involve complete immobility and it does not impair the mental faculties in any way. It is a change of state, a general rest which you can use for reading, listening to music, and letting yourself live at a slowed pace in calm and peace. It is a return to regenerating harmony.

Reading, like all activities during a fast, becomes an extraordinarily vivid experience. Becoming aware of the real makes us see our everyday life in a new light. You may even abandon your favorite magazines and plunge into books that nourish meditation! Some people continue physical or mental activity to some extent, but the longer you fast, the more rest you should have, to enable yourself to keep as much of your reserves as possible. The work of elimination should go on as long as necessary.

Preparation is an important phase. To avoid certain mishaps, it is better to prepare for a fast by eating wholesome, natural food for about a month and making sure that your intestines are in healthy condition.

The first day of fasting goes by without difficulty. On the second day you will have a few stomach pangs and a normal sensation of hunger which increases rather violently, unless you were sick before you began fasting, in which case you will already be feeling slightly better. The sensation of hunger diminishes considerably on the third day and often disappears on the fourth. From then on, your body no longer urges you to eat. The sight or thought of food often causes disgust, nausea, or even an impulse to vomit. But food does not always become repulsive; each person is a special case and reacts according to his own nature.

There is no need to drink more than you want to. A large intake of water does not necessarily increase elimination of poisons. Do not take sugar (even brown sugar) in anything you drink; it easily passes into the gums by osmosis and causes spectacular cases of gingivitis. A delicate balance must be found, based on previous eating habits; for someone who ordinarily eats a great deal of meat, drinking water is advisable, but it is less useful for someone whose diet is mainly or wholly vegetarian.

For the same reason, enemas are not advisable, except in cases of severe constipation caused by a diet consisting essentially of meat. It is better to trust the body, since enemas may contribute to a weakening of the nervous system. As far as hygiene is concerned, it is good to take a quick, warm shower every day. Long baths are inadvisable.

You will be surprised by the quality of your sleep during a fast. You may sleep much or little; you will sleep according to the exact need of your body. If you are suffering from nervous tension, you should concentrate on your breathing, exhale slowly for a long time, take a good posture, do relaxation exercises,* cover yourself warmly, with your feet against a hot-water bottle (it helps to increase circulation), and drink adequate herb teas.**

Do not be alarmed by dark urine, even if you are a vegetarian; elimination is running its course.

A renewal of sexual activity may be experienced during the first few days. But afterward, desire disappears. Physical compulsions and acts seem insignificant. Your clearheadedness then enables you to free yourself from any possessive or jealous feelings and reactions that you may have had with regard to others.

Perspiration is no greater than usual, but the hands are often moist, which gives a disagreeable sensation. A very bad taste in the mouth is another common annoyance. It can be diminished by a daily cleaning of the tongue, which tends to be heavily coated at first. Its coating is reduced as the days go by, and the

---

*See the chapter on "Yoga."

**See "Useful Herbs" in the chapter on "Healing by Plants."

taste becomes less unpleasant. After digestion of the last meal before a fast, the intestines practically cease functioning. In rare cases, there may be diarrhea, but in most cases fasting enables the intestines to rest and restore themselves.

As for exercise, it should be quite limited. The best position for a faster is lying or half lying, and he should make all his movements at a leisurely pace. He should take full advantage of the opportunity for great rest that is offered to him. He and those around him should carefully avoid doing anything that would dissipate his energy and reserves. The experience should take place under the best possible conditions, so that maximum benefit can be derived.

The impressions of the body react on the mind, just as those of the mind react on the body. A feeling of dejection, a useless discussion or emotion, or too many obsessive thoughts may affect the organs and functions of the body, hence the need for a relaxed, serene, and harmonious atmosphere.

If you are in the country, it is good to take long, soothing walks which soon brings a feeling of union with the living world around you. Sunbaths are always beneficial, but they should not go on too long and their length should be reduced as the fast progresses, to avoid depression and nervous irritation.

Having respected all these conditions, look at yourself in a mirror during your fast: Your eyes will be amazingly bright, your complexion will be clearer, and you will feel yourself existing in a new and pleasant way.

Nature will always indicate when a fast should stop. One may fast for thirty days or more without harming any essential tissues, says Dr. Shelton, if all the body's fatty tissues and other reserves are plentifully available to it.

Breaking the fast is the most important phase. Anyone who eats haphazardly when hunger returns is in danger of finding himself in a hospital. The food eaten at this time should be of the highest nutritional quality, with all its vitamins and minerals intact. But it is useless to take vitamin pills; nature contains what the body needs.

As a general rule, a fast should be broken with a liquid diet: fruit juice and vegetable broth, half a glass every two hours on the first day, then a full glass every two hours on the second day. Whole fruit may be eaten on the third and fourth days, then vegetables and cottage cheese. Impulses must be held in check because the urge to eat reappears by the end of the third day, but the intestines must resume their activity gradually. Eating too much and choosing the wrong foods will destroy the benefits of fasting; the body will develop congestions, swellings, and deposits of fat. Only wholesome, natural foods richer in protein than in carbohydrates should be eaten, with a gradual return to normal meals in about a week. One can then eat cereal if it is thoroughly chewed. Weight is often gained very rapidly. Thin people take on normal weight after a fast, since the body has been rejuvenated and now assimilates food better. It continues to react more strongly and the faster's receptivity is increased.

A fast is a pause, a break in the life you led before. It can enable you to look yourself in the face.

A man or woman who fasts is participating in a traditional, ancestral practice. A fast is not only a vast cleaning of the Augean stables; it can also be a journey to the wellsprings of the spirit. The whole person, feeding on himself, reverses the usual relation between his energy and the world around him. The body is pure; "it is light," as the American Indians say. It is like an empty bottle that can be filled with good wine. At all levels of his being, the faster makes himself more capable than ever of perceiving reality, the truth of things, the world as it is.

All over the globe, prehistoric peoples associated fasting with the use of sacred substances that were natural psychedelic drugs, as "primitive" peoples still do today. The Warao tribes of the Orinoco delta and the Huicholes of Mexico, for example, remind us that besides restoring his body to its original harmony and purity, a faster also puts himself in condition to "see." Always and everywhere, fasting appears as a necessary stage in the journey toward self-knowledge, a vision of one's true nature, and achievement of harmony with the cosmos.

Civilized human beings must relearn how to eat. The path of fasting leads to a clearer experience of Being. Understanding the act of eating allows us a deep, intuitive grasp of our total relation to the world around us.

healing yourself

Cast naked into a deafening, blinding world, on a planet alien to the gentle warmth of the womb, man, the weakest of animals, must learn to live among the elements. They engender death and life, and the West may be mistaken in its idea of mastering them. To be as healthy as possible, the wise man intervenes as little as possible. He lets things take their course. Life always reasserts its rights.

We may as well say at the outset that in our opinion the over-technical and overspecialized medical system of our time is based on a slight error of emphasis. "When a finger points out the moon to you, look at the moon and not the finger," says an old adage. The modern miracle worker concentrates on a machine that he isolates too much from its environment. Furthermore, even though the science of the unconscious has begun to filter through to them, doctors usually seem to disregard the mind in treating the body—and vice versa.

In the West, almost no one listened to the language of the body, the desiring body, until the work of a Viennese neurologist named Freud began attracting attention. And only then did a new kind of doctor, somewhat akin to the witch doctor, begin trying to decipher the enigmas formulated by the body in search of its life.

The way is now clear to men and women celebrating the rediscovery of their bodies to undertake the journey back to the self. We live in an age when the field of consciousness is widening. We are rooted not only in a fleshly mother; the abode of our rest is the mysterious Female of whom Taoism speaks, the Great Mother of all living things, Mother Nature. Her inexhaustible energy surges forth in perfect forms that cover the whole realm of manifestations: the animal, vegetable, and mineral kingdoms.

A few very simple but highly concentrated acts may be enough to restore or maintain a body's health. Natural medicines are a product, elaborated by long wisdom, of man's instinctive reactions to his environment. Bodily health and harmony with the world around us are completely interdependent.

THE BODY AND THE COSMOS

The Elements

In most traditions there are four elements—air, water, fire, earth—and they transform themselves by destroying or creating each other. The four elements are the four basic archetypes* on which the whole universe rests. Let us look at mythologies: Everything is based on conflicting and combining forces; it is up to man to know how to use them. The power of each of them is dangerous and can turn against the unskilled manipulator. By their perpetual movement they constitute the texture of the earthly world. This world, insofar as it is a ceaseless transformation, produces illusion. We are borne by the earth; air surrounds and penetrates us; water bathes us from the time of our conception; fire warms us, gives us light, and enables us to cook our food.

A handful of *earth* is not only a solid mineral mass of various colors; it contains all the potentialities of nourishing life. Earth is wedded to the active principles of air; it is the mysterious Female, the fecund element that gives rise to abundant rebirth. The wealth of nature is its fruit.

Man, a being possessing a particle of the sacred fire, stands with both feet pressed against the earth and takes his breath from the air. A connecting link between the sky and the earth, he delimits a free movement in space.

Water, another feminine element, is the substance in which nature is bathed. Plants are 95 per cent water, man is 80 per cent. Water is a source of life, and therefore it purifies.*

The body is constantly interrelating with all the elements. It is made to be used not blindly, but with full awareness of the different mechanisms affecting it. Overfed, overheated, and overprotected, many people in modern societies have lost contact with the elements. They regain it only briefly, when they are in the country, during moments of serenity and intense, immediate "hyperconsciousness."

Air and *light* are man's natural environment,** from which he receives a fit existence. But to draw the greatest benefit from them, he must play subtly with the atmosphere and the sun. An air bath allows the skin to breath; it invigorates the body and helps it to withstand harsh weather.

The *sun*, which illuminates and warms the

---

*Archetypes: collective patterns in the unconscious of all the world's peoples; discovered by Jung.

*See below, "Water and the Body."
**See below, "Air and the Body."

earth, is a source of light, heat, and life. It is good to expose your body to it, but you will sense its energy better if you add movement to your sunbath. Sunbaths taken while lying motionless can be beneficial, provided the body undergoes gradual exposure. The sun enables us to refresh and restore ourselves. It imparts well-being to our cells.

Like the sun with its rays, *fire* with its flames, both symbolize and produce the regenerative action of energy on our bodies. During the great plague in ancient Athens, only blacksmiths and corpse burners were spared. Hippocrates, the great physician, concluded that fire purified contaminated air. Fire can have beneficial effects by acting on certain centers of the body with its heat and radiation.*

Fire is not only flame, it is energy and warmth. In that sense, the act of love is a fire, and a life may be born of it, for energy permits the fusion of two opposites, a fusion that is found in the union of the ovum and the spermatozoon. Fire can be made by rubbing the end of a stick (yang) in a slot cut into the side of another stick (yin). Fire is not wood, ash is not fire. Yet, for man, wood is a promise of fire, it "contains fire." The two sticks are consumed by the flame that rises from them. Similarly,

the rubbing of the lingam (penis) in the yoni (vagina) breaks down barriers and the divine ambrosia flows in the two ecstatic bodies. Such is the profound wisdom, "old as the world," that is still conveyed by Tantrism and Taoism.

Living beings pursue their existence on a small lump of matter that has cooled through the ages; a moist atmosphere surrounds its fertile crust but the primordial fire still smolders in its depths. At night, the glittering vault of the sky radiates mysterious light: the inconceivable energy of supernovae, the white streak of the Milky Way, the faint glow of other galaxies. A handful of people still know, unconsciously, the acts of harmony with cosmic life: making fire, taking what nature gives them according to their needs, taking in the energy of prana to be like a bird in the air, communicating with each other in silence and solitude, purifying themselves at the vital sources.

All this was done mainly in prehistoric times, but in many ways we are returning to it today. It is amusing to see, for example, that the offspring of the most mechanized empire in history are rejecting the machine and striving toward a life in harmony with the cosmic order.

Air and the Body

Our bodies are penetrated and given life by energy, breath, prana. In breathing, we not only absorb oxygen, we also receive the vital atmospheric force, a fraction of the universal energy.

Man is made to live in air and light. All our vital activities are related to breathing. Intake of oxygen is more important to our life than eating. The lungs also play a part in digesting fats, perform an antitoxic defensive function, and are closely connected to the nervous system, the liver, and the spleen. There is no life without breath. When it is controlled, *breathing* can become an instrument of knowledge leading to self-transcendence and a physical and immaterial exchange with the cosmos. Tibetan hermits are capable of producing such

great body heat that they can meditate naked in the snow.

Everything that exists in creation inhales, exhales, and vibrates. But only in man does this natural process become conscious and capable of being perfectly controlled. Breathing is automatically regulated by the nerve centers of the medulla oblongata, but it can be voluntarily augmented or diminished. Its chemical and mechanical relation to the rate of circulation makes it the great regulator of the body.

Clothing should not hinder the expansion of the chest and abdomen. Free up-and-down movement of the diaphragm produces a deep, gentle, constant massage of all the abdominal organs and facilitates and regularizes the functions of digestion, assimilation, and elimination. Oxidation of the body's tissues depends on atmospheric oxygen, which feeds organic combustions. It is therefore good to live in the

---

*See "Making Fire" in the chapter on "Three Meditations."

open air, close to nature, close to the trees that transmit oxygen to the air.

The body has no reserves of oxygen. If we are deprived of air, death follows in a few minutes. Air is an essential element in the energizing part of the nutritional process. Breathing eliminates carbon dioxide, water, and sometimes volatile substances absorbed in the process of digestion. It takes in oxygen and other gases, as well as dust and moisture in the air.

Inhaling and exhaling should be done through the nose. Breathing through the mouth, which may serve as an extra resource for strenuous work, is not natural. It does not allow us to empty our lungs completely. Its weak exhalation quickens inhalation, which causes breathlessness. Breathing should be deep, to assure thorough irrigation of the surface of the lungs. Far from being limited to the volume of the lungs, deep breathing involves the whole trunk, from the nose to the anus.*

Breathing is not only a voluntary movement; it is essentially awareness of an inner phenomenon. There is no mechanism that must be voluntarily made to operate, only something that must be released.

Optimum breathing is seldom found among people who live in cities. The city dweller breathes polluted air: engine exhaust fumes containing carbon monoxide and lead, foul-smelling hydrocarbons, and various waste products from factories, so toxic that they can be lethal on a foggy, windless day.

In a city, the air is less dirty away from busy streets and the ground, and especially at night, when windows should be at least partially open, except in rainy and windy weather. If possible, choose an apartment on an upper floor. Take frequent walks in parks. Keep green plants in your apartment; besides gladdening your eyes, they will help your body function properly. Be careful of air that has been polluted and depleted by tobacco smoke, emanations from heating devices, or the presence of too many people in a room. Central heating dries out the air and favor inflammations of the respiratory tract. Put open containers of water under your radiators. Your flowers and green plants will help to give the air the right humidity.

We also breathe through our skin. The skin is made for air and light. Without fresh air, it becomes pale and dull, and often has a bad smell. A skin that breathes is ruddy, smooth, and lustrous. An air bath is beneficial for all, even a bedridden invalid.

Breathing exercises make it possible to bring about certain specific changes in the body.* The increased pressure of the cerebrospinal fluid stimulates the nervous matter of the brain and spine, thus augmenting the vital activities of the nerve cells. When a person is near death, his breathing indicates that there is still some vital force left in his body. The last breath is an exhalation in which the vital force abandons the body, leaving it lifeless.

Wind and breathing are manifestations of the same element: air. They represent the intermediate world between the sky and the earth. The two phases of breathing are yang and yin, evolution-involution, manifestation and resorption. According to Taoism, in the beginning there were nine breaths which gradually "coagulated and combined" to form physical space. Between the sky and the earth, space is filled with a breath (*ki*) in which man lives "like a bird in the air."

In India, this same subtle realm is that of the wind (*vayu*), the vital breath. *Pranayama* ("breath control") applies not only to material breathing, but also to its subtle effects. Breath awakens *kundalini* and sets off a prodigious potential of energy whose actualization depends on the meditator's concentration and mastery.**

In all times and places, this energy that makes man divine has been associated with the dragon or the power of the serpent. Control of breathing gives rise to control of the psyche and seminal energy.

Harmonious breathing is like one of those perfect spirals that are found abundantly in nature: seashells (like the conch of Neptune or Shiva), the molecular structure of DNA,† and the spiral nebulae. From the infinitely great to

---

*See the chapter on "Yoga," and "Breathing" in the chapter on "Zazen."

**See "Sex Life and Cosmic Life" in the chapter on "Sex."

†Deoxyribonucleic acid, the programmer of living matter at the cellular level. See the chapter on "Man/Life/the Cosmos."

---

*See "Breathing" in the chapter on "Zazen."

the infinitely small, the universe is a vast breathing, composed of myriads of breaths. *Ekspir* and *inspir* are the poles of pranic pulsation; ekspir is concentration on the interior and, ultimately, harmonization with *ku* ("the surrounding void"), while inspir is opening to the environment, to the outer air laden with all the vibrations of that environment. Like the ebb and flow of waves on a beach, ekspir and inspir are the dual expression of a single movement, the complementary pulsations of a single vibration, a sign of life under the blue of the sky.

Water and the Body

Water is a source of life, a means of purification, a regenerative element. It is extolled in one of mankind's oldest texts, the *Rigveda*:

> You, Water, who comfort,
> bring us strength,
> greatness, joy, vision! . . .
> Sovereign of wonders,
> Ruler of peoples, Water!
> I ask healing of you. . . .
> You, Water, take this away,
> this sin, whatever it may be, that
>   I have committed,
> this wrong that I have done to
>   whomever it may be
> this false oath that I have sworn.

In the Hindu texts, water is the *materia prima*. "All was water." In the Jewish and Christian traditions, it first symbolizes the origin of creation. It is the mother, the womb, the source of all things. "And the Spirit of God moved upon the face of the waters." (Genesis 1:2.)

The concept of the primordial water, the ocean of origins, is universal. Natural evolution, in its vast unfolding, its slow stirring of consciousness beginning with the inorganic, proceeds from the environment of the sea. Water is the original element of life. The deepest prenatal nostalgia and the farthest memory of the fetal age are reminiscences of that liquid womb. The Taoist primal dragon lives in the depths of the sea, even though he visits the highest mountains and travels through the air. The man and woman in Genesis are made of earth and water, with fire and air giving them energy and vital breath.

All that the heart desires can always be reduced to the image of water. Water is able to reunite everything; it contains cosmic power. It is a gift from the sky, a power of fertility. Water, an undifferentiated mass, contains the seed of seeds, all promises of development. The "return to the wellsprings" enables us to draw new energy, purify ourselves, be born again.

Treating springs as sacred is universal among mankind: A spring is like the mouth of living water.

Immersion in virgin water, or sprinkling with it, is found in the traditions of many peoples, often associated with rites of passage, mainly birth and death. Baptisms are initiatory operations of regeneration. In purification rituals, virgin water complements fire. A yin element, it corresponds to the north, cold, the winter solstice. The ritual water of Tibetan initiations symbolizes the vows and commitments of the candidate for admission.

The song of a stream is also fresh and clear. The sound of water announces limpidity and purity. Water gives life.

A stream evokes natural feminine nudity. A person who comes out of water is a reflection that gradually materializes. But feminine plasma water, fresh water, lake water, is different from male, foaming, fecundating ocean water.

Cool water awakens and rejuvenates the face. The eyes are refreshed. Purity and coolness combine to give a special delight known to all lovers of water. Water is creative and destructive, a source of life and a source of death. In the desert, springs are meeting places for nomads and places of joy and wonder. Water becomes a center of peace and light. Without water, man cannot live. Rivers are agents of fertilization; rain and dew make the soil fertile. Traditionally, a visitor receives cool water and his feet are washed so that his peace and rest will be assured.

Water is part of our daily comfort, but we tend to forget that for three quarters of the human race it is still a gift from the heavens. It is urgent for us to rediscover the elementary truth that some things are priceless, and to realize that elements like water and air are not a dumping ground for the deadly wastes of our civilization.

PURE WATER, NATURAL WATER

In nature, water has its cycle. It emerges from the earth to become a brook, a river, an ocean. The sun warms it; its vapor rises into the atmosphere, where it is recharged with ozone, and returns in the form of rain, snow, or hail. Rainwater is a veritable medicine. One can bathe in it, splash in it. It has a high specific heat and can convey or absorb a large number of calories.

But today we live far removed from nature and drink tap water, which is radically different from rainwater. It is water that has already been used several times, but filtered, treated, and "regenerated," it becomes harmless. But it is not really pure and it no longer contains certain microorganisms that are useful to the body. Long live the rainwater that grandmothers used to gather in their barrels in the country!

Water is a good conductor of electricity; it transmits electric charges and can discharge their potential. It is also a solvent that cleans. Hydrotherapy utilizes its properties in different ways in which temperature contrasts play the main part.

Water or water vapor makes possible varied and powerful therapeutic effects. Any hydrotherapeutic procedure causes a functional imbalance that increases as the treatment is prolonged and is also greater in proportion to the difference between the temperature of the water and the body. To this unbalancing stimulation, the body responds with a regulating effort to restore metabolic balance.

BATHING

In Europe, baths and particularly warm baths were frowned upon for centuries as an indication of excessive attachment to sensuality and care of the body. The Fathers of the Church forbade Christians to go to public baths, which they regarded as places of debauchery. Only women could take baths, and even then infrequently. Immersion in cold water, however, was recommended as a mortification for subduing the flesh.

A bath enables a person to purify his mind and his whole being, and it refreshes his mind.

The Huichole people, who live in the heart of the Sierra Madre in Mexico, still experience their relations with nature in a profoundly prehistoric way. They look on nature as a mother who provides them with forces: springs, water holes in the desert, volcanic geysers, waterfalls. Water (either associated with fire or not) concretely represents, on certain occasions, the place of a second birth.

The various properties of water are transmitted to anyone who impregnates himself with it. Washing is a means of communicating with the invisible force of water, a spiritual discipline whose vehicle is the physical bath.

Whether ritual or not, a bath satisfies a need for relaxation, security, and tenderness. It stimulates the conditions of fetal life. In bathing, we expel the residues of strain and fatigue.

In Russia and Siberia, physicians of the common people regarded medical baths as an essential part of general therapeutics. They all had oaken tubs and even in small towns there were steam baths, recommended for rheumatism and arthritis. They often added hay dust to the bath water (about two quarts of hay dust boiled for half an hour in a pint and a half of water, then poured into a warm bath) or prepared baths with birch leaves (two pounds of birch leaves in a cotton bag, boiled for half an hour in a quart and a half of water).

BATHS AND SHOWERS

A warm bath (98° to 100°) is the most powerful means of warming a person. Below that temperature it is soothing, and if it is prolonged it reduces blood pressure. A hot bath (101 to 104°) can decongest one region of the body by drawing blood into another. Congestive disorders of the upper part of the body can be treated in this way. A foot bath in hot water is recommended for relieving certain kinds of headaches, colds, and asthma attacks.

Water can also act as a decongesting agent by heating the surface of a painful, swollen region. Baths can thus be used for treating arthritis, asthma, bronchitis, and kidney and liver disorders. Decongestion can be produced by hot showers or poultices composed of a mixture of water and linseed meal, starch, or natural mud. But a poultice must not be applied too hot, because that could cause serious burns and the formation of permanent scars.

Sauna baths and turkish baths open the pores of the skin and allow it to be cleansed thoroughly. Washing and bathing in sulfurous water are good for all skin diseases and lung disorders. If you are near a place that has sulfur springs, go there often to bathe in the water, sprinkle it on yourself, and drink it; all these activities will be beneficial to you.

Warm or hot water relaxes and yinifies the body, while cool or cold water invigorates and yangifies it. A cold shower is a kind of shock treatment whose strong, lasting effects stimulate and develop the body's reactive and healing powers. But do not take one if you are already shivering. A cold shower has a strong, harsh action. It is even more effective after a sauna or a hot bath. Goaded by the spray of water, the skin reacts strongly, causing the body to warm itself, constricting the pores, activating the circulation, and stimulating the nervous system. An invigorating shower dispels muscular fatigue, gives a feeling of well-being, and supplies great energy. Applying cold water to the legs and feet with the hand or a natural sponge has an invigorating effect and is a good treatment for varicose veins. Repeat it several times a day.

Hydrotherapy offers a rich array of treatments. But like any therapy, it must be individualized, making allowances for the season and the person's age and vitality.

It is not enough to know the powers of water; we must also know how to take advantage of them in our daily physical care. The way to attend to our body—though this does not mean that we should be preoccupied with it—testifies to the image we have of ourselves. Always, and especially in the presence of fire and water, it is important to be absorbed in what we are doing. It is therefore good to concentrate in the bathroom as well as in the kitchen.

The skin is the frontier between the inside and the outside. It requires daily washing, especially if you live in a city. Surrounding impurities are deposited on it and block its pores. The skin is not only a tough, supple, impermeable envelope that is always being renewed; it is also a sensory and vascular organ, and a lo-

cus of energy exchanges. The individual is linked to the external world by that organ of perception and information. Equipped with a dense network of nerve endings, it enables us to perceive with great precision and constantly acts on the whole body. It is one pole of the body's heat balance. External heat penetrates through the skin, which contains pigments that prevent the sun's radiation from going in too deeply.

The skin is also an organ of elimination. A good sweat relieves the kidneys of part of their work.

That organ of protection and communication deserves to be well maintained, so that its natural functions will not be hindered.

In hard water, most soaps form invisible salts which impede secretion of sebum, and this may cause chapping and eczema. Use a soap made with clay, olive oil, and honey. Protect your skin from detergents, because they dry it out too much. Take saunas and steam baths as often as possible.

Dry skin, the most delicate and fragile kind, needs fatty substances. But do not use a cream chosen at random. Good massages with dairy products (milk, fresh cream) are preferable to bad-quality creams containing nonnatural products. Oily skin can be cleansed of the fat and sebum contained in its pores by simply washing it in warm water, with or without the astringency imparted by such plants as thyme, rosemary, blackberry leaves, and hawthorn.

The skin of the face is the most delicate and also the dirtiest when it is covered with makeup. In the past, women removed their makeup with cow's milk, either plain or mixed with fruit or berry juice.

If you have dry skin, cover your face once a week with an egg yolk beaten with a spoonful of olive oil. Leave this mixture on for fifteen minutes, then remove it with cotton dipped in warm milk. For best results begin by exposing your face to the vapor from water boiled with a pinch of dried linden blossoms, thyme, rosemary, or sage. This will disinfect the skin and dilate its pores. A face pack made of vegetables or fruit, with a spoonful of fresh cream, nourishes and moistens dry skin.

Wrinkles always appear in skin dehydrated by bad health or a sudden loss of weight. It is good to bathe the face morning and evening in a lotion made with a quart of spring water, a pinch of chicory, and a pinch of celandine.

To invigorate, revitalize, and firm your skin, and remove wrinkles and blackheads, apply lotions made with carrot juice and raw tomatoes and cucumbers, and, if you have dry skin, packs made with an egg yolk and a spoonful each of honey, rye flour, and olive oil; beat the ingredients together and apply for twenty to thirty minutes.

If your skin is oily, omit the olive oil and replace the egg yolk with the juice of half a lemon or the white of an egg to narrow the pores and make the skin's texture finer. Another ideal lotion for oily skin: a pinch each of red rose petals, sage flowers, walnut leaves, and scouring rush, soaked for twenty-four hours in a quart of spring water.

Do not squeeze out blackheads; that injures the skin and continues the irritation. Rub them with slices of fresh tomato or ripe pumpkin. It is also good to use the following lotion: a pinch of fresh celandine and a pinch of couch grass soaked overnight in a quart of spring water.

Plants and water enable the skin to regain its softness and luster. In season, use fresh herbs, vegetables, and fruit to give your skin the means of absorbing all the nourishment and vitamins it needs. Earth, clay, mud, and sand can also transmit their virtues to us. Along with sunlight, air, and water, whose vital principles it receives, earth is one of the most powerful agents of physical regeneration.

When you get up in the morning, splash cold water on your face and eyes. It will make it easier for you to become wide awake.

Compresses of linden-blossom tea remove rings around the eyes. Several times a week, apply a flower infusion: one pinch of mallow flowers, one of camomile, and two of rose or violet petals. For conjunctivitis, use celandine: soak a pinch of it (leaves and stalks) and three or four pinches of red rose petals, which are soothing, overnight in a quart of natural water.

Brush your teeth every day. Use, for example, a good toothpaste made with clay and alternate it with one made with seaweed or other plants. Pressing a piece of lemon peel against the teeth whitens and strengthens them.

If your gums are irritated, rinse your mouth with mint tea. For painful canker sores, rinse it with a decoction of mallow, thyme, sage, and blackberry leaves, or rub it with lemon or onion juice.

HAIR

Hair (especially long hair) is a beautiful natural ornament that deserves good care. Brush it vigorously several times a day with a hard brush (made of pig's bristles, for example) with a wooden handle. To prevent hair from falling out less rapidly, and to avoid breaking its delicate fiber, cut it only during the new moon. It is good to nourish it beforehand by rubbing in olive oil and wrapping warm towels around the head for several hours before shampooing.

If your hair is too oily, soak it for twenty minutes in two egg yolks beaten in a small glass of rum. For softer hair, add a decoction of burdock roots to the rinse water. To lighten its color, use camomile tea. Henna will nourish it and give it beautiful red glints.

You can make your own toilet water to perfume your body and hair. Plants will provide you with everything you need. To make toilet water with lavender, roses, jasmine, violets, or any other flowers or herbs whose fragrance you like, soak an ounce of flowers in a quart of brandy for a month, then strain. An easily made toilet water consists of a quart of 90 percent alcohol mixed with an eighth of an ounce of the essential oil of each of the following: orange blossoms, rosemary, citron, and bergamot. Let the mixture stand for twenty-four hours, then strain.

Such preparations have always been known and valued for making oneself attractive and seductive. Aromatics have also had important uses. In ancient religious ceremonies they were sprinkled over statues of the gods.

Incense not only serves to purify and perfume the atmosphere: Its smoke rises toward the heavens like an offering and facilitates meditation. In Tantrism the Shakti, before uniting with the principle of Shiva (the phallus), is anointed with perfumes on special points of her body.

"Jasmine for the hands, *keora* for the neck and cheeks, *shampa* and *luira* for the breasts, spikenard in the hair, musk on the pubis, sandalwood along the thighs, saffron or *khus* for the feet."

(*Tantra Asana*.)

The spirits of plants and minerals penetrate the subtle channels and prepare the transfigured body for the cosmic act.

In the *Tao Te Ching* we find this prescription for cosmic well-being!

> *Know the masculine,*
> *and therefore adhere to the feminine.*

The wise man knows solar energy and therefore adheres to the water that gave birth to him: From it he daily draws the strength to renew his life. In the cycle of his day, fire (power of the Father, yang) and water (Mother, yin) are in conflict and harmony. It is not surprising that one of the most common metaphors in the intuition of cosmic life is that of the moon's reflection in water. A mineral mirror of the sun, the full moon casts its rays on the nocturnal water. The sun is not affected by moonlight. The moon and the water are not contained in the reflection. The play of light on the primordial waters is also the image, as fleet and delicate as human life, of the harmony of yin and yang.

> *It is found again.*
> *What? Eternity.*
> *It is the sea united*
> *with the sun.*
> Rimbaud

Rest and Action

God rested on the seventh day of creation. That rest is not related to a static state. The seventh day joins the first, perfection is achieved, the cycle begins again, beginning and end are joined. Rest does not mean that the process of development stops. It is a new transfer of energy to creation, an elevation to another level, a greater awareness. Energy circulates in its totality.

REST

The body needs a state of balance and unity in order to pursue its effort. Today, people are tired and overworked, and they even lose awareness of the need for a pause that enables the body to catch its breath and recharge itself. The activity-rest cycle has been disrupted.

Rest is even better in silence, the silence that closes a door and allows the passage of something else. In silence, body and mind regain their natural unity. "In silence, the immortal spirit rises," says the *Shodoka,* a thirteenth-century Zen text. Life might be described as silent effort. Today, people have often forgotten what effort is. Everything is made easier for them. Yet is is effort that makes the human race progress. Without it, we regress.

Modern man is overwhelmed by a feeling of fatigue, strain, and uneasiness. Fatigue may be the expression of a physiological disorder or a psychic imbalance. We must learn to rest in relaxation. Strain arises from an accumulation of vibrations that lead to an impoverishment (nervous, mental, auditory, or visual strain) of the body, which is not given time to restore itself. It is healthy for the will to be manifested in an activity requiring effort in order to perform a creative function.

SLEEP

Natural sleep is a source of health. In our time, sleep is often artificial. Insomnia is combated with sleeping pills or tranquilizers that disrupt the natural process. Medical science recently rediscovered sleep and has been using it as a treatment for nervous depression. But in this case it is artificially induced sleep, whereas the body ought to feel that special sensation of lassitude on its own and abandon itself to it naturally.

The amount of sleep required varies with individuals. A newborn baby's sleeping schedule is exactly patterned on his eating schedule. Yogis can function quite well with only a few hours of sleep each night. But follow the duration of your sleep, which you can determine for yourself.

Sleep passes through various phases: falling asleep, complete sleep, awakening. The onset of sleep is often facilitated by fatigue, darkness, calm, silence, muscular relaxation, a comfortable position, and warmth.

Sunlight has an influence on all our cells.

They are thus altered at sunset and again at dawn. In daylight they become active, and at night, more receptive to external life, they are recharged. It is good to follow the cosmic cycle, to go to bed early (before midnight as much as possible) and get up early, in order to acquire more energy.

Sleep in a quiet, cool room (use several blankets if necessary), on a hard bed, lying on your back or preferably on your right side, to facilitate the functioning of the organs and avoid putting pressure on the heart.

SLEEP AND DREAMS

The best rest consists essentially in sleeping well, but for many people that is not easy. We now have a certain understanding of the processes and rhythms that govern sleep. The powerful charge of dreams is being discovered and many questions are being raised about that mysterious world parallel to the world of our active life. The average person spends about a third of his life sleeping; it is a basic need. Deprivation of sleep causes very serious physical and mental disorders. A human being can do without food for three weeks, but if he is deprived of sleep for that length of time he is on the verge of madness and death.

It should be said at the outset that sleep, however brief, always brings a beneficial disconnection from reality. Who has not had the experience of feeling ill at ease, worried, tired, and depressed, then feeling much better after a short nap? We have the impression of cutting ourselves off from the external world when we take refuge in that reassuring torpor. It is important, however, not to slip into facile laziness, into a soft, womblike cocoon whose security is illusory.

Sleep is a void (in the eyes of consciousness), disconnected from time and space; we gravitate into another universe, we unconsciously connect ourselves to unknown inner circuits which recharge us with energy. On awakening, the mind is clearer, the body is stronger, action is simpler.

The duration of sleep varies with individuals, places, and situations. The body does not always require the same amount of sleep, but it does need balanced amounts. Very short nights of sleep (four hours, for example) require a long, restoring night within three days at the most. During that night, let your body recuperate naturally, without limitation. If it is in its normal state, you will wake up rested.

What happens to us during sleep? First of all, sleep is not a single state, but different alternating ones. We can distinguish two types of sleep. "Slow" or shallow sleep takes up most of our sleeping time. During it, our brain waves are slower than when we are awake. It is hard to give the name of "dreams" to the thoughts and images which occur in this state. The muscles relax, the heartbeat slows, and there is a gentle floating sensation. In this phase the sleeper often moves and sometimes talks or snores. He reacts to stimuli in his environment. His suggestibility is unconsciously awake.

REM (Rapid Eye Movement) or deep sleep always occurs in short periods during which brain waves are different and more rapid than in the waking state. An electroencephalogram shows them becoming broader and slower until an abrupt change takes place. The eyes move in their sockets. This phase is the most important. It is accompanied by dreams; the sleeper has little sensitivity to external stimuli, but he can describe his dreams precisely if he is awakened at that exact moment. This phase is essential to proper functioning of the whole vital system. The first phase is like a preparation for this one. The sleeper slowly descends the steps of sleep until he reaches a state that contains certain essential keys to the mysteries which underlie nature.

These two phases of sleep form a cycle of ninety to a hundred minutes, with only a few minutes of deep sleep. Then the sleeper awakes to some extent, stirs, changes position often, shifts to another part of his bed, and, normally, begains another cycle.

Sleeping difficulties are frequent nowadays. People often sleep badly. Nearly everyone has periods of insomnia because of anxiety, depression, fatigue, tension, or simply bad digestion or breathing. This is a common experience, but chronic insomnia is a more serious matter. Not getting enough sleep gives rise to excessive reactions of nervousness, guilt, mental disorder, and aggressiveness. The slightest disturbing factor seems to prevent the insomniac from sleeping, whereas he actually creates a whole array of obsessions for himself.

Insomnia can take various forms, but people who spend several consecutive sleepless nights are very rare. An insomniac may say and believe that he "didn't sleep a wink," and remember only the anguished times when he was waiting for sleep. Agitated and depressed, having built up a veritable psychosis of sleeplessness, he goes to his doctor and asks for a prescription.

Sleeping pills and tranquilizers have become the most frequently used drugs in the world. They are now known to be dangerous, because there is no pill that can induce sleep identical to natural sleep. Some of these "medicines," such as barbiturates, may even lead to serious addiction, while at the same time accentuating the disruption of normal sleep. Deep sleep becomes rare; the brain waves are different, broken by "mini-awakenings." The biological clock is out of order. The insomniac sometimes begins taking mixtures of drugs that do still more damage to him. While he is awake, he must keep himself going with other pills. He can no longer function without the influence of artificial chemical processes. He becomes sick without them, yet they make him deteriorate steadily.

Insomnia is not a disease, however, but a degenerating disorder. Before trying to sleep, we should know how to fall asleep and realize that insomnia can be caused by any excess in eating, physical or mental exertion, or various irritations. We should therefore learn to relax before going to bed, by means of a walk, an herb tea,* a few relaxing exercises. Everyone can find his own solution: a warm bath, reading, listening to music, yoga postures, making love. . . .

And if, in spite of all this, you still wake up during the night, you must try not to struggle against insomnia, or think about its consequences or dangers, or use pills. Do not desperately try to sleep, feeling more and more upset as you toss and turn in your bed. To change the atmosphere, light a candle, read, listen to music, or meditate on light and fire. If you still feel upset, drink a cup of hot, relaxing herb tea and savor the calm and lucidity of the night, which is propitious to meditation.

Night, that "dark brightness which falls from the stars," consoles the afflicted, protects

---

*See "Useful Herbs" in the chapter "Healing by Plants."

lovers, and is the great rest of nature. Intuition flows better at night, and whether you are asleep or kept awake by the magical brilliance of the full moon, you will be unconsciously impregnated by the vibrations of the universe around you. We are here referring to night animated by the sighing of the wind and the cries of birds. In a city, night is the time of greatest calm, but nature remains absent, unless you know how to make silence within yourself. Depending on how you have prepared for it during the day, your night will be either a restful oasis or a destructive no-man's-land.

DREAMS

The world of sleep plunges us into a mysterious part of life. Many people say they cannot remember their dreams, yet everyone recalls a few nightmares or revealing dreams. The images and symbols of dreams have their roots in an unconscious structure common to all mankind.

Religion, art, legends, and myths all convey archetypes, those essential symbols such as the father, the mother, the serpent, the river, the cave, water, the egg, the sword, the tree, the forest, the spring, and so many others. Certain waking concerns are found in dreams, deformed, dramatized, fragmented into a kind of jigsaw puzzle that seems incomprehensible. Time and space no longer have the same values. We travel along a chain of dreams. The journey may seem endless, but it lasts only a few seconds.

In dreams, we attain another state of reality. Will and responsibility no longer come into play. We are brought into situations which we really experience, in another dimension of consciousness. We may identify ourselves with anything. The philosopher Chuang-tse wrote, "I, Chuang Chou, once dreamed that I was a butterfly, fluttering and contented with my fate, not knowing that I was Chou. Suddenly I awoke and realized with amazement that I was Chou. But how can I tell if I was then a man dreaming he was a butterfly, or if I am now a butterfly dreaming I am a man?"

A mirror is held up to the mind, reflecting its inner truth. Each dream has a meaning; we now know that it expresses the sleeper's deepest yearnings and that, with all its strange aspects, it says things about him in a language rich in teachings for those who know how to interpret it.

The presence of the state of dreaming in life poses a question: What is a total person? Waking consciousness may be like the visible part of an iceberg. Dreams immerse us in a cosmic sea. A dream may be telepathic, premonitory, whimsical, terrifying by its realism or monstrous aberrations, or fertile in implausible situations, but it is surely decipherable on one level or another.

The importance of this part of our lives must be emphasized: to know it better is to have a greater awareness of our own inner wealth.

AWAKENING AND VITALITY

Awakening is the final phase of sleep, and it is often sabotaged. Anyone can feel the difference between a spontaneous, natural awakening and one caused by an alarm clock, a telephone, or someone calling him. Cerebral activity does not stop during sleep, however, and it is easy to decide in advance when sleep should end. When a person wakes up, his organs take on new activities and his metabolism changes. He often stretches, thus enabling muscular tonicity to be restored. His eyes are bathed in light; he again enters the cycle of the day.

It can be said that silence and effort are the natural dimensions of rest and activity. Make silence without fleeing from noise. Strive without forcing yourself. In rest from all agitation, life follows its natural course: vitality awakens. Rest, sleep, activity, and communication with others become the right expressions of our being in the cosmos if they are bathed in silence and governed by effort. Breathing should be stressed here again. The body's discovery of its center of gravity, the secret "golden flower" of the Chinese, *ch'i* (the ultimate life force), depends on breathing, on deep exhalation pushed by the belly.

Silence is the nakedness of being, an opening to the vibration of the totality. Silence is not the absence of sound, it is a chance for the body to regain its natural condition. Silence is on both the near and the far side of words. Plunged in inner experience, it is also the natural vehicle of communication. Make silence before speaking. Eat in silence. Arrange for moments of silence—"spaces" of silence—in the course of the day. Silence abolishes the illusion of time. And of course it is necessary for us to leave the feverish agitation and tainted air of cities, the disquieting hum of electronic centers and mechanized daily life, so that we can go and communicate with the silence of nature, the silence of blowing wind, flying birds, and growing grass.

But silence is not reserved for Robinson Crusoe. Making silence is not fleeing from noise. Making silence means concentrating here and now. We can truly speak of a "way of silence," a course which enables man to discover his original face. Silence is the most powerful natural means of expanding the field of consciousness. It is not by chance that Soto Zen is called the sect of silence in Japan: seated facing the wall, silence . . . the sound of the wind in the pines and the murmur of a stream.

HARMONY IN MOVEMENT

Bodily expression reflects the whole person. Body and mind are inseparable in a living human being. Energy animates the body's involuntary functions as well as its system of relations. The state of health is reflected by the extent to which circulation of that energy is proper and balanced. Energy animates the body.

Like all physical objects, the human body has a center of gravity. Whether a person is standing, sitting, or lying, his center of gravity, that point at which the forces of the Sky and the Earth converge, is approximately in the middle of his abdomen, a little below the navel. The force of this center should be developed. Inside the abdomen are all the organs of assimilation and elimination, a veritable internal factory. Operations are regulated by involuntary mechanisms that control production of the energy which nourishes our action.

The spinal column is the axis of the body. It binds the trunk together and gives it structural unity. It combines several systems: a bone system (the vertebrae), a muscle system that enables it to move and remain erect, the central nervous system (spinal cord) surrounded by branches of the parasympathetic system. The neck, highly mobile, enables the head to make extremely delicate movements. To hold all this up, the muscles at the base of the column must be powerful.

The whole body is coordinated in relation to the vertical line of the spinal column. Any deformation or blockage of it causes weakness and premature deterioration of the body. When we hold ourselves erect, standing or in the lotus position, energy flows up and down the spinal column. With a straight back, if we concentrate on exhalation we feel energy (warmth and vibration) at the base of the back.

By its verticality, the spinal column is an ascensional symbol, an affirmation of oneself. Straighten your spine to receive energy better. Bend it to pay homage. The long story of human evolution is the story of a progressive verticalization freeing the forelimbs and giving much greater development to the brain.

MOVEMENT

The body is traversed by a continual exchange of matter and energy with the surrounding world. Its health depends on what it is capable of acquiring and rejecting. Most of the energy received by man is expended in the form of movement and heat. Everything that lives moves. Any movement requires the action of a large number of the muscles and nerves. Feeling and thought, conscious or unconscious, are embodied in acts.

Movement gives the individual the possibility of developing his muscles, improving his shape, and increasing his litheness and vitality. The form of each species is determined by the movements necessary for its life. Movement cleans the body by burning the by-products of its metabolic activity, and stimulates it by producing a multitude of muscular, cutaneous, articular, and visceral sensations. It invigorates the organs by strengthening the muscles that support them. It gives the spinal column constant support and a certain litheness. It plays an essential part in the functioning of the digestive organs.

The city dweller leaves home in the morning and goes straight to his car or bus or subway. Lack of exercise makes him weak and tense, flabby and rigid at the same time. He may be led to a renewal of his life and his being by rediscovering his body, regaining his strength and energy, and coming to know the necessity and joy of physical effort.

If movement is to impart all its benefits, it must be performed in a concentrated way; it must be real and complete. In the course of hundreds of thousands of years, it has given the human races their forms and aptitudes. An adult can regain at any age what a child discovers and acquires as soon as he is in the midst of nature: the spontaneous ability to use his body harmoniously.

To maintain and strengthen his health, civilized man must take exercise. But to learn how to exercise well, he may have to begin by doing nothing! His body is disordered. To restore a better balance of forces, he must first relax tensions and strengthen fundamental energies. Any tonic imbalance produces a series of compensations necessary for maintaining the ability to act. Restoring tonic harmony in the body permits action without tension. A proper movement must have maximum effectiveness with a minimum expenditure of strength, and it always results from a rhythmic alternation of tension and relaxation, permitting long work without exhaustion.

Rest enables us to catch our breath and prevents movement from becoming more and more tense, to the point of blockage and exhaustion. A person whose body has regained its tonic balance perceives his efforts as an overall application of his strength and not as painful tension here and there. The "centering" of strength in the belly assures maximum economy of movement and maximum concentration in each act. The tautness resulting from this double movement of downward support and upward surging is comparable to the tautness of a bowstring at rest, ready for action in dynamic equilibrium.

While proper movement requires coordination in the posture of the body, it also involves relative abandonment of our voluntary action in favor of reflexes governed by unconscious elements. Since birth, many external influences have grafted a mask of deformations onto our deep nature.

Listen to your body attentively. Correct posture enables you to achieve a good state of mind, which is lined to concentration without tension, and attention available at the precise moment, here and now. Children have that attitude when they play freely. Once an adult has regained it, it becomes spontaneous again.

Each human attitude and act has a meaning. Proper movement permits very rapid and delicate adjustment to the present situation, since sensitivity is not blocked by any excessive tension. It makes the whole body participate in each act. The human being regains his or her beauty.

In their movements, men and women should never be hampered by clothing that constricts the body and prevents them from breathing and acting freely. Clothes may be the visible form of the inner person (in the best of cases, when they are not the dreary garb of a joyless society). Thus the attire of a Zen Buddhist monk does not merely evoke detachment from the world, dust, and rags picked up along the way. A white robe is native purity, a black robe is a veritable accumulator of energy (light, heat, etc.).

Subjected to the influence of climate, man had to learn how to sew animal skins to make clothes and shoes for himself. He also learned to spin and weave plant fibers and animal hair. In winter, clothes must keep the body warm to avoid losing its stored heat, which would cause a general chill. Cold creates conditions favorable to diseases of the respiratory tract. It is particularly important to keep the feet and the back of neck warm (when the latter is not protected naturally by hair). Wool and natural silk provide a good temperature for the body; they are good thermal insulators. In summer, thin, light-colored clothes let the body receive filtered sunlight. It is then good to leave the neck and feet uncovered.

Natural plant fibers (flax, cotton, hemp) are made of cellulose, a carbohydrate. Some artificial fabrics also have a base of cellulose, but it is taken from wood. The most modern synthetic fabrics are made from petroleum.

Silk is made of long chains of simple amino acids with peptide links. More and more synthetic fabrics, such as nylon and acrylics, are now being made. Although their use does not seem harmful to health, it is still true that traditional fabrics, admirable joint achievements of man and nature, such as broadcloth, silk, linen, velvet, wool, and cotton, give the whole body a greater feeling of well-being.

Rest is to movement what silence is to speech. The voice detaches itself from silence and then returns to it (there is a quality of silence in speech), and, similarly, a right act is detached from a background of concentration. Still more deeply, silence is present in sound, immobility in movement, emptiness in form. Experience shows that the rightness of our movement (of our body and our mind) is a function of our concentration. The man or woman who lives naturally thinks with his or her body.

The Territory of the Body

Each of us lives at the heart of an empire and is capable of being its enlightened sovereign. The body is our territory. We can harmonize it with the cosmic order. Or, more exactly, there are techniques of ancient knowledge which, properly used, enable the body to rebalance itself.

In our time, this practical wisdom of the body is particularly well preserved in the Far East. The roots of Far Eastern philosophy and medicine lie in a prehistoric heritage. The principles that animate them, whatever their particular formulations may be, have a universal character. We can approach Far Eastern philosophy and medicine properly if we intuitively understand the seven following points:

1. Man is a whole, functions as a whole, and must be treated as a whole.
2. This whole (microcosm) is a product of the influence of the environment. It is an element of the Great Whole (macrocosm).
3. Consciousness is a manifestation of life. Life is a manifestation of energy.
4. Consciousness, life, and energy are in complete interdependence.

Far Eastern wisdom and medicine (see Fig. A) concentrate all their efforts on energy, E, letting alterations take place naturally, spontaneously, and unconsciously at the level of bodily health, L, and psychic life, C. The West, however (see Fig. B), categorizes and makes

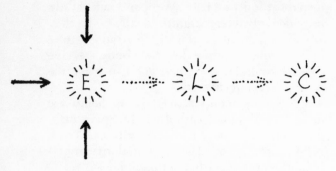

Fig. A—Far East

frequent use of compartmentalized or specialized interventions.

5. Energy, life, and consciousness are a combination of two opposed currents of concentration and expansion, evolution and entropy, yang and yin.
6. Energy—*ch'i* in Chinese, *ki* in Japanese—circulates along the fourteen meridians of the body and between the points on them.
7. Several kinds of action are possible on a single area:

   With the hands or feet: massage.
   With fire: moxas.
   With needles: acupuncture, in the strict sense.

ACUPUNCTURE

Although this practice goes back at least to the third millennium B.C., the West has begun to know it better only in recent years. Acupuncture is officially recognized now that scientists have proved the validity of its basic laws by electronic means: the presence of a form of energy has been shown by the use of devices which, when moved over the body, are able to detect and measure the frequencies of that energy in relation to the points indicated by Chinese tradition. The effect varies according to the polarity of the metal used. Gold and copper, for example, have a stimulating effect, while silver and zinc have a calming effect. Steel is said to be neutral. Doctors in China recently aroused great interest in the West when they allowed reporters and study groups to witness treatments and operations performed with the aid of acupuncture. One patient who underwent a tumor operation, smiling and insensitive to pain, was a striking example.

We must not forget that in the Orient the universe has not been fragmented into distinct parts and that man is a reduced image of the universe, subject to the laws that guide the movements of life as well as the stars. In China, medicine and philosophy are one.

The ancient Chinese thus noticed that everything was governed by two antagonistic and complementary principles, yin and yang, the "absence of light" and the "light of the sun." Both elements—feminine and masculine, yin and yang—are found in each of us, usually with one predominant, according to sex. These two forms of energy cannot exist without each other. The total balance of energy in the void permits the movement of atoms among themselves.

> Thirty spokes converge on the hub,
> but it is the emptiness between
> that makes the wagon move.
> Clay is shaped to make vases,
> but it is on the inner emptiness
> that their use depends.
> A house has openings for doors and windows,
> and it is emptiness
> that makes it inhabitable.
> Being has aptitudes
> that nonbeing uses.
>
> *Tao Te Ching*

The expansion and concentration of galaxies is found in the pulsations of the heart, in the inspir and ekspir on which life is based. Conforming to the Tao, the Middle Way, is living in harmony, harmonizing yang energy and yin energy, since an excess of either causes imbalance in the body.

The single law: The universe is the oscilla-

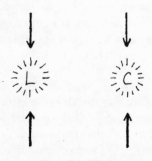

Fig. B—West

tion of the two activities, yin and yang, and its vicissitudes.

The first observation made by the Chinese was that pulsations can be felt at specific points of the body. They also discovered that pressure, heat, or a pinprick gave a sensation of energy flowing along a certain course, as though that energy went all through the body along exact lines.

These lines, known as meridians, do not follow any physical pathways known in the West, such as nerves or veins. Yet the alignment of points on them, far from being imaginary, is a precise reality.

The meridians are divided into two groups: those on the inner side of the limbs (yin) and those on the outer side (yang). They are connected to each other at their ends and by secondary vessels. Soulie de Morant, who in 1934 was the first to describe the practice of acupuncture in the West, situates them as follows:

OUTER SIDE	INNER SIDE
ARMS	
Small intestine meridian	Lung meridian
Triple warm-ing meridian (digestion, breathing, reproduction)	Heart meridian
	Sex and Blood meridian
Large intestine meridian	
LEGS	
Bladder meridian	Liver meridian
Gall bladder meridian	Spleen and pancreas meridian
Stomach meridian	Kidney meridian

Besides these twelve meridians there are two median lines: the conception vessel, on the front of the trunk and head, and the governing vessel, on the back. They communicate with each other but not with the twelve other meridians. They form a separate circulation, acting directly on the organs. The conception vessel acts on the respiratory, digestive, and urogenital systems. The governing vessel acts on the motor and cerebrospinal systems. Energy rises along the conception vessel and descends along the governing vessel. This cycle can be activated; it is the secret pathway of the subtle Taoist alchemy.

The Chinese also concluded from observation that vital energy circulates without interruption, returning to the lungs, the "masters of energy," each morning, and then departing from them. It passes from one organ to another according to a precise schedule.

Lungs	3 A.M. to 5 A.M.
Large intestine	5 A.M. to 7 A.M.
Stomach	7 A.M. to 9 A.M.
Spleen	9 A.M. to 11 A.M.
Heart	11 A.M. to 1 P.M.
Small intestine	1 P.M. to 3 P.M.
Bladder	3 P.M. to 5 P.M.
Kidneys	5 P.M. to 7 P.M.
Heart governor (blood circulation)	7 P.M. to 9 P.M.
Triple warmer	9 P.M. to 11 P.M.
Gall bladder	11 P.M. to 1 A.M.
Liver	1 A.M. to 3 A.M.

Knowing this schedule makes it possible to act with maximum effectiveness, depending on which part of the body is diseased and which organ is unbalanced.

Acupuncture can be regarded as an exercise of great concentration in which knowledge of the patient's psychic, emotional, nervous, and muscular characteristics is essential to the physician.

THE POINTS

Depending on the type of action exerted at each point, the process induced is centripetal or centrifugal, stimulating or soothing. The Chinese distinguished from twenty-seven to forty-seven aspects in the beating of each pulse. The main aspects are defined by regularity or irregularity, slowness or fastness, amplitude, and certain characteristics such as hardness or softness. A slow, small, and/or soft pulse beats in a yin manner. A hard, large, and/or rapid pulse is a sign of yang.

It must be determined whether an injured organ is suffering from too much or too little yin or yang. To restore balance, the patient must be soothed by dispersing the principle of

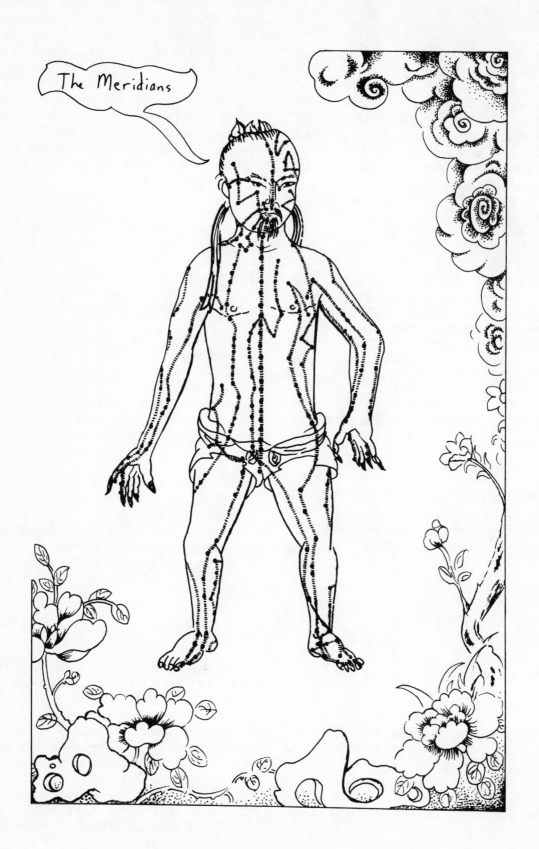

which there is too much, or stimulated by strengthening the principle of which there is too little. If, for example, the pulse related to the stomach is large and swollen, it is a sign of swallowed air and insufficient energy in the stomach. If it is soft, small, and weak, digestion is too slow; if it is rapid, small, and hard, it is a sign of general hypertension, cramps, spasms, and burns that may develop ulcers.

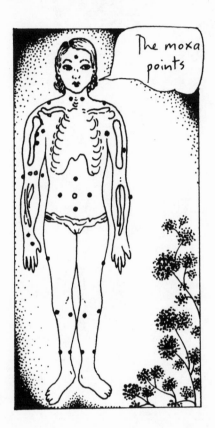

The moxa points

Once these points have been situated (and that is the hardest part), how is one to act on them? By massage and pressure, as we will see later, by fire in the form of moxas, or by acupuncture needles.

Before going on to the techniques of massages, let us examine the action of moxas. Through fire and its radiation, they transmit energy capable of soothing or stimulating. For this purpose the Chinese use a little ball of burning powdered mugwort resting on a thin slice of garlic and a leaf, placed over the point to be treated. The Indians use cones of incense. You can use a glowing stick of incense as a form of moxa: Gradually move it as close to the skin as possible, above the point to be treated, and leave it there a few moments. The effect of moxas is beneficial for weakness, rheumatism, and anemia, but farmful in cases of inflammation and congestion. For that reason their use should be avoided just before or after a hot bath.

Using a small number of moxas (three to five) on a point usually has a calming effect. Using a larger number produces stimulation. Moxas can be used effectively only at certain specific points.

THE MERIDIANS

The following drawings show three important meridians—those of the lungs, stomach, and kidneys—as well as the governing vessel and the conception vessel.

Lung meridian

7: Master point of the conception vessel

Lung meridian. A yin meridian which starts below the collarbone and ends at the thumb. It acts on the respiratory tract.

   Point 2: cough, sore throat
   Point 3: cerebral congestion
   Point 6: laryngitis
   Point 8: cough, vomiting
   Point 10: dizziness, shivering, tension

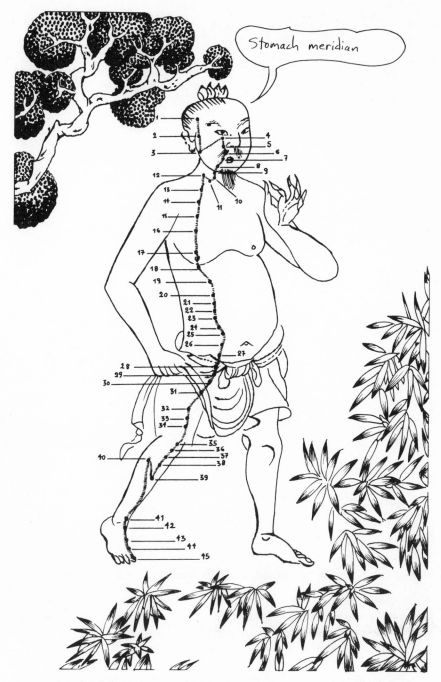

Stomach meridian. A yang meridian, with 45 points, which begins at the temple and ends at the second toe. It regularizes general energy.

    Point 9: angina

    Point 19: cough

    Point 22: gastritis, incontinence of urine

    Point 36: a very important point which acts on nervous and psychic disorders, pain, general fatigue, stomach spasms, and low blood pressure

    Point 41: tonification point; acts on rheumatism and constipation

    Point 45: sedation point; indigestion, insomnia, bilious attacks

Kidney meridian. A yin meridian, 27 points. Begins at the sole of the foot and ends under the collarbone. Acts on general energy and the fluidity of the blood.

 Point 1: sedation point; heart palpitations, high blood pressure, cough

 Point 3: heart pain, constipation, angina, vomiting

 Point 4: overemotionalism

 Point 6: insomnia, mental disorders

 Point 7: inadequate kidney functioning

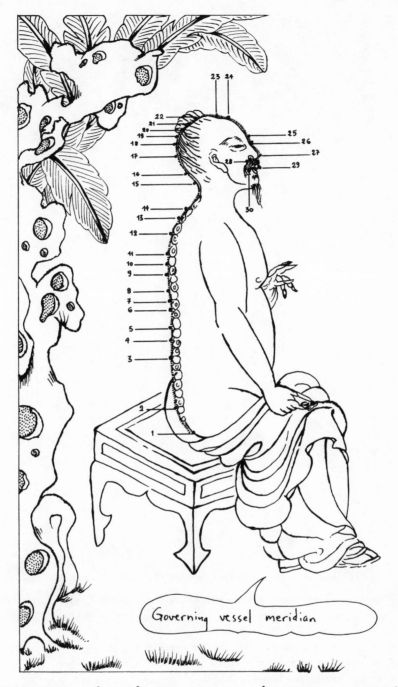

Governing vessel meridian

Governing vessel meridian. A posterior, cerebro-nervous, yang meridian, 30 points. Begins at the point of the coccyx and ends at the upper
gum. In its lower part (up to the sixth cervical vertebra) it acts on physical energy, while in its upper part it harmonizes mental energy and
strength of character.

   Point 2: disorders of menstruation and the uterus
   Point 4: headache, ringing in the ears
   Point 11: heart disorders. This point must not be needled; mox-
ibustion or massage must be used instead.
   Point 13: nervous depression

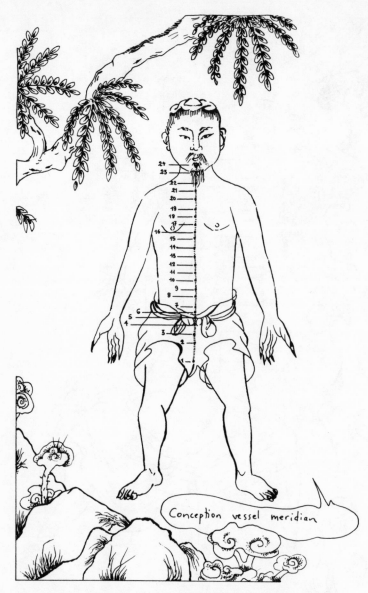

Conception vessel meridian

Conception vessel meridian. An anterior, yin meridian. Begins at the coccyx and ends at the chin. From the navel to the coccyx, the points act essentially on the urogenital organs; from the base of the sternum to the navel, on the digestive functions. The most important points are:

Point 5: the "genital center"

Point 6: general disorders of energy, irregular menstruation, dizziness

Point 13: stomach disorders

Point 15: fatigue, nervous prostration

Point 17: the essential point at which all energy is concentrated

Point 22: cough, pharyngitis

MASSAGE

The activities of the body-mind are engendered and maintained by the vibrations of the environment. Certain vibration frequencies are picked up by our sense organs. Colors, light, sounds, and the resistance of matter are manifestations of the same energy, segments perceived in a continuous range of waves.

We are sometimes conscious of these phenomena, and sometimes not. The same can be said of the waves picked up by our skin, the palms of our hands, and the soles of our feet. Not all human beings pick up energy in the same way, because many receive vibrations from the environment badly or incompletely.

When we awaken, we often instinctively rub our eyes and stretch. We unconsciously perform acts that enable energy to flow and activate numbed organs or points. We can perform them on others as well as on ourselves. They undoubtedly represent one of the oldest and most widespread forms of therapy and maintenance of the body-mind. In our time, certain gestures have at least partially preserved a charge of symbolism: the laying on of hands, for example. And do schoolchildren still know that when a man was dubbed a knight he was given a colossal blow on the top of his head?

When a person is in good health he draws energy from his environment in an invisible form and redistributes it in a visible form.

The opposite is also true, since we "burn" food. The human body picks up the electromagnetic vibrations of cosmic energy at points along the meridians.

When an element of the body is not in is normal condition, the points of the corresponding meridian become hard and painful even before the internal organ is sensitive. The network of meridians is an essential part of the body's mechanism of self-defense and self-regulation. As long as it is alive, an organism always contains energy. But that energy often circulates badly. The "blockage" of a point causes congestion of energy and a shortage downstream. When a point is painful, it generally indicates an excess of energy there. Proper functioning of the circuits can be restored by massage in the form of rubbing, striking, squeezing, or pressing on the point and in the painful area.

When a point suffers from an excess of energy, it is calmed by dispersing energy into the meridian. The action of massage can be compared to that of removing a stone that hinders the current of a stream, and just as stagnant water loses the properties it had as running water, excessive energy reverses its effect on the body.

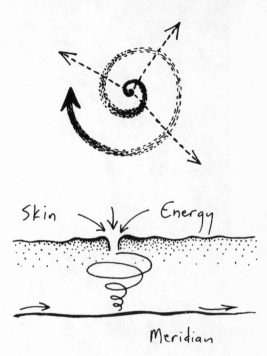

We can relieve a painful point and unblock energy by massaging the point deeply and continuously, using the fleshy part of the thumbs and synchronizing the thrusts with exhalation. If necessary, the point is massaged with a movement away from the center.

If a point is too painful, it is possible to act along the meridian, gradually moving up to the point. When energy is deficient at a point or in a meridian, it is pressed rapidly and lightly with the fingertips rather than the thumb, moving toward the center in spirals if necesary.

It goes without saying that breathing plays a fundamental part when one gives and receives a massage. If one person massages another, they should synchronize their breathing. Exhalation should be deep, always directed toward the region of the intestines, with inhalation taking place naturally. The kind of food you eat conditions the effectiveness of massage. And during massage you will be better aware of your body if it is not overfed or overladen with toxins.

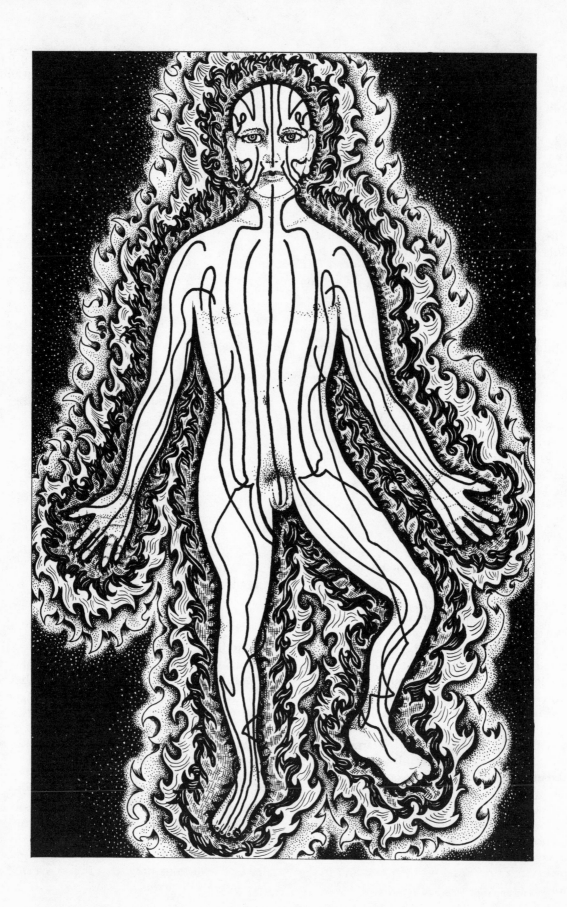

MASSAGE YOURSELF

You can massage yourself, and it is a very good way of becoming better acquainted with your body. You can also give the same massages to someone else (or receive them from him), which is an excellent way to make energy circulate.

Seated lightly on your heels, with your spine straight, your pelvis tilted, your chin drawn in, and your hands resting on your thighs, take the posture which, along with the "cross-legged" one,* is the basic posture. If you breathe correctly and if your body is relaxed, there will be a self-massage of the internal organs.

Salutation-exhalation. The hands flat on the floor form a triangle (yang). Lean forward, exhaling deeply, and place your forehead in the triangle. Remain in this position for a few moments, then straighten up while you inhale deeply and naturally.

When you take the posture, concentrate on it.

Your hands are tools. Here is how to prepare them: Rub or shake them to stimulate circulation of the blood, nervous energy, and *ki.*

---

*See the chapters on Yoga and Zazen.

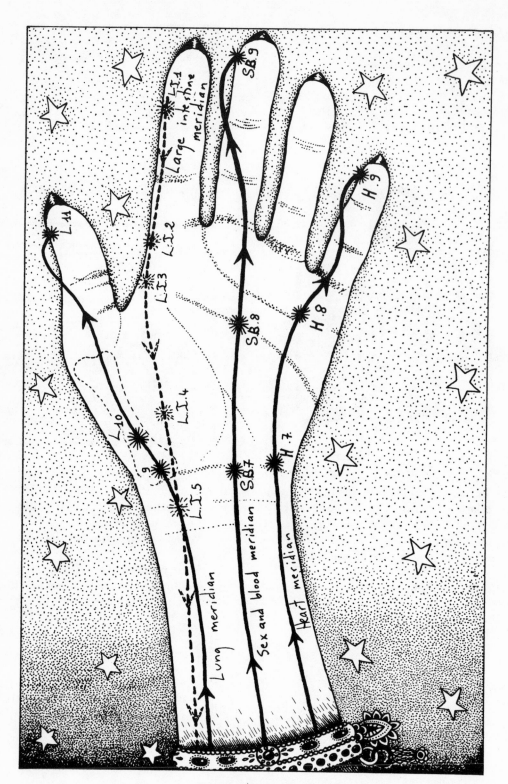

The hand meridians

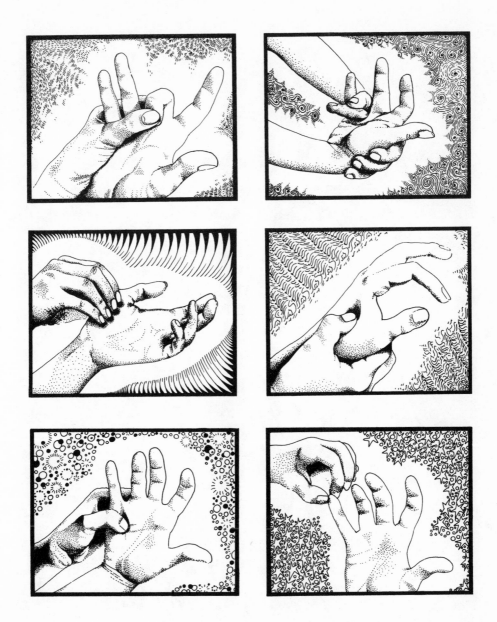

THE HANDS

Pull on the end of each of your fingers, pinching them and giving them a slight rotary movement, in order to stimulate the meridians that "end" there and change polarity.

Bend your fingers at their joints—and so much the better if they crack! Energy accumulates briefly at the "breaks," then flows more forcefully when pressure is relaxed.

Press one thumb against the fleshy part at the base of the other, at the lung points (L9, L10).

The large intestine point should not be painful. Massage it in the morning to stimulate the large intestine if you are in pain.

Massage point H3 (on the heart meridian) with your thumb. If you are with someone who has had a stroke, strongly pinch point H9 on each of his hands, synchronizing your breathing with his.

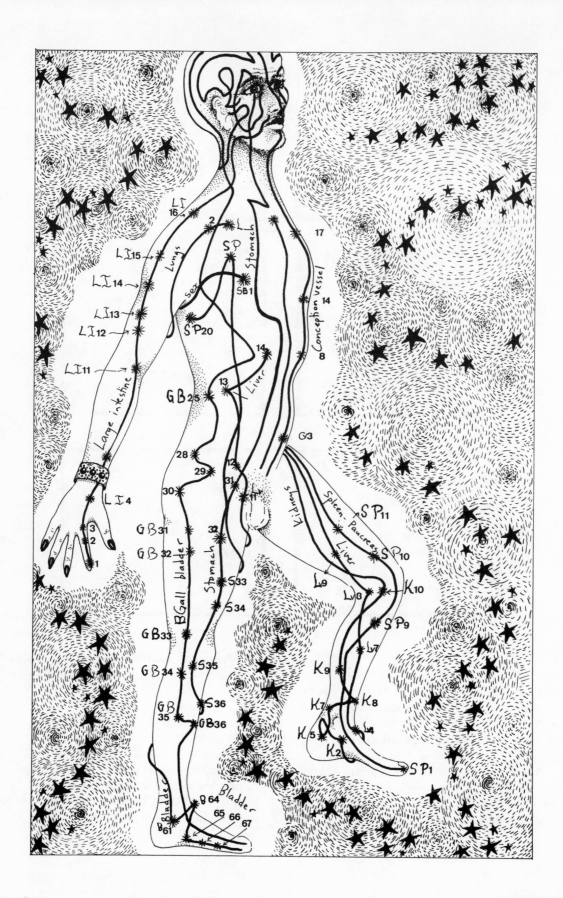

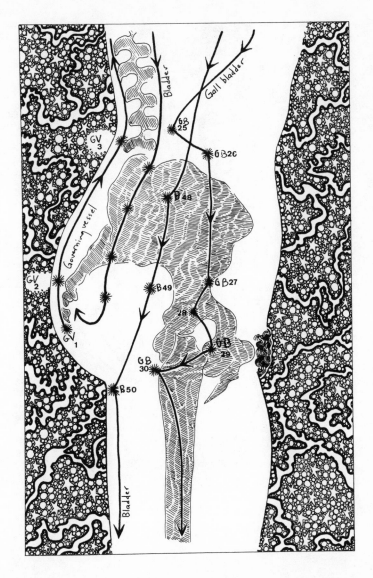

THE DIGESTIVE ORGANS

Press on the armpits, rub and press on the chest, ribs, and belly. You may also strike the belly lightly. Check the state of your digestive organs, particularly the liver and spleen, locating the points that lie along the meridians. It is preferable, however, not to press too much on the whole region of the sternum, the plexus, and the throat.

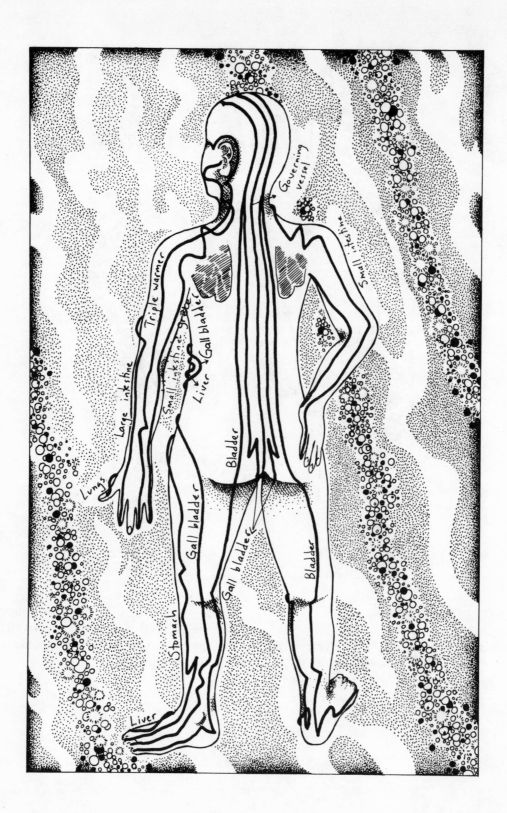

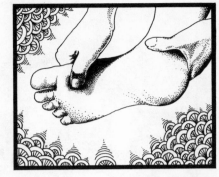

THE GOVERNING VESSEL MERIDIAN

The governing vessel, bladder, and gall bladder meridians run along the back and hips. You can hammer them vigorously with your fists. Massage the spine, pressing with your thumbs on both sides of the spaces between vertebrae. This massage must obviously be given by someone else; you can then return the favor. If you are alone, lie on the floor with a firm cushion under your back, directly below your navel. Relax, breathe deeply, and roll on the cushion from side to side.

THE FEET

The heel bones influence the regeneration of bone cells. Stretch out your legs and strike your heels together. By pinching the Achilles tendon strongly, you will regularize the activity of the kidneys, bladder, and sex organs.

To influence the activity of various organs of the body, press the corresponding points indicated in the following drawing.

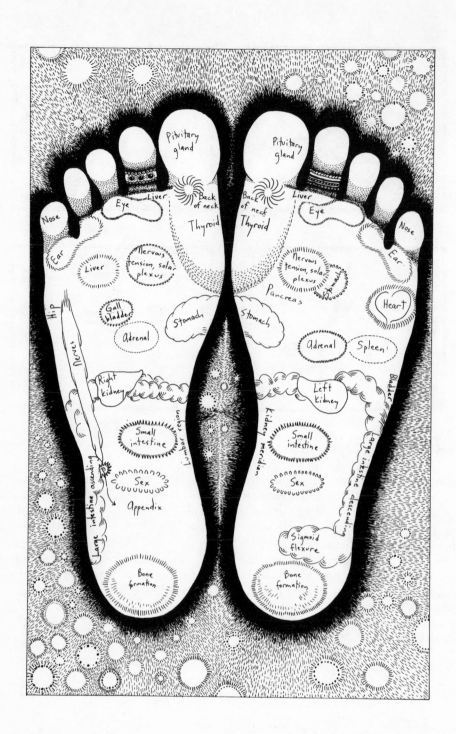

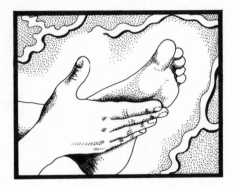

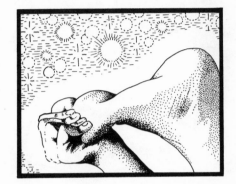

Pinch the big toe strongly (at point SP1) to activate the spleen and liver meridians, as well as the intuition center.* To stimulate the reflex points (eyes, sinuses), walk barefoot on pebbles, or vigorously slap the soles of your feet.

If you grip your toes tightly and make them crack, you will activate all the meridians in the legs. To stimulate the digestive organs, lie on your stomach and have someone step on the soles of your feet with his heels.

*According to tradition, the "third eye," or organ of light, situated in the middle of the forehead a little above the eyebrows, is related to the pituitary gland.

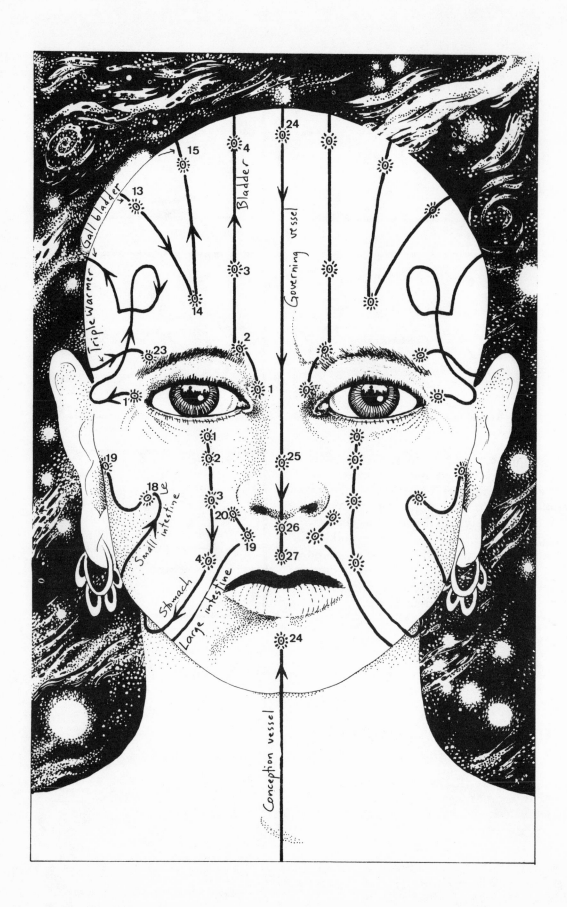

THE HEAD AND FACE

The fists form wonderful little hammers for lightly striking the scalp and thus stimulating the governing vessel, bladder, and gall bladder meridians, as well as the triple warmer above the ears.

You can pull your hair rather strongly, gripping it in handfuls. Normally, you should not feel pain. You will thus stimulate the meridians. Pull very strongly if you have drunk or feasted too much the night before.

If you have done some intense mental work and your head feels heavy, massage your temples and press your thumb against point TW16, behind and below the ear. With your fingers, massage along your brow ridges from the bridge of your nose outward, lingering over your temples.

Our ears are antennae that pick up vibrations from the infinite. Pinch the rims of your ears and pull and massage their lobes—you will live better and know wisdom!

You can give yourself (or have someone else give you) a beauty massage. Gently pinch and pat the skin of your face after passing your fingers over your eyes as you do when you are tired. If you concentrate well, at the end of a good massage you can completely relax the person you have massaged; he will stand up with his body and mind completely renewed and you will have communicated your *ki* to him.

When you massage someone, have him adopt the basic posture (see drawing) or sit cross-legged, preferably in the half-lotus position, or sit on a stool. Place yourself behind him and let his head rest on your chest. Close his eyes with your fingers and his ears with your palms. Synchronize your breathing with his. During an exhalation, press his eyes gently and his ears more strongly. Relax the pressure during inhalation, without removing your hands. Repeat the sequence several times.

There is also a massage that will deeply relax xomeone who is tired. Have him lie on his back with his muscles slack and his arms along his body. Sit on your heels and place his head on your lap. Put your left hand under the back of his neck and the forefinger and middle finger of your right hand just above his eyebrows. Synchronize your breathing with his. During exhalation, lightly press down your

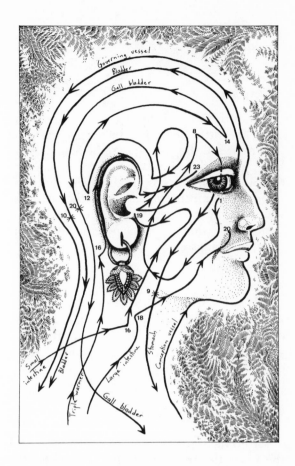

fingers and lift the back of his neck a little. Release the pressure during inhalation. If you continue this massage for a certain time, you may even put him to sleep.

SELF-HELP

Determining the points to be massaged is a matter of practice and intuition. Depending on the type of disorder, you should rub (press the end of the thumb down strongly, with a circular motion), or massage (press less strongly), or lightly stroke (in a little circle with one fingertip). You can also pinch the skin lightly. If the point is very painful, massage may last several minutes.

Here are ways in which some common disorders can be treated:

Anxiety

Rub the inner side of the arm below the wrist, then the inner side of the wrist, the shin, and the middle of the skull, at the junction of the three bones.

Asthma

Rub the inner side of the wrist, near the edge; the little finger just below the nail; the lower edge of the collarbone; the inside of the knee, just at the joint. Lightly stroke the top of the big toe; the biceps, at about the center of the upper arm; the inner side of the wrist, toward the outer edge; the point of the breastbone; both sides of the spine, between the shoulder blades.

Chronic Bronchitis

Rub the inner side of the wrist, toward the outside; the inner side of the arm above the wrist, also toward the outside. Massage along each side of the spine.

Constipation

Rub the top of the instep, in the hollow of the joint; the front of the leg, just under the knee; the inner edge of the outer side of the arm, just below the elbow; the inner side of the knee. Lightly stroke the inner side of the leg, just below the knee; the inner side of the foot, above the instep; the outer side of the leg, below the knee.

Mental and Physical Depression

Rub below the navel and above the pubis; the front of the shin; the inner side of the big toe joint; the spine, between the shoulder blades; the center of the skull, above the occiput.

Heart Pain

Lightly stroke the ends of the ribs at the edge of the stomach; the inner side of the foot, above the heel, and above the big toe joint.

Tired Legs

Rub the front of the leg, just under the knee; the upper part of the calf; the top of the instep, at the angle formed by the leg and the foot.

Impotence and Frigidity

Rub the spine at the level of the fourth lumbar vertebra; the inner part of the thigh, at the height of the groin; the inner side of the calf and the knee.

Insomnia

Rub at the angle of the foot and the leg. Massage the inner part of the wrist, above the thumb joint.

Headache

Rub the inner side of the foot at the base of the big toe. Pinch the skin at the top of the nose several times. Massage the back of the hand toward the middle of the outer edge; the base of the thumb joint; the inner side of the forearm, toward the outer edge; the inner side of the foot, below the ankle; the front of the leg, below the knee.

Painful Menstruation

Massage the back of the hand toward the middle of the outer edge.

Nervous Cough

Locate the sensitive points on either side of the spine (around the fourth thoracic vertebra) and massage them.

The "bodily contact" of massage is a way, probably a primordial one, of treating the total person. It takes on its full meaning when it is combined with the other ways of natural medicine: ways of healing (and maintenance of the body) by minerals and plants, and also the homeopathic taking of elements from the environment.

HEALING BY MINERALS

> If I pick up a stone
> or a lump of earth
> and look at it,
> I see in it the superior and the inferior,
> I see in it the whole world.
>
> Jacob Boehme
Mysterium Magnum, II, 6.

> In my hand the illuminated stone.
> *Zen Koan.*

There is every reason to believe that, consciously or not, man has always associated the energies of the earth with the concept of a primordial maternal power. Impregnated by the celestial semen of sunlight and by all manifestations of energy from above (cosmic rays, for example), dry land emerges from the original waters and brings forth lichens, mosses, mushrooms, and all its progeny of plants. It gives birth to all living beings. Each day the wise man celebrates the eternal wedding of the earth and the sky.

The mineral world is rich in infinite potentialities. The nourishing soil that sustains us receives seeds and turns them into plants that seek sunlight; but the fertile surfaces of the planet are only a thin crust. The inner fire (the "inferno") still burns in its depths. Awesome and sacred forms of energy surge up from the bowels of the earth.

Western civilized man has been too much inclined to regard natural sources of energy as a boundless reserve from which he can draw without restraint, not caring about balances of the effects of his acts—some of which are irreversible. It is not surprising that he has almost entirely lost intuitive knowledge of the regenerative and curative powers of clay, the substance from which, according to the Bible, he was originally drawn. He receives the vibration of the mineral world so badly that stones become dead objects for him. Yet stones breathe, and they act on us.

Clay

The earth gives life and takes it back. In harmony with sunlight, air, and water, whose vital principles it receives, earth—clay, mud, sand— is a powerful agent of physical regeneration. The ancient Egyptians used it for mummifying their dead and knew its purifying abilities.

Clay, that living element, transmits powerful virtues to man. By its antiseptic action it hinders the proliferation of parasites and pathogenic microbes and bacteria, and favors cellular restoration. It also has the property of going to the seat of a disorder: When it is swallowed, it automatically makes its way to the focus of the ailment, fixes itself there, then takes the harmful agents with it when it is evacuated. Placed on the body, it eliminates bad odors and efficiently draws out impurities. By stimulating radioactivity, it restores balance and protects the body from dangerous ionizing radiations.

Not all kinds of clay have the same properties. It is best to get curative clay from an herbalist or a dietitian. It may be green, red, yellow, gray, or white. Different varieties of it traditionally have been prized for treating particular ailments. Before using it, make sure it has undergone no transformation after being extracted. The more clay has been exposed to sunlight, air, and rainwater, the more effective it is reputed to be. Choose a smooth clay, without sand, preferably from the region where you live, and take no more than one teaspoonful a day, or half a teaspoonful for children under ten.

The action of clay varies with individuals, the method of preparing it, and the way of applying or drinking it. Clay may not be accepted well by your body. Begin by drinking only water in which clay has been soaked; it should then become progressively easier for you to absorb it.

It is better to prepare the clay in advance, which also facilitates homogenization of the mixture. Let it rest awhile before using it either internally or externally. Apply it directly to your skin as often as possible. For maximum effectiveness, it is important for the clay to cling closely to the part of the body to be treated. To make sure of this, press down firmly on the poultice.

CLAY TAKEN INTERNALLY

Because of the diastases it contains, clay cleanses and enriches the blood. Its diastases fix free oxygen. Composed mainly of aluminum silicate, it also contains lime, magnesium, sodium, potassium, iron, and calcium. It stimulates a deficient body and contributes to restoration of proper functioning by permitting assimilation and fixation of minerals that are present in food but could not be retained by the body without the aid of clay. It is a catalyst which acts more by its presence than by the substances it contains. It is thus a powerful agent of transformation and transmission of energy.

It takes part in the symbiosis that enables the organs to function in harmony. It naturally absorbs toxins and neutralizes chemical acids and other poisions. Traditionally, it is an excellent remedy for mushroom poisoning.

Take clay in the morning on awakening, at bedtime, or an hour before meals. Never leave a metal spoon in contact with clay. Use a thick glass: Clay emits or refracts strong radiations. At the beginning of a course of treatment, it may cause constipation. Dilute it in a little more water and spread the dose over several different times during the day. If constipation persists, replace the clay with a laxative herb tea.

To soothe inflammation of the gums, chew a spoonful of powdered clay. Clay is inadvisable for anyone with high blood pressure. It can be used in relatively large doses or in homeopathic doses. It is useless to take a great deal of it, however, since its action is due mainly to its magnetism. It should be taken for a week at a time, alternating with a week of abstention, over a period of one or two months. *If you are following a course of medical treatment, even a homeopathic one, do not take clay.*

Clay is a good remedy, but it must be used with care and discrimination, especially when taken internally. It is also effective when used externally.

CLAY USED EXTERNALLY

If you gather clay yourself, before using it you must dry it well and handle it properly. Do not touch it with a metal that rusts. Dry it in sunlight, preferably, and never in contact with a source of heat. When it is thoroughly dry, crush it into little pieces and clean it by removing pebbles, roots, and other impurities. Put it in an enamel, earthenware, wooden, or porcelain container (never use metal or plastic). Level its surface and add water that has not been boiled. The clay will gradually absorb it. Stop adding water when the clay is covered. Let the mixture rest a few hours. You should obtain a homogeneous paste that is not too thick.

Clay can be applied cold, warm, or hot. To treat a feverish, congested part of the body, make a cold poultice; it will gradually absorb the heat of the ailment. Renew it as soon as it is warm. To revitalize the kidneys, bladder, or liver, the clay must be warmed before it is applied.

To invigorate or revitalize, the poultice must be warm; but to treat an inflamed part of the body it must be cold; oxidation and blood circulation are thus accelerated in the body, and the ailment is rejected more forcefully by the stimulated defensive functions.

Clay can be warmed in a double boiler. Leave it on the stove until the clay paste is of the desired temperature. A better method is to expose the clay to sunlight or place it near a wood fire. It is better not to warm clay more than once, so prepare only enough for a single application.

The poultice should be larger than the area to be treated. With a wooden spoon, spread an even layer on a piece of cloth, whose thickness varies according to the ailment involved. Sometimes a mud compress is better than a poultice. In such cases, make a thin paste and dip a cloth into it. Put the poultice or compress in place and attach it with a bandage of soft, warm cloth. If it is placed on the back of the neck, wrap the bandage around the forehead, not the neck.

Application varies with the ailment. For a festering sore or wound, renew the application every hour until suppuration stops, then leave the last poultice on for about two hours, to let the tissues restore themselves better. To treat organs, such as the liver, kidneys, and stomach, leave the poultice on for two to four hours at a time. To revitalize an organ or restore decalcified bone tissue, the poultice can be left on overnight, but it must never cause discomfort or a painful sensation. The clay is almost dry by the time it is taken off. It comes off easily if everything has been done correctly. Rinse with warm water without soap, alcohol, or eau de cologne.

Clay can be used in enemas and douches. Put four tablespoonsfuls of powdered clay in a quart of unboiled water. Warm it slightly and stir well. Finely powdered clay is effective for diaper rash and children's minor injuries. It exercises a disinfecting action on all cuts and sores and favors restoration of the damaged tissues. It also increases the effectiveness of massage.

Sprinkle it on the skin for blotches, eczema, and other skin ailments. But treating eczema solely from the outside strengthens its internalization. It may sometimes be caused by an ordinary emotional upset and its treatment varies according to the state of the skin, but there are few cases in which it is not necessary to insist on draining the liver and clearing the intestines.

The action of clay is very powerful and releases a great deal of energy. It is therefore preferable not to apply it to two organs at once. It spreads its effects through the body in a kind of chain reaction. Once a clay treatment has begun, it is better not to interrupt it, even briefly.

Before treating yourself with clay, clean out your body with natural laxatives, take lemon juice regularly over a period of several days, and also drink water with powdered clay in it. At the beginning of the treatment, the ailment seems to become worse: The clay treats in depth. Pain increases at first, then diminishes, and finally disappears. The ailment is "leaving the body." If there is an open sore, it closes and healthy tissue is formed.

A special treatment: Each morning swallow a small teaspoonful of clay in half a glass of water, alternating every other week with a small teaspoonful of olive oil in the juice of half a lemon. Take a cold hip bath for three or four minutes. In the evening, place a thick clay poultice over your lower abdomen one day and over your liver the next.

Dry eczema can be treated with a mixture of clay and olive oil (two large spoonfuls of olive oil and one of water, beat, add a large spoonful of powdered clay, and mix thoroughly). Coat the affected part and cover with a bandage. For weeping eczema, simply sprinkle on powdered clay. If the eczema is infected, alternate clay poultices with compresses moistened with a decoction of boxwood leaves (an ounce and a half in a quart of water, boiled ten to fifteen minutes).

Eczema often comes from deep-seated disorders. Its treatment first requires a calm life and complete cleansing of the body by means of a wholesome diet, preferably with little meat. It is a long-range treatment which must restore the unbalanced body to proper functioning, but manifestations of the disease can be quickly relieved and diminished by external applications.

Acne, a skin ailment characterized by a lesion or functional disorder of the sebaceous glands, occurs in several different forms. Although it does not seem to be very serious in itself, it embarrasses those afflicted with it and may be accompanied by other disorders such as bad functioning of the sex organs or intestines.

Treatment of acne also acts on the liver, which is related to it. An acne sufferer is poisoned and devitalized. He should eliminate meat, animal fat, alcohol, white sugar, and denatured foods from his diet, and eat a great deal of fruit, fresh raw vegetables, dried fruit, honey, and yogurt. He should also drink a glass of water with a spoonful of clay in it every morning before breakfast for a week, then alternate for a week with olive oil in the juice of half a lemon.

An acne sufferer should clean the face every morning with lemon juice, or a mixture of lemon juice and olive oil, or an infusion of half an ounce of wormwood and half an ounce of geranium steeped in a pint of boiling water for ten minutes. Treatment of acne requires perseverance, since it often takes several months for signs of recovery to appear.

Clay can be used extensively in beauty care. Puffiness under the eyes can be diminished by the application of clay. Most beauty packs consist mainly of clay, though unfortunately it is often mixed with unnatural substances which lessen the power of its action. Make a paste of powdered clay, water, and an equal quantity of cucumber, tomato, and grape juice. Spread it on and let it dry. Very thick clay can be applied locally to pimples and wrinkles and left overnight. Treat all excrescences, warts, and blotches with clay.

Anything that affects the nose (head colds, hay fever, sinusitis) can be treated by rinsing with clay water (one small spoonful of clay in a cup of water). Once, twice, or three times a day, put your nose into the cup, close one nostril with your finger, and gently inhale to draw water through the open nostril. Some of the water may run down into your throat. Repeat the procedure five or six times for each nostril, and also breathe the vapor of thyme in boiling water. In cases of persistent sinusitis, apply cold clay poultices to the forehead and the wings of the nose.

A good toothpaste can be made with pure, finely powdered clay from which all sand has been removed, flavored with crushed dried mint leaves. If your teeth are in bad condition or are becoming loose, rinse your mouth alternately with powdered clay and salt water, and suck little pieces of clay, impregnating your gums with it. To relieve a gumboil, put a cold clay poultice to the cheek and apply half a dried fig, cooked in a little milk, to the affected gum. Renew the clay poultice every two hours.

Clay is an excellent remedy with which ever man and woman ought to become acquainted.

MUD BATHS

All treatment with mud requires a natural diet and is even more effective if it is preceded by fasting and applications of clay and water. A course of treatment is a cleansing that enables the body to regain its natural balance; it involves the totality of the individual.

You can make a mud bath for yourself by digging a hole wide and deep enough to contain your whole body. But the clay must not be cold, and open-air baths must be taken only during periods when the sun warms the ground sufficiently.

Make a thin mixture of clay and water. Before each use, add a little cold or hot water, as needed. Begin by remaining in your mud bath five to ten minutes a day, then gradually increase the duration. If you feel tired, space out your baths. A course of treatment should not last longer than a month. Allow an equal amount of time to pass before beginning again.

In the same way, you can take foot baths and hand baths as treatments for rheumatism.

Mud baths can be used for bone ailments, certain forms of paralysis, rheumatism, and arthritis.

It is good to wallow in mud, something which children and animals love to do. Clay is good for animals in the same ways as for human beings.

In some rural areas, seriously sick animals were once coated entirely with a mixture of clay and salt water (unrefined sea salt). Add a little clay (four or five teaspoonfuls per quart of unboiled water) to the drinking water of animals.

To dress a tree wound, apply a layer of clay paste thick enough to hold itself in place. Before replanting small plants in your garden, soak their roots in a mud bath. Spread clay paste on the roots of trees, shrubs, and large plants. Clay improves the acidity of the soil and, when added to organic waste, increases production of humus and the amount of carbon retained in the soil.

Because of the heat it stores, sand is a good remedy for the body. Warm beach sand contains radioactive substances. Sand baths are an excellent remedy for bone ailments; they can be used for treating rheumatism, lumbago, sciatica, arthritis, decalcification, and rickets. Lie on dry sand and cover yourself with a thick layer of it, except for your head, which must be protected from the sun. Begin with sessions ten to fifteen minutes long, after which you quickly plunge into the sea. Gradually increase their duration until you are spending an hour or two under the sand each day, divided into two or three periods. A sand bath quickly causes heavy sweating. As soon as the sand is wet, replace it with dry sand.

Sand can also be used in poultices to treat the same ailments treated by mud baths, but less effectively. Heat sand from a beach or river bank in an oven or a pan. Apply it hot, about an inch thick, for a few hours by means of a bag made of fine cloth.

Sea Salt

Go to the seaside to bury yourself under the sand and gather salt. Salt is necessary for the balance, in volume and osmotic pressure, of the extracellular fluids. Everyone must have his daily dose of it. In therapeutic treatment, by strengthening the action of other elements, unrefined sea salt combats a number of deficiencies that cause humoral, glandular, and nervous imbalances.

The natural magnesium contained in sea salt is a precious remedy. Iodine in its natural state acts favorably on the thyroid gland. Bromine soothes the serves without weakening the nervous system. Salt, intermediate between earth and sea water, also contains traces of catalytic elements, such as gold, copper, nickel, and cobalt, as well as particles of clay. It goes very well with treatment by clay. Like clay, it attracts and absorbs sickness and is a pole that attracts substances with negative radiation.

Its healing and antiseptic properties have long been used in washing wounds. Gargling with salt water soothes a sore throat, and a salt water mouthwash is an excellent remedy. A tablespoonful of sea salt in a large glass of unboiled water relieves toothache and inflammation of the oral mucous membranes. To invigorate yourself, take a twenty-minute bath in salt water (about two pounds of salt in a tub of hot water) once a week. Washing in cool salt water and soaking your feet in hot salt water will reinvigorate your whole body. If you have varicose veins in your legs, soak your hands instead of your feet.

Since the action of salt strengthens that of clay, it is good to make clay paste with salt water. A boil or abscess can be treated with unrefined salt. Put two tablespoonfuls of sea salt in a container (not made of aluminum) and add enough water to dissolve it. Heat while stirring with a wooden spoon. Add powdered clay until the mixture has the consistency of an ointment. Enclose it in a piece of cloth, apply it to the boil or abscess in the morning, and change it at night. When pus appears, stop using salt during the day and replace it with cold clay poultices.

In your garden, the sodium chloride in sea salt will balance the addition of potash to cultivated soil, and the magnesium in it will slightly reduce the harmfulness of chemical fertilizers.

Other Mineral Salts

Sea salt is not the only mineral salt found in nature. Soil, water, vegetables, fruit, and all plants contain various salts, such as calcium, magnesium, phosphorus, iron, and silica. Let us recall that when vegetables are boiled, half of their mineral salts passes into the water. Each mineral salt has a specific action that is precisely known. When they are taken in food, no excess is possible because they are present in small amounts.

Treatment by biochemical salts is possible, but it is important to know that overly large doses of them are harmful because they are not entirely eliminated; they become fixed and may cause an actual sclerosis of tissues. Assimilation is thus necessary, and it is best to make use of homeopathic dilution.* The biochemical salts sold in pharmacies are often in that form and are prepared as either powders or little pellets whose mineral elements have been diluted to the third centesimal (3C).** One can make use of twelve biochemical salts prepared in this way:

  Calcarea phosphorica

  Calcarea sulfurica

  Calcarea fluorica

  Ferrum phosphoricum

  Kali muriaticum

  Kali phosphoricum

  Kali sulfuricum

  Magnesia phosphorica

  Natrum muriaticum

  Natrum phosphoricum

  Natrum sulfuricum

  Silicea

To take a salt in the form of a powder, stir about a quarter of a gram in a glass of water and swallow a mouthful every half hour, after making sure that the whole inside of your mouth is in contact with it. Several salts can be used at once; put a measure of each of them into a glass of water and drink it in the course of a day. For a salt in pellets, take three of them and let them melt in your mouth as slowly as

possible. As with any homeopathic remedy, you must avoid drinking coffee, tea, or infusions of mint or camomile. A light diet is also advisable during the course of treatment, which should not last longer than about two weeks.

Let us now examine some of the properties of the twelve salts listed above.

Calcarea phosphorica. Excellent for the bones. Rickets, fractures that are slow to knit, bad or late-growing teeth. Some forms of rheumatism are helped by this tonic salt.

Calcarea sulfurica. A specific for suppurations of all kinds: bronchial, nasal, inflammatory, etc.

Calcarea fluorica. Helps to restore bones, ligaments, glands, and blood vessels.

Ferrum phosphoricum. A very effective fever remedy when taken in high homeopathic dilution (9C). Used in a longer course of treatment, it helps the body to combat anemia and all kinds of inflammation. Iron, which is one of the main components of blood, has the ability to attract oxygen, hence its great usefulness in cell life and blood exchanges at the level of tissues.

Kali muriaticum. Effective against whitish mucus, apthae, dysentery, sinusitis, colds, and all other diseases of the nose, throat, and ears.

Kali phosphoricum. A constituent part of the brain, nerves, muscle cells, and red corpuscles, potassium phosphate is essentially recommended for nervous depression and insomnia, neurasthenia, incontinence of urine, and diarrhea.

Kali sulfuricum. Soothes all eruptions of the epidermis and chronic inflammations of mucous membranes. It can therefore be used to treat eczema and all kinds of skin disease, and also various forms of nasopharyngitis, colds, obstructed ears, and phlegmy coughs.

---

*See the chapter on "Homeopathy."
**These are homeopathic terms of measurement.

Magnesia phosphorica. An integral part of muscles and nerves, this salt can be used to treat cramps, convulsions, acute neuralgia, asthma, and chronic bronchitis.

Natrum muriaticum. A regulator of the liquid contents of the body, this salt is essential in treating growth and heart disorders. It is also good for fever, headache, hives, hay fever, and diabetes.

Natrum phosphoricum. Combats acidity, and so can be used for treating colic, rheumatism, gout, aerophagia, angina, and diabetes, since it reduces an overabundance of sugar.

Natrum sulfuricum. Also influences the liquid contents of the body, and facilitates eliminating any excesses of the organs. It is therefore a specific for calculi and diseases of the liver and bile ducts. It also improves rheumatism, malaria, and nasopharyngitis.

Silicea. Silica is found in connective tissue: hair, nails, skin. This salt hastens the end of suppuration by bringing abscesses and ulcerations to a head. It revitalizes brittle hair and nails and can be used for treating warts, bronchitis, and chronic rheumatism and asthma.

Mineral salts, basic components of our body and of nature, are essential to psychosomatic equilibrium. They are normally provided by a wholesome diet and a healthy life. But the loss of energy caused by pollution and a hectic life may periodically require brief courses of restorative treatment with mineral salts. When one is ill, they help the body to reestablish its natural functions.

Salts of the earth, salts of life.

Man and Minerals

Ever since man's first appearance on earth, two forms of the manifestation of energy have particularly attracted his attention as reserves of magic power: the plant world and the mineral world. Among the first traces of mankind are ashes and chipped, then polished, flint tools. Wood gave the bow, the stick, and fire. Stone gave arrowheads and also sparks.

But stone and wood are not only tools. The primordial forest is a mysterious reserve of plant prana. The bowels of the earth (the central fire) and mountains (crystal) contain a particular energy that is manifested, for example, in very slow geological movements: a mountain moves, lives, breathes. Certain places on the planet—beaches, deserts, deep mountains—are like "cosmic chimneys." Magnetic influences and messages from celestial space/time are received by mineral masses as by a photographic plate. The outstanding places in human history are nothing other than accumulators of cosmic energy. The medicine man makes a pilgrimage to the desert or climbs the magic mountain.. He fasts and/or takes natural psychedelic substances; he sings, dances, and puts himself into a complete state of receptivity. He communicates with the elements, he is unconsciously penetrated by the flow of telluric energy that has been stored in the sacred space in the course of billions of years. (The breathing of inorganic matter is incalculably slower than that of plants!)

Man left traces of his passage on the planet in the days when he did not alter its basic balances. He made piles or rows of stones: mounts, tumuli, ziggurats, winding lines in the desert. The first magic signs of communication with the spirit of the earth were drawn in sand or carved into the sides of inaccessible cliffs. Erect stones, lingams, and menhirs are mineral replicas of the pillar-tree of the cosmos; like it, they are symbols of the energy of the phallus, which has always been associated with lightning. Springs, water holes, caves, and underground lakes, on the other hand, are reserves of yin energy.

Clay serves to make forms (containers, houses) and flint gives fire; gemstones, particularly crystals, represent an even more concentrated form of mineral energy, the end product of a process of very slow purification by fire. Sand, flint, and quartz, for example, represent three successive states of the same mineral substance: silica.

Stones that Heal

Precious stones, the essence of stone, are born of the mother rock after maturing in it. Stone is alive, in its fashion, with its very slow movement, from formation to wearing away.

Celestial activity is exercised on stone, a strong receptive substance. In Masonic symbolism, a cubical stone expresses the idea of stability, balance, and completion, and corresponds to the alchemical salt. A cubical stone surmounted by a point symbolizes the philosopher's stone: The pyramid above the cube represents the spiritual principle resting on the base of salt and the ground.

In the past, meteorites fallen from the sky were regarded as instruments of fertility. Offerings were made to them during droughts or in the spring to assure a good harvest. The ancient Mexicans called them "rain gold" and believed they could cure all sorts of fevers. Upright stones, such as the Indian lingams and the Breton menhirs, symbolize fertility; with similar rites, sterile Indian and Breton women seek help from them.

These stones were worshiped from the time when they were quarried until they were made into statues. They were believed to have supernatural properties and magnetic virtues capable of healing. Hard stones with multiple angles and facets aroused curiosity and respect. They were made into amulets, fetishes, and talismans.

Precious stones are the result of a transmutation from the opaque to the translucid, from shadows to light. They act as charms and remedies.

Coral, mother-of-pearl, and amber are said to give protection against the evil eye. Coral, carnelian, and ruby are signs of rejoicing and prosperity; agate is a sign of respect and fortune, turquoise of victory and longevity, emerald and topaz of courage.

In primitive societies the jewel has always been a talisman. Necklaces of animal and human teeth, pierced flints, and seashells provide magic protection. Rings, clasps, earrings, and ankle rings have prophylactic properties.

In Arab traditions, stones have curative and talismanic values. They act by their presence and heal. Diamonds give protection from poison and drive away care; rubies heal wounds; sapphires help in making escapes; emeralds make one immune to venom; pearls prolong youth; galactite gives milk to nursing mothers and strenthens fruit trees.

The medical science of the Middle Ages and the Renaissance, closely linked to magic and astrology, concerned itself with the virtues of stones. Famous physicians and earnest pharmacologists extolled the therapeutic power of stones, included them in subtle preparations, and stated that their wondrous properties were due to the influence of the heavenly bodies.

Stones of the sun are related to that heavenly body: The diamond wards off heart disease, the topaz prevents bad dreams. Stones of the moon impart its virtues to the opal and the pearl, whose milky whiteness seems to be a reflection of the moon. They cure disorders of the nerves and brain, and fevers. Stones of Mars, formed under its influence—ruby, garnet, red agate—are tonic stones which cure anemia and give protection from wounds. Stones of Venus, such as the emerald, protect women from diseases of the belly and kidneys, favor conception, and give long life. Stones of Mercury—onyx and jade—soothe the nerves and reduce fever. Stones of Jupiter—turquoise, sapphire, aquamarine—protect against baldness and liver diseases. Stones of Saturn—amethyst, black agate, jet—combat deafness and disorders of old age.

Later, science also concerned itself with stones. Cardan, a great sixteenth-century scientist, wrote, "No precious stone lacks virtue. They favor longevity. Some favor health, others wisdom, others wealth, others love, others divination, others bodily strength, and others good fortune. Still others have a bad influence: Some make people lazy, some make them timid. . . ."

Precious stones and pearls were used in various ways. They were ground to a powder which was swallowed either by itself or mixed with other powdered stones or substances such as gold and silver. These strange mixtures eventually came to be regarded as precious medicines, potions, and elixirs.

Knowledge of the mineral world has been almost totally lost in civilized societies: Even less is known about the virtues of stones than those of plants. Yet all the elements of creation can be consciously used as elements of a subtle alchemy that transfigures the human body in unison with cosmic vibrations. The Taoist sage is like a log or a pebble, and he flies on the wings of the wind. Precious stones, particularly the diamond, amethyst, turquoise, and quartz, are to the mineral world what the sage is to the world of human beings. The power of the diamond is the great wisdom that surpasses everything, the state of the *immortal mortal*.

HEALING BY PLANTS

Man soon realized the healing power of plants. No plant is lacking in powers. They all have a specific character that is manifested in their varied shapes, their colors, and the places where they grow. Each has its own special virtues. There is ancient knowledge of the way to harvest plants and herbs. Knowing how to describe their properties is a treasure. The Vedas of India, one of the world's oldest sacred texts, praise the power of plants, extol the origin of herbs, and glorify their ancient source; these hymns honor plants as the firstborn of the divine lineage.

Their roots draw vigor from the couple formed by Father Sky and Mother Earth; they come from the flow that gave birth to the form of the universe and all living systems. A blessing for man, plants can rebalance everything if they are used properly. In the Vedas, the healing sage also sings a ritual hymn whose magic power was intended to prepare the patient and rouse the plant kingdom to struggle against illness.

I know these plants by eye, I see them,
The unknown as well as those we know,
And those in which we know assembled virtues.
May all herbs together appreciate my magic
*   power.*
My we be able safely to bring this man out of
*   distress.*
Dasvattha, the fig tree, Soma, the queen of
*   plants, the drink of immortality,*
Healing Rice and Barley, immortal twin sons of
*   the Heavens.*

Saraka Samhita

Elsewhere, in South America, on the desolate high plateaus of the Andes, women gather plants to be used in preparing remedies prescribed by *curanderos* ("healers"). There, the earth provides most of the ingredients used in therapy. Decoctions of leaves and flowers are the main remedies, but wood, resin, and bark, whose powders are often highly active, are also used.

115

For mild ailments, intense fatigue, and food poisoning, Incan healers usually prescribed purges made from the white roots, resembling small turnips of the *Euphorbia huachanchana*. Then the patient lay in the sunlight on a stone slab, so that vasodilation could set off the therapeutic process and accelerate its progress. The patient felt himself weakening as a tingling sensation spread through his body. He then expelled all the bad things that had come into him.

Most of the plants in the Incan pharmacopoeia are still used by the Quechua Indians in the Andes. They grind green corn leaves to obtain a juice that helps wounds to heal. A fermented liquid that is spread on painful lesions is made from cooked and ground seeds. Potato poultices were once used for gout. Toothpaste was made from the bark of the cinchona tree. An infusion made from the grated wood of this tree relieves fever and liver congestion. The oil extracted from its fruit heals wounds. As is done in modern medicine, each treatment was prescribed with a diet poor in fats, meat, or starch, to obtain better results. There were plant remedies for all the everyday ills. Many medical laboratories are now sending teams to study and gather those plants. One of them recently brought back a still-secret plant decoction reputed to cure skin cancer.

All over the world, whether used by Siberian shamans, African witch doctors, the bonesetters of the Alps, or the healers of Islam, plants are still one key to healing and well-being. Some of them are hallucinogenic and provide initiation into "nonordinary states of reality."

It is regrettable that man is no longer familiar with a certain magic of nature. Forces work through it, forces that animals know well. Everything is there, around us. All we have to do is look, gather, and prepare.

Useful Herbs

The wild plant is always better than the cultivated one, because nature has given it a place in a particular climate, where it contains its maximum amount of energy, especially if it takes full advantage of the soil and air by growing at a distance from other plants. We should choose those plants having the greatest smell, taste, and color.

They should be picked when they are fully ripe, in summer for many plants, at those solstices which have always been regarded as propitious times. The eternal rhythms of the cosmos exert an influence on our world here below. Furthermore, when you pick a plant you must also consider its stage of development. It is advisable to choose a dry, sunny day and not begin picking too early in the morning or finish too late in the evening. Damp flowers and leaves deteriorate rapidly and thus lose some of their powers. After a rain, however, you can pull up roots and rootstalks without breaking them. At the beginning of spring and the end of fall, the sap has not yet risen into the stalk.

All these operations require great concentration in order to respect the life you have just suspended: Leaves and flowers should be plucked and put down gently. If you want to gather a large quantity of leaves and stems, it is better to take them from several plants; if a plant is deprived of too many of its leaves or stems, it cannot reproduce. Roots should be pulled up in a place where the species grows abundantly. The harvest is a gift of nature that should not be wasted.

Drying your harvest is an important phase. It must allow the proper changes to take place in the substances contained in the plant, which are much more fragile and delicate than the "dead substances" of remedies that come from a laboratory. Plants must be dried in a place that is easy to aerate, always in the shade (with rare exceptions): The warmth of the sun destroys the volatile substances and essential oils of aromatic plants, and bright light takes the color out of flowers.

As soon as you come back from picking plants, spread them out to avoid the fermentation that would take place if they were left in your basket. It is not necessary to wash them, since they must be picked far from roads, in a place where they are not covered with dust and have not been treated with insecticides or other chemicals.

With roots, the procedure is different: Wash them soon after pulling them out of the ground, because water will not then penetrate them and dissolve their curative parts. Expose them to sunlight for several hours and cut them into pieces before you dry them, since it is hard to do afterward.

Spread all your plants in a single layer, to avoid mildew and fermentation. To assure even drying, it is good to turn them over now and then during the first few days. When drying is finished, cut the leaves, stems, and flowers into small pieces ready for storage. Remember that they will be spoiled by the slightest trace of dampness. They must be really dry, so that the essence of each one will be kept intact until steeping in hot water releases it to invigorate tired organs.

When you have cut your plants into pieces, put them in an airtight container made of wood, tinned iron, or glass and store them in a closet or some other dark place to avoid letting contact with light make any change in their molecular structure.

If you lack the will or the opportunity to pick your own herbs, you can buy them at special stores, although these are rather rare. Our industrialized society prefers to market expensive and uselessly complicated medicines rather than remedies that are natural and therefore inexpensive. Yet such remedies are effective and less toxic to the body.

Plants, water, fire—those are the only elements needed for your personal alchemy. Plants, the vital sap of life; water, the fundamental liquid in which everything is bathed; fire, heat, the source of transformation and movement. How does one bring about that transformation?

For an infusion. Put the plants in a teapot and pour in the desired amount of boiling water. Cover and let steep for the time required, which varies with the plants used. Strain.

For a decoction. Put the plants in water, slowly bring to a boil, and continue boiling on low heat. Use a stainless steel or enameled pot; aluminum has a bad effect on plants.

You can also prepare plants by maceration. Put the prescribed quantity of them in a liquid: water, oil, wine, or alcohol. Let them soak for several hours or several days, depending on the plants involved; then strain.

In all three cases, follow the prescribed dose exactly; too much may be worse than none at all. The herbs set off a mechanism in us, and we must not tire our organs by stimulating them more than necessary.

We can also treat ourselves with essences of plants or aromatic essences called essential oils. They can be found in a few pharmacies, especially homeopathic ones. They are extracted from plants in various ways: steam distillation, tapping, separation by heat, pressing. Use them carefully, because they are highly concentrated. Here are some examples of the yield from a hundred pounds of plants: three ounces of essence of thyme, three pounds of essence of eucalyptus, a pound and a half of essence of sage. Such essences are the basic ingredients in all traditional toilet waters.

They are used a few drops at a time: swallowed with sugar, inhaled as vapor (mixed with hot water), rubbed on the skin, or applied in compresses. The first time someone treats a cold, for example, by taking essences of eucalyptus, thyme, and cinnamon on a lump of sugar, he is unpleasantly surprised by a burning sensation. But the relief which quickly follows makes up for that drawback. Besides being antiseptic, essential oils have antitoxic properties and a powerful energizing effect. "Physicians," said Montaine, "ought to make greater use of odors than they do, for I have noticed that they change me and act on my spirits in accordance with their nature."

In everyday life, herbs can also be a useful and delicious accompaniment of your cooking. Our ancestors preserved their cooked foods by means of a cluster of thyme, parsley, bay leaves, and cloves. That was enough to ward off microbes.

And why not add a small spoonful of honey to your evening herb tea? In ancient times honey was regarded as a gift of heaven, an elixir of life. In a whole day, a bee can make only a drop of honey weighing about a tenth of a gram. This precious food has all the elements necessary for the body's functioning and maintenance.

Bees gather nectar and make it into honey. When it is brought back to the hive, the nectar is distributed to many worker bees, who regurgitate it several times in the form of little drops.

A large part of the water it contains is evaporated. It is placed in the cells of the honeycomb, where it continues to thicken. The bees add a product of glandular secretion to it.

All the sugar in honey comes from nectar and its fragrance comes from the flowers that provide the nectar. No human being would have the patience to gather the minute drops of nectar found in flowers. The amount of nectar that a bee brings to the hive is no larger than a pinhead. To gather that booty, the bee has to visit more than a thousand clover flowers, for example. Imagine the work of a colony of bees that make more than two pounds of honey a day, as they often do in summer.

Bees are our friends. They are in the process of disappearing because of the chemical treatment of soil. We must protect them!

The stimulating and regenerative powers of beebread and royal jelly have always been known. Honey is a living food. Because of the action of its sugars combined with mineral salts, active diastases, and vitalized flower energies, it can often replace chemical sugar. But while it is very good for many people, it often proves to be too strong when one is sick. It can then be taken diluted after being boiled, or in cake or gingerbread.

The properties of honey vary according to the place where it was gathered, the nature of the local plant life, weather, and the procedures used in preparation. Never buy honey that is old or has been treated. Insist on honey made from wildflowers. Liquid honey is good, but it is even better when eaten with the honeycomb. Carefully chew the wax, which contains vitamin A.

Besides being an excellent food, honey is also a medicine. The ancient Egyptians attributed magic powers to it and used it for treating coughs, wounds, and diseases of the eyes, kidneys, and digestive tract.

To relieve an abscess, take a little honey, an equal quantity of flour, and a little water; mix well and apply to the abscess.

For inflammations of the throat, use a gargle made by boiling a spoonful of honey in a half-pint of water for five minutes.

The same preparation, applied at night in compresses, is recommended for eye ailments.

Honey relieves and reduces the swelling of rheumatism. For sinusitis, to clear the nasal mucous membranes, chew a honeycomb for a quarter of an hour and spit out what remains in your mouth. Honey is the only preventive remedy for hay fever.

THE MAIN USEFUL HERBS AND HOW TO USE THEM

If we become familiar with useful herbs, we see nature around us in a new light. The man who walks in the country and takes herbs is not the man who drives seventy miles an hour on highways and takes aspirin. The country ceases to be merely scenery and becomes a wonderful regenerative organism surrounding us.

Basil

Besides its digestive properties, basil has a calming and antispasmodic effect.

It relieves the most stubborn constipation and puts the stomach and intestines in good condition again: Soak a handful of leaves in a quart of wine for three or four days, then add a quart of olive oil.

The juice of fresh basil leaves relieves inflammations of the ears.

Blackberry Bush

Blackberry leaves, crushed between the fingers, immediately stop bleeding from scratches. They have an astringent, tonic, and restorative effect on the mucous membranes. They promote healing of inflammations of the intestines and mouth.

A decoction of them is recommended in treatment of urogenital diseases and to decongest the female organs.

Blackberry jam, an excellent dessert, relieves sore throats, hoarseness, diarrhea, and enteritis. Slowly eat a tablespoonful of it several times a day.

Blackberry syrup (cook blackberry juice with an equal weight of sugar until it takes on a syrupy consistency) taken in the amount of two or three tablespoonsfuls is recommended for bronchial catarrh and sore throats. A tablespoonful in a glass of water makes a refreshing drink for people who are sick or convalescing.

Borage

Borage relieves the heart, dispels melancholy, and engenders gaiety. It is a soothing plant when it is young, and refreshing, purifying, and sudorific when it is flowering. Drinking a small glass of fresh borage juice (pound and squeeze the plant) every morning before breakfast will put your kidneys back in good condition.

Borage is used in infusions drunk at bedtime, and in decoctions (a quarter to a half an ounce of the dried plant in a quart of water, boiled two or three minutes) for fever. The fumes from a stronger decoction (three to three and a half ounces per quart of water) can be breathed to treat bronchial diseases.

Fresh borage leaves combined with watercress and dandelion provide an excellent purifying herb juice.

Borage flowers can embellish your salads. The leaves can be used in soups and cooked as a vegetable.

Burdock

Burdock roots and leaves can be used to treat rheumatism, acne, lingering colds, and chronic bronchial diseases.

A decoction of one and one-half ounces of fresh roots boiled ten minutes in a quart of water lowers the proportion of sugar in the blood. A burdock decoction can be used to treat measles: an ounce of fresh roots in a pint of water, strain, add honey, and take in small spoonfuls every five minutes.

Burdock poultices relieve bruises and contusions.

To prevent falling hair, soak four ounces of burdock root and two ounces of nettle root in a pint of rum for a week, then massage the scalp with this lotion every day.

A concentrated burdock infusion is very yang.

Eucalyptus

Eucalyptus trees were once used for purifying marshy areas where fevers were common.

When eucalyptus leaves are scorched on a hot stove during winter evenings, they impregnate the air of the room and give protection against contagious diseases.

An infusion of eucalyptus leaves (a half ounce in a quart of water) is recommended for people who cannot tolerate quinine. It can be used for treating diseases of the respiratory and urinary tracts. It is a powerful antiseptic. Breathing its vapor combats sore throats and clears the bronchi. You can take essence of eucalyptus alone (three or four drops on a lump of sugar) or in combination with the essential oils of pine, thyme, and lavender. For sinusitis, influenza, or bronchitis, put a tablespoonful of it into a bowl of boiling water and breathe the fumes; do this two or three times a day for about a week.

Eucalyptus stimulates the appetite and aids digestion. It can be taken before or after meals in a drink made by soaking an ounce and a half of leaves in a quart of good wine for two weeks.

Geranium

Wild geranium traditionally had the power of healing fractures and relieving tumors. Gathered in May or June, it is recommended for gastric ulcers, diarrhea, internal hemorrhages, diabetes, and retention of milk in the breasts.

Ground geranium leaves applied to a cut or sore help it to heal.

A concentrated decoction (four ounces of plants in a quart of water) can be used for treating angina and inflammations of the eyes or skin.

Essence of geranium can be part of the treatment of burns, cuts, sores, and shingles.

There are excellent geranium teas.

Horsetail

Horsetail is a plant that does not flower, but reproduces by its spores, like mosses. It is an excellent source of minerals, containing silica, calcium, sodium, iron, manganese, potassium, sulfur, and magnesium. It is also a diuretic and a blood purifier, used for treating diseases of the kidneys and bladder, general swelling, rheumatism, and skin diseases.

An excellent internal and external cicatrizer, it is recommended for tuberculosis and inflammation of the mucous membranes of the stomach, intestines, and genitourinary organs.

It can be taken in a decoction: Place one

ounce in a quart of water, soak for several hours, then heat slowly, boil for twenty to twenty-five minutes, and let steep. Drink three or four cups a day. This decoction makes white spots on fingernails disappear and strengthens brittle nails, after about two weeks of treatment. A stronger decoction, with twice as much plant for half as much water, can be used for hemorrhoids, aphthae, certain skin diseases, eczema, and slow-healing cuts and sores.

Tincture of horsetail is made by soaking the plants in alcohol for two to three weeks. Spreading this on the feet every day prevents them from sweating.

The young sprouts, tonic and restorative, can be eaten in salads.

Lavender

The ancient Romans mixed lavender with their bath water. Grandmothers often put it in their closets to perfume linen and keep away moths. Lavender heals, soothes, disinfects, invigorates, and regularizes.

A weak infusion (a fifth of an ounce of flowers in a quart of water) cures insomnia and indigestion. A stronger one (an ounce in a quart of water) is sudorific, tonic, disinfectant, and soothing. It relieves diseases of the respiratory tract, fever, influenza, and fatigue. It can also be used in vaginal douches as a treatment for leukorrhea.

The essential oil obtained by distilling the plant is a powerful antiseptic. It kills the tuberculosis bacillus at a dose of 0.2 per cent. Its vapors destroy pneumococci and streptococci in twelve to twenty-four hours.

For insect bites, rub on a mixture of equal parts of alcohol and essence of lavender.

Lavender baths have a sedative effect; best to take them in the evening, alternating them with rosemary, pine, and seaweed baths.

Linden Blossom

Dedicated to Venus, the linden tree has always been used in medicine and sorcery. Gathered in the middle of summer, its blossoms have calming, cooling, and antispasmodic properties.

An infusion (two pinches of blossoms per cup) relieves nervous indigestion, headache, palpitations, and insomnia.

Linden blossoms are an excellent remedy in the treatment of arteriosclerosis, for fluidifying the blood.

A decoction (one ounce of blossoms per quart of water) applied daily as a lotion removes impurities from the skin, takes away wrinkles, and favors the growth of hair. For nervous, agitated children, double the strength of the decoction and mix it with their bath water.

Marjoram

Marjoram relieves the stomach, spleen, and liver. It is a sedative, an antiseptic, and a stomachic, used for treating menstrual pain and rheumatism. To make an ointment, mix four ounces of fresh marjoram with a pint of olive oil and strain through a cloth. Rub it on areas of the body where rheumatic, muscular, or nervous pain is centered. To relieve headache, spread it on the forehead and temples.

An infusion (a quarter ounce of flowers per quart of water) sweetened with honey combats digestive spasms, insomnia, and migraine headaches. Marjoram can also be taken in good wine (two ounces of fresh plants soaked in a quart of wine for ten days) after meals.

Essence of marjoram (five or six drops) neutralizes the tuberculosis bacillus at a dose of 0.4 per cent. It is a powerful antispasmodic.

Marjoram flowers, with their marvelous fragrance, can also be used in cooking: salads, stews, vegetables, pizza.

Marsh Mallow

The marsh mallow, with its tall, fuzzy stalk, grows in uncultivated, marshy ground. It is the most emollient of all plants. Its root soothes irritations of the gums and facilitates the loss of baby teeth.

In infusions, it soothes colds, bronchitis, and laryngitis.

A decoction made by soaking an ounce of roots in a quart of water for two hours, then heating over a low flame, soothes irritations and inflammations of the mucous membranes.

A stronger concentration (five ounces per quart of water), used as a gargle, treats angina and inflammation of the tonsils. As a mouthwash, it soothes abscesses and aphthae. In warm enemas it is an excellent remedy for constipation. Marsh mallow can also be used for treating sinusitis: Put it in hot water and inhale its fumes, and place compresses of it on the painful areas.

Mint

There are many varieties of mint. Peppermint is the richest in both medicinal and culinary virtues. The fragrance and cooling powers of mint have been used in all times. It is a help in combating lice, fleas, and mice. But above all it is cooling, an aid to digestion, an antiseptic, an antispasmodic, and a tonic.

Taken in infusions (five leaves per cup of water), it combats general fatigue, indigestion, aerophagia, poisonings of gastrointestinal origin, and liver diseases. It invigorates the nervous system and cures headaches, palpitations, and dizziness. Taken in strong doses, however, it may hinder sleep.

A good remedy for cough, asthma, and bronchitis: an inhalant made by soaking two ounces of fresh or dried mint leaves in warm water. A mint decoction is an excellent vermifuge for children.

If you are taking homeopathic medicines, it is better not to take mint at the same time as a dose of one of them.

Essence of mint is a powerful remedy for general fatigue. It kills staphlococci and neutralizes tuberculosis bacilli at a dose of 0.4 per cent. To keep mosquitoes away, put a few drops of it on your pillow.

Here is the recipe for an aphrodisiac bath worthy of the *Satyricon*. Ingredients: two ounces of ground nutmeg and a handful of each of the following: mint, rosemary, sage, marjoram, camomile flowers. Put in boiling water, let steep for twelve hours, then add four ounces of tincture of juniper and four ounces of tincture of cloves.

Moreover, I advise you to add mint leaves to your salads and raw vegetables.

Multiple uses are made of mint in all countries of the world. The Arabs combine it with green tea to make a drink that is both cooling and invigorating, well suited to the heat and light of the desert.

Mugwort

The mugwort, a tall plant, grows on slopes and uncultivated land. It protects women in their ailments, regularizes their cycle, and aids in childbirth.

It is advisable to drink an infusion of it (one-third of an ounce per quart of water) ten to twelve days before the expected start of menstruation. It is a vermifuge and an excellent general stimulant. In small doses, it has a powerful antispasmodic and sedative effect.

Its aromatic qualities make it good to use in cooking. It stimulates the digestive functions.

Rose

The rose, the flower of lovers. Rose petals, delicate and velvety, can be used fresh or dried for infusions.

For cough and bronchitis, drink a rose infusion (a half ounce per quart of water). As a gargle or mouthwash, it treats aphthae; as a lotion, it eliminates blotches on the face.

A handful of petals put into a bath soothes rheumatic pain; a handful of fresh petals soaked in lemon juice makes the skin healthier, disinfects small cuts and sores, and relieves pain.

Excellent in jam, roses soothe the throat.

Rosemary

The herb of the troubadours, rosemary is a shrub common in southern France. It is a good healing agent, an antiseptic, a general stimulant, a heart tonic, and a remedy for rheumatism and neuralgia. Its effect on the liver is important: It modifies and thins the bile. A preparation made by distilling rosemary branches in brandy relieves rheumatism and many ailments of digestive or nervous origin. It keeps the skin fresh, reduces puffiness under the eyes, invigorates the scalp, and prevents loss of hair.

Rosemary makes good infusions. Use a pinch of it per cup, several times a day, especially after meals. To treat a sick liver, it is better to drink this infusion in the morning before breakfast. For those who tend to overeat, I recommend rosemary wine: It is a tonic, an aid to digestion, an antispasmodic, and a strong diuretic. Soak two ounces of rosemary in a quart of your best wine for several days and drink a glass of this mixture with each meal.

A decoction of rosemary flowers (two

ounces per quart of water, boil two minutes, steep fifteen minutes) is a good daily lotion for combating wrinkles. A handful of rosemary boiled fifteen minutes in a quart of water makes a decoction that can be used in hot compresses placed directly over areas of rheumatic pain.

Used in salads, sauces, and vegetables, rosemary adds a delightful fragrance and facilitates digestion.

For muscular pain, rub three or four times a day with three or four drops of essence of rosemary mixed with olive oil. Rosemary baths are an excellent tonic, recommended for those who suffer from fatigue.

Sage

Sage was once a sacred herb. It sometimes grows along roads and reaches a height of three feet in some places. Outside of areas where it grows naturally, it loses a large part of its virtues. In the past it was harvested with great respect, without the use of iron tools, by barefoot people wearing linen tunics. It is the king of medicinal plants, the plant that saves. It not only serves to protect life, but also aids in giving it. Its hormonal properties are beneficial to girls in the period of puberty, women disturbed by the menopause, and women who want to have a child. In the Middle Ages, it was an ingredient in all miraculous mixtures and rejuvenating potions.

Sage is an antiseptic, an aid to digestion, an appetizer, and a tonic; it combats food putrefaction, stimulates the nervous system, activates circulation, and aids the heart.

A sage infusion is an advantageous replacement for coffee. Mixed with milk and honey, it can be used for treating colds at their inception. It cures diarrhea in babies.

A sage decoction (half an ounce of leaves and flowers per quart of water) is excellent for sore throats and angina. As a mouthwash, it relieves inflammations and irritations.

In vaginal douches, it eliminates leukorrhea. It heals and effaces pimples. A mixture of sage decoction and rum in equal parts, rubbed into the scalp every morning, will clear up dandruff and prevent loss of hair.

Taken in the form of essence, two to four drops three times a day, sage increases the strength of the whole body.

It is used in cooking because of its delicate flavor. It can replace cinnamon in flavoring hot wine and is excellent in soup and on cheese. It is always good to have sage in your home.

Savory

Savory, a small aromatic plant, whose smell and appearance are similar to those of thyme, enjoyed great prestige in ancient times. It is an ingredient in many love potions. Men who eat savory experience a marked increase in amorous ardor.

Savory has important digestive properties. It is good to use in cooking, especially in stews, beans, and starches that are hard to digest.

In an infusion, it combats stomach pain, chronic diarrhea, flatulence, and mental and sexual debility. Lotions made with strong infusions (two ounces per quart of water) can be used for treating skin diseases. Savory has a revitalizing effect; it is beneficial to rub the spine with a decoction made by boiling a handful of savory in a quart of water.

Essence of savory can be used to treat dental neuralgia and deafness (one drop in each ear).

You can also use savory like thyme, sage, and rosemary, by putting a handful of it in your bath water.

Scotch Pine

Scotch pine is valuable for its ability to disinfect the bronchi, the respiratory tract, the urinary passages, and the bile ducts. Its buds, gathered in spring, are used in decoctions: a half ounce per quart of water, soak for two hours, heat slowly and boil one to two minutes, steep ten minutes. This preparation is also recommended for rheumatism and skin diseases. As an inhalant, it treats head colds and sinusitis. It can be used in vaginal douches for leukorrhea, and as a gargle for sore throats.

Essence of pine is obtained by distilling fresh pine needles. It is good for all diseases of the respiratory tract and urinary passages. It stimulates the cortex of the suprarenal gland and is a tonic. To ease rheumatic pain and drive away skin diseases, add a decoction to your bath water: Boil two pounds of chopped pine needles and cones in four gallons of water for two hours; take this bath warm, about 95°, for fifteen minutes.

Thyme

Thyme has always been regarded as a veritable panacea. It is a preeminently antiseptic plant, a general stimulant, and a good remedy for difficult digestion, tired intestines, and disorders of the respiratory tract (cough, bronchitis, influenza, chills). It aids recovery from physical and mental fatigue and relieves menstrual disorders.

To make an infusion, use a handful of thyme per quart of boiling water and steep for ten minutes. Drink three or four cups a day. It can also be used as a gargle and as a lotion for washing infected cuts and sores.

For a decoction, use four ounces of thyme in a gallon of water and boil down. The resulting solution is more powerful and is recommended for fits of coughing. For anemia, disorders of the joints of circulation, or skin diseases, pour this decoction into your bath water. Rubbed into the scalp every day, it is good lotion for preventing falling hair.

An inhalant containing the maximum dose of five or six drops of essence of thyme is an effective remedy for bronchitis and other diseases of the respiratory tract. Taken on a lump of sugar, it allays diarrhea and dysentery, and also clears the bronchi. It is the best remedy for all disorders caused by chills.

Thyme, a wonderful herb that has been used since the dawn of history, should also have a place in most of the dishes you cook.

Vervain

All over the world, vervain has been regarded as having magic powers. It is the herb of witches and spells, the herb of the liver and the blood. The vervain cultivated in Mediterranean regions differs in appearance and components from that of India, Madagascar, and the West Indies, which contains a bitter glucide; it acts on the liver, is a tonic, aids digestion, combats neuralgia, and reduces fever.

Vervain can be taken in a light decoction (a half ounce per quart of water). Soak in cold water for fifteen minutes, heat, boil only for a few seconds, steep for ten minutes. Prepared in this way, vervain is a gastric stimulant, an antiseptic, and a regulator of the vagus nerves. It is also a remedy for liver diseases, fever, and painful and irregular menstruation. It can be applied in compresses for cleaning cuts and sores and for relieving the pain of sprains. As a gargle it combats sore throat and, as a mouthwash, bad breath and inflammation of the gums. Spread on the temples and forehead, it relieves headache.

If you want to relax and refresh yourself, pour a concentration decoction (two ounces in a quart of water) into your bath.

Woodruff

Woodruff grows in damp woods and its little white flowers, with their delicate fragrance, can be used for decorating your house, scenting your linen, and protecting your clothes from moths.

Fresh woodruff leaves applied to the forehead relieve neuralgia. An infusion (a sixth of an ounce per quart of water) is recommended for menstrual disorders and diseases of the liver, kidneys, and bladder. It soothes the nerves and ought to replace many of the chemical tranquilizers used today.

HEALING HERBS USED IN COOKING

Bay Leaves

Bay leaves act as a stimulant, an antispasmodic, and an aid to digestion. The berries of the plant help reduce fever and act as a diuretic, an expectorant, and a remedy for rheumatism.

An infusion (a half ounce of fresh or dried leaves per quart of water) can be drunk immediately after meals to help digestion, or about three hours after meals to treat influenza, chronic bronchitis, and pains in the stomach or intestines.

Dried and powdered bay leaves are a good remedy for intermittent fevers: soak one thirtieth of an ounce of powder in a glass of cold water for eight to ten hours; drink every two hours.

Bay leaves are used in pickling liquids and cooking for aroma and flavor. They are part of the traditional French cluster of herbs for seasoning soups and stews. In some rural areas, hams are smoked over a fire of bay leaves to preserve them better and give them a special taste.

Chervil

The ancient Greeks called chervil "the leaf that gladdens." It is a plant very rich in vitamin C. Excellent in the treatment of all liver diseases, and jaundice in particular, it is cooling, purifying, laxative, and diuretic.

It is always used fresh, since drying causes it to lose a large part of its active properties. Do not cook it, because that destroys its flavor and aroma.

Chervil can be taken in an infusion (a half ounce per quart of water, steep ten minutes) between meals.

In compresses or lotions, a decoction (boil an ounce in a quart of water, steep half an hour) relieves inflammation of the eyes. But be careful to keep your eyes tightly closed to avoid getting any of the liquid in them. Chervil softens the skin and delays the appearance of wrinkles. In a hip bath, a decoction of ground fresh chervil boiled for ten minutes eases the pain of hemorrhoids.

A remarkable treatment for biliary colic: Squeeze equal amounts of the leaves of chervil, chicory, lettuce, and dandelion, collect the juice, and drink some of it every morning before breakfast. Applied to the breasts in poultices, chervil will, like parsley, stop the flow of milk.

Above all, use chervil abundantly in your cooking. Chop it fine and sprinkle it over your salads, vegetables, soups, and omelets.

Parsley

Parsley is easily cultivated. Do not neglect to grow some of it in your garden, because it is one of the most useful of all medicinal foods. All parts of the plant are usable.

An infusion (an ounce of dried leaves per quart of water) relieves painful menstrual cramps, aids digestion, stimulates blood circulation, and treats jaundice and other liver ailments.

In an emergency, apply crushed fresh parsley leaves to a wound. They also soothe insect bites. Nursing mothers used to put chopped parsley on their breasts to stop the flow of milk.

A parsley infusion relieves toothache, joint pains, and inflammation of the eyes. Applied to the face morning and evening, it decongests and clears the complexion. To prevent loss of hair, rub the scalp with powdered parsley seeds on three consecutive evenings.

Parsley is rich in iron, calcium, and vitamins A and C. Use it raw, sprinkled over your salads, vegetables, and omelets.

Tarragon

Tarragon grows easily in gardens. It is recommended for difficult digestion, flatulence, nausea, aerophagia, and rheumatic and neuralgic pain.

An infusion (a half ounce per quart of water, steep ten minutes) should be drunk after meals.

But above all, use it in cooking. Like parsley and chervil, it can accompany meats, vegetables, and salads. Its gastronomic virtues make it one of the best seasonings. It stimulates the digestive organs and is recommended for people on a saltless diet.

Nature contains everything we need for healing ourselves, yet most of these marvelous plants have lost their prestige, except in rural areas where women carry on the traditions of the old empirical medicine and still see herbs as wonderful remedies for all ills. We must relearn how to know plants, love them, respect them, and use them.

Vegetables that Heal

Vegetables and fruits are the main source of iron and other minerals that can be directly assimilated by the body, and the vitamins that defend us against disorders caused by malnutrition. These substances, combined with cellulose, tannin, and a large variety of gums, acids, and essential oils, give vegetables and fruits remarkable therapeutic properties. The pharmaceutical industry extracts active substances from many species of fruits and vegetables for the manufacture of certain medicines. Aside from the beneficial diets of which they are an essential part, vegetables and fruits—if they are grown without chemical fertilizers and insecticides—provide us with valuable remedies in the form of infusions, lotions, and poultices. All vitamins come from plants.

A sterilized food is a dead food that can have many harmful effects; its smell and taste can tell us nothing about its real freshness. Fear of germs is our most serious disease. In trying to eliminate germs from food, we deprive it of its revitalizing substances.

Boiled for a long time in a large amount of water, foods lose flavor and most of them lose a large part of their vitamins and about half their minerals.

Plants take in solar energy, store it, and give it to man to maintain his life. Eat vegetables and fruits as often as possible, raw or cooked in a small amount of oil or water, and salted at the last moment. Do not throw away the water in which vegetables have been cooked. It can be used as the base for good soup.

Learn to know, love, and take care of your vegetables. They will transmit their powers to you.

Artichokes

The artichoke, rich in vitamins A and B, is a nourishing vegetable that whets the appetite, purifies the blood, fortifies the heart, and restores strength.

Eaten raw, it relieves intestinal diseases and stops diarrhea. Diabetics should eat artichoke hearts often.

A decoction of fresh artichoke roots in water or white wine is diuretic and relieves rheumatism, gout, jaundice, and gravel. Prepared as a maceration or an infusion (two ounces per quart of water), taken alone or with oak or willow bark, artichoke roots relieve fever.

Artichokes are, along with carrots, the best natural remedy for liver ailments. Take a cup of the following decoction before meals for twelve consecutive days: Slowly boil four fresh artichoke leaves in a quart of water until a fourth of it has been boiled away, then add a little cane sugar. This preparation relieves rheumatism, gout, and all manifestations of arteriosclerosis.

Artichokes are perfectly digestible and well suited to delicate stomachs. They are good to eat raw, but must be chewed thoroughly.

When cooked, they should be eaten immediately because microbes soon develop in them.

Asparagus

Asparagus is not very nourishing, but it is refreshing and wholesome. It is rich in vitamins A and B and easily digested, even by delicate stomachs. Rich in phosphorus, it is recommended for weak people and sedentary workers. It should not be eaten by anyone suffering from acute rheumatism, cystitis, or gonorrhea.

Do not throw away the scales of asparagus when you cut them off; they are the part richest in vitamins. Use them for making soup.

Cabbage

Cabbage is one of the oldest vegetables. History tells us that the ancient Romans consumed a great deal of it. Wild cabbage is edible, and hybridization has given rise to many varieties. But red cabbage is the richest in curative and nutritive properties.

Rich in vitamins A, B, and C, cabbage is a plant with great food value. Because of the arsenic and iodine it contains, it stimulates the appetite, gives strength and vitality, and improves the complexion. Among its components are a very active oxidase, organic salts, a substance that protects the digestive mucous membranes, vitamin V, and vitamin K, which is an antihemorrhagic. It aids the healing process and stimulates intestinal functioning. It also contains iron, copper, magnesium, and chlorophyll. Well supplied with nitrogen and carbohydrates, it is a tonic and an energizer.

For a cough, drink as much as you like of a concentrated decoction (six leaves boiled for forty-five minutes in a quart of water and sweetened with honey) or a syrup made from red cabbage leaves: pound them, squeeze out the juice, and add honey.

Applied externally, cabbage leaves give excellent results in cases of headache, rheumatic pain, gout, sciatica, bronchitis, sprains, and swollen glands. Take the greenest, freshest leaves and wash them thoroughly. After flattening their veins, warm them over a source of heat. Apply them to the painful area and keep them in place with a bandage. Change this poultice once or twice a day.

Cabbage leaves dipped in milk can be used to treat blisters, lumbago, and neuralgia.

Rather indigestible, cabbage must be cooked a long time, and it disagrees with people who have liver ailments. It is preferable to cook it slowly with a little oil in a closed pot.

Sauerkraut made by natural methods—fermentation in a wooden barrel or an earthenware pot, with the aid of sea salt—is beneficial to the human body.

To clean your carpets, cut a cabbage heart in two and use it as a brush.

Carrots

The nutritional value of carrots became widely known when research on carbohydrates was undertaken. Because of their glucose and sucrose content, they should not be eaten by diabetics. They are rich in vitamins A, B$_1$, B$_2$, and C, and contains a provitamin, carotene, which the liver converts into vitamin A.

Carrots also contain iron, calcium, phosphoric acid, sodium, magnesium, and potassium. They are useful in cases of anemia, growth disorders, and humoral acidity, and their cellulose permits cleansing of the intestines. Eat raw carrots in the morning before breakfast. They are also recommended for constipation and diarrhea. For constipation, make a soup with two pounds of carrots boiled two hours in a quart of water. For diarrhea, even in babies, boil a pound of scraped carrots in a quart of water until they become soft. Strain them so that no residue remains. Add boiled water to make a quart of mixture, stir in a tenth of an ounce of salt, and keep in a cool place.

Having the ability to fluidify bile, carrots are, along with artichokes, the preeminent natural remedy for liver ailments and bilious temperaments.

Raw carrot juice is purifying and diuretic. Drink a glass of it every morning before breakfast. To prepare it, grate and squeeze the carrots, let the juice rest a few hours, then strain. When it is pure, it favors expulsion of secretions that clog the lungs and bronchi, and it remedies loss of the voice.

Carrots can be applied directly to the skin. The vitamin A they contain facilitates development and reproduction of cells. To rid your complexion of blotches and pimples, make a face pack of grated carrots and a little lemon

and leave it on for half an hour. To soothe the pain of burns and prevent blisters from forming, and to diminish the pain of abcesses, tumors, and inflammation around fingernails or toenails, apply a poultice of fresh carrot pulp enclosed in gauze.

Remember that the tastiest and most nutritious part of carrots is around the outside. Never peel them; instead, scrape or brush them.

Eat carrots often, especially raw ones. You can even give raw carrots to a baby as a substitute for a teething ring.

Chicory

Chicory, a bitter vegetable, grows wild on slopes and along roads. It is a friend of the liver. Its leaves, rich in vitamin C and potash, are tonic, purifying, laxative, diuretic, and a stimulant to the appetite.

An infusion of chicory leaves (one ounce per quart of water) relieves congestion of the liver and spleen, intestinal colic, and jaundice. It purifies the blood and restores vigor to the body.

The root has the same properties as the leaves. It should be dried in an oven. It contains inulin, a kind of starch which the body converts into fructose, a natural sugar that can be assimilated directly. Inulin is also found in salsify roots and the tubers of Jerusalem artichokes, which are excellent calorific foods for winter, and beneficial for people with liver ailments.

A decoction of chicory roots (one ounce per quart of water) cures intermittent fevers and skin diseases.

Dried and roasted chicory root is sometimes mixed with coffee. It is a beneficial tonic for the intestines. A root infusion (an ounce and a half per quart of water) stimulates bile secretion. Drink a cup of it before breakfast and at bedtime.

Cucumbers

Cucumbers are cooling and rich in vitamin C, but not very nourishing. Eaten ripe and well cooked, they are suitable for people subject to intestinal irritations and colic, and for bilious and sanguine temperaments. They are rather indigestible, however, and it is good to soak them in water before preparing them. Peel them, cut them into thin slices, cover them with unrefined sea salt, and let them marinate for several hours. Cucumbers are good in salads, with oil, lemon juice, and burnet. Do not salt.

If you have oily skin, wash your face with unsalted water in which cucumbers have been cooked. To narrow dilated pores on the face, take equal amounts of cucumber, pumpkin, and melon seeds, reduce them to a powder, mix a spoonful of this powder with milk or fresh cream, spread the mixture on your face, leave it on for about half an hour, then wash your face with warm rose water.

The following preparation is also recommended for facial care: Crush two ounces of shelled sweet almonds in a half-pint of cucumber juice that has been boiled and cooled, strain, and add a half-pint of alcohol and a thirtieth of an ounce of essence of roses. It is an excellent lotion.

Garlic

Garlic holds the first rank among plant medicines. It contains allyl, volatile sulfurated essence, sulfur, iodine, and silica, which contribute toward maintaining the body in good condition until an advanced age.

Garlic strongly stimulates the appetite and favors disgestion by activating gastric secretion and the motivity of the stomach wall. It eliminates fermentations of intestinal gases. Drink a light infusion: a sixth to a third of an ounce per quart of water. A first-rate antiseptic, garlic gives protection against infectious diseases. By disinfecting the air cells of the lungs, it quickly reduces purulent expectorations. It is therefore recommended for asthma, bronchitis, whooping cough, and pulmonary tuberculosis.

Garlic activates and regularizes blood circulation, strengthens the heart muscles, lowers blood pressure, and purifies the blood. It relieves arteriosclerosis, hypertension, rheumatism, arthritis, difficult menstruation, varicose veins, and hemorrhoids. For all these ailments, eat a clove of garlic every morning before breakfast. The strong breath it causes can be attenuated by chewing a piece of parsley or a few roasted coffee beans. The sulfurated essence it contains is then dissipated through the respiratory tract.

Here is a good way to prepare garlic: In the evening, chop it fine, mixed with parsley, and add a few drops of olive oil, then spread this mixture on a piece of bread for breakfast the next morning.

You can enjoy the benefits of garlic by giving it a large place in your daily meals—preferably raw, because cooking costs it part of its volatile substances. Chopped fine, it is good in soups and salads, on vegetables, and rubbed on bread. It is also used in the preparation of some cheeses. Garlic dried in the oven and powdered is an advantageous substitute for pepper, which is a dangerous stimulant. But it should not be eaten by people with skin diseases or by nursing mothers, since it spoils their milk and gives colic to their babies.

An ointment made by grinding garlic with olive oil will relieve sprains, rheumatism, and neuritis when rubbed on the painful area. For corns, calluses, warts, and small cysts, apply a hot clove of garlic that has been baked in an oven or under glowing embers. For deafness and earache, wrap a clove of garlic in gauze and insert it in the ear. For wasp or bee stings, remove the stinger, then rub with a clove of garlic cut in two. For toothache, apply crushed garlic mixed with fresh butter to the tooth. For greater virility, rub your spine with a clove of garlic.

Garlic can replace paste. Rub both objects to be attached with a clove of garlic cut in two, them hold them together until the juice is dry.

The vapors given off by garlic retard food spoilage. If open receptacles containing cloves of garlic peeled and cut in half are put in a room where fruit is stored, the fruit will keep better through the winter.

Leeks

Rich in vitamins B and C, leeks also contain iron, lime, sulfur, magnesium, potassium, and phosphorus. They are diuretic, antiseptic, and emollient. They improve the health of those suffering from anemia or rheumatism. Their laxative properties are well known. The cellulose they contain helps in the elimination of intestinal residues. They correct disorders of the intestines, such as diarrhea.

The presence of a sulfonitrogenous essence in leeks makes them a good remedy for rheumatism and diseases of the kidneys and bladder. Take two pounds of the white parts of leeks, cut them into pieces, boil them in two quarts of white wine until the mixture is reduced by half, filter it, and drink a glass of it every morning.

For congestion of the bronchi, take a tablespoonful of leek syrup whenever you have a fit of coughing, morning and evening. Cook several leeks, extract their juice, and add a tablespoonful of honey for each pint. As a mouthwash or gargle, a strained decoction (boil two or three finely chopped leeks for fifteen minutes) can be used for treating angina.

The pain of pleurisy can be relieved with hot poultices of leek and cabbage leaves cooked in a frying pan, with a cup of vinegar added. Leeks are a healing food suitable even for someone whose stomach makes it difficult for him to eat anything else. Eat them often, preferably cooked slowly in a closed pot. Regular use of them will enable you to stay in good health.

Rubbed raw on the skin, the white part of leeks relieves the pain of insect bites; the acid in them decomposes the venom.

Lettuce

Containing vitamins A, B, and C, iron, magnesium, sodium, and copper, lettuce is very beneficial. Lettuce gone to seed has been known since ancient times for its sedative properties, which facilitate sleep and have a calming effect on the genital organs. Because of its cellulose, lettuce favors elimination of the contents of the intestines.

Apply a poultice of cooked lettuce to a boil or a burn.

For acne, rub the face with water in which lettuce has been cooked.

Lettuce is cooling and it whets the appetite by stimulating the digestive glands. A salad of it should always be served at the beginning of a meal.

Nettles

The herbaceous plant, nettles, is an excellent vegetable. Its hairs secrete a liquid containing formic acid which irritates the skin, and this has unfortunately given it a bad reputation. It is a general tonic, it purifies and regenerates the blood, and it can be used for treating dry skin troubles, eczema, nosebleed, and hemorrhages. It stimulates the digestive functions and cures rheumatism and diabetes by facilitating urinary secretion.

Its leaves and roots, fresh or dried, are used in light decoctions (an ounce and a half of leaves in a quart of water, boiled two to three minutes; two ounces of roots in a quart of water slowly brought to a boil for five minutes, then allowed to steep for ten minutes). Nettle syrup has the same properties. Nettle seeds are used in making a drink that stimulates sexual activity and combats impotence.

Applied externally, the juice of the fresh plant immediately stops nosebleed. The roots invigorate the scalp: Make a decoction of three and a half ounces of roots in a quart of water.

As a food, nettles can be used in making tasty soups. Wearing gloves, pull of several stalks and wash them thoroughly, then brown them in oil with a chopped onion, add a quart of water, and cook for fifteen minutes. You can put this soup in your blender, the result will be creamy and delicious.

Onions

Rich in vitamins A, B, and C, onions also contain iron, lime, phosphorus, potassium, sodium, sulfur, iodine, silica, and sugar.

The phosphorus in them facilitates brain activity. They are also good for treating nervous or physical depression. An energizing food, onions help old people, growing children, and anyone who has lost his appetite. Cut a large onion into pieces, boil it in three cups of water until only one cup remains, and drink this liquid in the morning before breakfast.

Because of their sulfur, onions are a blood antiseptic and they purify the respiratory tract. To treat influenza, asthma, or bronchitis, make a decoction of three onions boiled for ten minutes in a pint of water sweetened with honey or syrup. Add a tablespoonful of honey and heat over a low flame until the liquid thickens. Take two to six spoonfuls a day.

The iodine in onions makes them beneficial in cases of scurvy and diseases of the lymphatic system. Like garlic, they have antibiotic properties. Drink onion wine: Put into a bottle three and a half ounces of finely chopped onions, an ounce and a quarter of honey, and seven ounces of wine; let soak at least forty-eight ours, shaking often. Or mix a spoonfull of honey and a finely grated onion in a glass of wine.

Because of their silica, onions help make strong bones and elastic arteries. They are a powerful diuretic and can be used to treat cystitis, cirrhosis, and articular rheumatism. Eat finely chopped onions in bouillon or spread on pieces of buttered bread. This treatment is also recommended when the body needs to eliminate not only toxic waste products, but water invading the tissues.

It is preferable to eat onions raw. To peel them without getting tears in your eyes, hold them under water while you work. They are an incomparable health-giving food that can be used to enrich your salads, vegetables, and soups. Their purifying properties improve the complexion. If you find your breath displeasing after eating them, chew parsley or roasted coffee beans.

Unlike most other vegetables, onions keep their properties when they are cooked. Onion soup is known for its ability to ease the stomach when one has eaten and drunk too much the night before. But the onions must only be "melted," without being burned. The tops of white spring onions contain large amounts of vitamin C. Do not throw them away. They can be used to make good soup.

For diarrhea, boil a handful of onion skins for ten minutes, strain, and sweeten with honey. Drink this mixture three or four times a day.

Applied to the temples, onions relieve congestion; on a bee or wasp sting, they soothe the irritation; and on a dog bite, they heal the wound and combat infection. For a burn, apply crushed onion with a pinch of sea salt to ease pain and prevent blisters from forming.

For earache, make a paste of baked onion and butter, enclose a little of it in a piece of thin cloth, and insert it in the ear.

Inflammation around a fingernail or toenail can be quickly cured by putting onion skin over it. To get rid of a wart, rub it morning and evening with the liquid obtained by hollowing out a big white onion and filling the cavity with sea salt.

Onions can also be used in housework. Onion skin cleans light bulbs. An onion cut in half will restore the shine to a patent-leather belt or handbag, make windows clear, and clean even slightly rusted knife blades. To make woodworms disappear, rub the infested wood with an onion every day for two weeks. A mixture of moist earth and crushed onion is good for cleaning copper pots.

If you want to write to your secret love, use onion or lemon juice. The invisible writing will appear as soon as the paper is heated.

Potatoes

Potatoes are rich in vitamins B and C, irons, fats, and potash (nearly a tenth of an ounce per pound). Baked or boiled, they are included in the diet of diabetics. We are so used to seeing them on our tables that we often overlook their therapeutic properties.

For neuralgia, put a piece of raw potato on each temple. Raw potato juice combats excess gastric acid in cases of stomach ulcers and chronic diarrhea, and is recommended for diabetics. Drink it sweetened with honey, or mixed with carrot or tomato juice.

For puffy eyes, chapped skin, and the pain of burns, apply a poultice of raw grated potato for a quarter of an hour.

For cooking, peel potatoes very thinly, since the most nutritious part is just under the skin.

To preserve their taste and alkaline salts, it is better to bake them unpeeled.

A few pieces of raw potato can help you to withdraw excess salt from a soup. As they cook, they absorb it.

Water in which peeled potatoes have been boiled is a good cleaner for silverware. Rub your mirrors and windowpanes with slices of potato.

Spinach

Spinach contains vitamins A, B, and especially C, iron, lime, phosphorus, magnesium, and potassium. Favoring the formation of red corpuscles, it is beneficial to anemic people, convalescents, children, and old people. They can take it in a mixture of four parts wine and one part spinach juice, drunk before meals. Pregnant women should eat a great deal of spinach; some of the iron it contains passes into the liver of the fetus and enables it to make its own red corpuscles.

The iron and lime in spinach help to keep your teeth in good condition. To remedy a deficiency, prepare the following drink: Chop a handful of spinach and a handful of parsley, grate a carrot, mix, soak two hours in a little water, squeeze, and add an equal amount of grape, apple, or pear juice. Drink it with an afternoon snack. The juice obtained by squeezing one handful of spinach and one of the watercress brings recovery to people suffering from physical or nervous depression.

The chlorophyll in spinach stimulates the muscles and intestines, and its cellulose favors elimination of waste products. It is a good laxative. It is recommended for those afflicted with rheumatism or liver ailments.

For a bad cut, a sore, or a burn, apply a poultice of spinach leaves cooked in olive oil.

Do not keep cooked spinach very long because it soon begins to ferment. You can make good soup with the cooking liquid.

But eat young raw spinach in salads as often as possible.

Sorrel has the same virtues as spinach, but do not eat it if you have rheumatism, asthma, or a lung disorder.

Tomatoes

Tomatoes, rich in vitamins A, B, and C, contain iron and many other minerals, such as phosphorus. They stimulate the appetite and are cooling. They are recommended for bilious and sanguine temperaments and people suffering from arthritis, nephritis, kidney stones, bladder or liver ailments, or constipation. For chronic constipation I recommend a mixture of finely chopped raw lettuce, celery, carrots, and cauliflower, seasoned with raw tomato juice, taken during meals.

Tomato juice is also a good diuretic. Mixed with an equal weight of celery juice, it becomes restorative.

Tomatoes are not very nourishing. They should be eaten only during the season in which they grow, in the place where you are. They are then recommended even for children, eaten raw to clear waste products from the intestines. But they do not agree with all stomachs. Cooked in their own juice, they facilitate digestion of starches and are a good accompaniment for pasta and dried beans.

For blackheads, gently pat the affected area with a tomato cut in two, then rinse with water. Do the same thing with raw sorrel the following day. Tomato leaves ward off wasps and mosquitoes. Make a string of them to hang in your bedroom.

Turnips

Rich in mineral salts, sugars, and vitamins A, B, and C, turnips also contain arsenic (which fortifies the body against contagious diseases), phosphorus, iodine, and sulfur. Their emollient qualities make them a good remedy.

A decoction made with three and a half ounces of turnips boiled in a quart of water with a little honey can be drunk as often as needed for soothing colds and lung irritations. Turnip syrup has the same properties. Hollow out a turnip and fill the cavity with cane sugar. A concentrated syrup will soon be formed. You can take four or five spoonfuls of it a day.

To soothe itching, chilblains, and abscesses, bake an unpeeled turnip and apply it while it is still warm. People subject to acne and eczema should chew a piece of raw turnip every day to get the sulfur they need.

Turnips are cooling and can be used in broth given to invalids. But because of their high sugar content they must not be eaten by diabetics.

Watercress

Watercress is one of the vegetables richest in vitamin C. It acts strongly against liver congestion. Eat it in moderate amounts, however. It is recommended for diabetics because it eliminates the sugar contained in urine. Being an antidote to nicotine, it is good for smokers. In salads or soups, or in the form of juice (extracted by crushing large green leaves), it is cooling, purifying, diuretic, and stimulating, and it whets the appetite, provides needed minerals, and combats scurvy. It contains iron, sulfur, iodine (combats anemia), copper, and calcium.

Chewed raw, it makes the gums firmer and prevents them from bleeding. It also cures apthae. Children should occasionally be given finely chopped watercress, seasoned with lemon juice, on a slice of buttered bread.

When watercress has been kept too long after being cut, it turns yellow, begins to ferment, and becomes toxic. It should not, of course, be eaten in that condition. Also avoid watercress that has flowered.

Watercress is part of a folk medicine for making hair grow back: Rub the scalp with a lotion composed of four ounces of watercress juice, four ounces of alcohol, and half an ounce of essence of geranium.

Fruits that Heal

At the beginning of his evolution, man could eat only fruit and roots. Today, fruit is often neglected, or is used only as a dessert to provide a change of taste after a meal and refresh the breath and palate. Yet each fruit is rich in vitamins and minerals. Restoring fruit to its proper place, and using it periodically for courses of treatment to correct certain imbalances in the body, cannot be recommended too highly.

Instead of blindly following advertising that makes great claims for processed sugar as a source of energy, why not get real natural energy from fruit? Fruit contains pure sugar—glucose, fructose—that can be directly assimilated by the body. Nowadays, of course, it is hard to find tree-ripened fruit in good condition.

But how are we to recognize good fruit? By its taste. Weak taste shows artifical or inadequate ripening.

The best fruits are those that grow in the country without insecticides and that we pick ourselves. They provide the body with such minerals as iron, lime, phosphorus, magnesium, potassium, sodium, sulfur, silica, iodine, and arsenic, all vitalizing and directly assimilable substances that serve to build tissues in children and maintain them in adults.

Aside from the minerals it provides, fruit has various effects on the body that make it a remedy for many ailments.

A healthy person, with his gastrointestinal organs in good condition, should be able to tolerate all kinds of fruit. Most of them have a laxative effect because of the cellulose and water they contain. They therefore ward off self-poisoning and enable the organs to function well. Compare the complexion of someone who eats a great deal of meat with that of someone whose diet contains a large proportion of fruit.

Fruit also has a diuretic effect. The acids in it destroy themselves by burning in the body, leaving alkaline salts which increase the secretion of digestive juices, regularize the flow of bile, and enable urine to become neutral if it is too acid. It is a good remedy for rheumatism and diseases of the stomach and liver.

Fruit contains a large amount of water that has its own vitality, like mineral water from a spring.

Some fruits, such as oranges, lemons, and grapefruit, contain various acids—malic acid, tartaric acid, citric acid—which do not decalcify the body even if they are taken in large amounts. Unlike chemical acids, they are oxidized and burned in the cells, dissolving impurities and giving off usable energy in the form of nitrogenous and fatty substances. Alkaline carbonates are the only residue they leave, and they favor fixation of lime in tissues.

Unless it has been taken directly from the tree, fruit should be carefully washed, especially if you do not know exactly where it came from. The skin of fruit, exposed to the action of sunlight and air, is richer in vitamins (especially vitamin A) than the inside. It also contains diastases that make the inside of the fruit more assimilable. Eat the skin with the rest of the fruit whenever possible, and chew it thoroughly.

There is no nutritional advantage in cooking ripe fruit. Heat can only diminish its taste and the amount of vital elements in it. When it is cooked, however, it can be tolerated even by delicate stomachs.

Extract the juice of fruit and vegetables yourself. This "plant blood" is a powerful energizer that contains vitamins, enzymes, amino acids, essential minerals, and valuable trace elements.

You can put yourself on a health regimen with a single vegetable or fruit, or with a mixture, provided you respect the individual qualities of each kind. The amount to be taken is variable. You can drink half a glass of carrot juice before breakfast, for example. But for greater effectiveness, take a glass of juice twice a day: before breakfast and in the course of the day. Taken before meals, fruit or vegetable juice whets the appetite by its stimulating effect on gastric secretion.

Almonds

There are two kinds of almonds: sweet almonds, which are edible, and bitter almonds, which contain a poison, hydrocyanic acid, used in external medicine.

Almonds contain vitamins A and B, sugar, gum, oil, calcium, and phosphorus. They are a tonic for fetuses and newborn babies, and so are recommended for pregnant women and nursing mothers.

Almonds are a very nourishing food, either fresh or dried. When they are well chewed they whet the appetite and aid digestion. But eat them only in moderate amounts.

For children and convalescents, and to treat coughs and irritation of the digestive tract and urinary passages, almond milk is recommended: crush two ounces of shelled almonds to a smooth paste, mix with a quart of water, and strain through a fine cloth.

For inflammation of the urogenital organs, take orgeat syrup: two pounds of crushed almonds and a pound of brown sugar mixed in a quart of water. It is also a good, refreshing drink.

An infusion of an ounce of almond leaves and half an ounce of blossoms is a diuretic, a purgative, and a vermifuge.

For fever, cough, and sore throat, use a decoction made by boiling a handful of crushed almond shells for half an hour, with a little sugar and a few drops of rum or lemon juice.

Burns, contusions, and sores can be treated by applying a poultice of crushed fresh almond leaves.

For constipation and abdominal inflammations, rub the lower abdomen with almond oil.

Bitter almond poultices soothe headache, rheumatism, and biliary colic.

If the skin of your hands or breasts is rough, apply a lotion made as follows: slowly heat almond oil and cocoa butter together, stirring the whole time, then take the mixture off the stove and continue stirring until it cools.

Apples

Rich in vitamins A, B, and C, fats, tannin, and cellulose, apples also contain iron, calcium, phosphorus, magnesium, potassium, sodium, and silica.

If an apple has come from your own garden, eat it with its skin. If you buy apples, choose the ugliest ones, those that are spotted and wrinkled: they have not been chemically treated. Make your own fresh apple juice, grated apple for babies, baked apples, and apple butter.

Apples are one of the best medicinal fruits. Ohsawa regarded them as the most yang of fruits in the West. They nourish nerve and muscle fibers. They dissolve uric acid and other poisons in the body and stimulate the salivary and gastric glands. They are recommended for diarrhea in children, arthritic diathesis, chronic rheumatism, diseases of the bronchi and liver, and dysentery. They also help dissolve gallstones and kidney stones. Since their sugar content is low, they can be eaten by diabetics.

To combat constipation, eat an apple at bedtime, chewing it thoroughly. This will also help you to sleep.

Keep the peels and cores of homegrown apples to make infusions for the heart, lungs, intestines, and disorders of rheumatic origin. For a stubborn case of influenza, eat nothing but one to two pounds of apples a day for two or three days.

If a child has diarrhea, feed him only raw, very ripe, finely grated apple at the rate of one tablespoonful every hour.

Apples combat fatigue, mental strain, and mineral deficiencies.

A poultice of grated apple soothes the pain caused by a blow to the eye. A pulp of cooked, peeled apples relieves sore eyes and inflammation of the eyelids.

For falling hair and itchy scalp, comb your hair every morning and evening after dipping your comb in a glass of water with a teaspoonful of apple cider vinegar stirred into it.

The juice and meat of apples makes body tissues firmer and constitute a good beauty treatment.

Apricots

Apricots are richer in vitamin A than any other fruit. They build bones and tissues, extend the life of cells, increase the ability to be active, and favor longevity. They also contain vitamins B and C and sugar.

Apricots should be avoided by people with liver ailments, but otherwise they are recommended for mental workers. They strenthen nerves and help an anemic body to regain its health.

When eaten raw they should be very ripe, especially for delicate stomachs. Cooked in the form of marmalade, they become perfectly digestible and can therefore be recommended for convalescents.

Blackberries

Blackberries are rich in vitamins A and C, sugar, and essential oils with disinfecting properties. A handful of them, eaten in the morning before breakfast, acts as a laxative and purifier. A syrup made from green blackberries can be used to treat diarrhea in babies. Blackberry syrup is also effective against angina and lung diseases.

A decoction of leaves picked before flowering (one ounce per quart of water) combats diarrhea and retention of urine. Drunk with honey, it soothes the throat and relieves angina. In a douche, it is effective agains leukorrhea. It should be strained thoroughly.

If you have inflamed eyes, apply warm compresses made with an infusion of blackberry leaves in barley water.

Blueberries

Not only can blueberries be used to make tasty pies, syrups, and jellies, but they also have therapeutic properties.

Rich in tannin, they are astringent and antiseptic. They purify the intestines, relieve skin diseases and disorders of the liver and throat, improve faulty circulation, and increase visual acuity, espeically at night.

A decoction of blueberry roots (three quarters of an ounce per quart of water), used in compresses, helps to heal cuts and sores.

Cherries

Cherries contain vitamins A, B, and C, sugar, iron, calcium, magnesium, sodium, zinc, and a great deal of potassium.

A good way to purify your blood is to eat large amounts of fresh cherries for two or three days. The disinfecting power of cherries on intestinal fermentations makes it possible for them to cure not only constipation but also diarrhea and dysentery. Even diabetics can eat them, since fructose, the sugar in cherries, can be directly assimilated.

Cherries are a diuretic and are recommended for rheumatism, arthritis, and bilious and sanguine temperaments. Since they are low in calories, they are a fruit that you can eat abundantly even if you want to lose weight.

If you have a delicate stomach, soft, easily digested black cherries are the only kind you should eat raw. The harder varieties can be eaten in compotes.

Cherry-stem infusions (a third of an ounce per quart of water) and wine, in which five handfuls of crushed cherry seeds have been soaked, are highly regarded diuretics. They increase the amount of urine and diminish its acidity. Taken in a decoction, cherry stems (one ounce per quart of water) relieve jaundice, influenza, and kidney disorders. If you use dried stems, soak them half a day before boiling.

A decoction of cherry leaves in milk provides a gentle purge, without colic. For headache, apply crushed cherries to the forehead and temples. A face pack of crushed cherries will give increased vitality to the tissues.

Chestnuts

Chestnuts contain vitamins B and C, cellulose, fatty and nitrogenous substances, magnesium, and sodium.

Eaten ripe and sufficiently cooked, they are a nourishing, complete winter food that helps to give the body the heat it needs. Because of their high starch content, they should not be eaten by diabetics.

Because of their tough shell, they keep their vitamins and nutritive substances even when they are boiled for three quarters of an hour or roasted for fifteen minutes. Convalescents and old people should often eat chestnut purée made as follows: shell the chestnuts and boil them slowly with a sprig of celery; strain and place over high heat, stirring often; add vegetable stock or milk, a little butter, and sea salt.

Currants

Black currants, one of the fruits richest in vitamin C, which does not deteriorate, are used for making wines and creams reputed to favor longevity. Few plants can be used for treating such a large number of ailments. They will relieve arthritis pains, liver diseases, inflammations of the stomach and intestines, chronic diarrhea, fever, urinary inflammation, and general fatigue.

An infusion of black currant leaves cures heartburn and all disorders caused by an excess of uric acid. Drunk cold, it will quench your thirst in summer. Make it by soaking two ounces of fresh or dried leaves in a quart of cold water for an hour. Drink three or four glasses of it a day.

Black currant juice, raw or cooked, will relieve colds and angina. An infusion of an ounce of fresh or dried leaves and an ounce of licorice in a quart of water is a refreshing drink and can be used for the diseases mentioned above, as well as inflammations of the stomach and intestines. Rub the jagged little leaves of the black currant plant on insect bites.

Red currants have the same properties as black currants, but to an appreciably smaller degree. They contain vitamins A, B, and C, sugar, iron, mineral salts, and citric, pectin, and tartaric acids.

Red currant jelly has all the vitamins of the raw fruit because its acidity reacts in such a way that cooking destroys neither vitamins nor mineral salts. Here is the recipe: squeeze out the juice and put it on low heat in a pot with an equal wieght of brown sugar, slowly bring to a boil, and skim often until the right consistency is obtained.

A pound of red currants and two ounces of raspberries make a delicious mixture. You can also add strawberries and black currants.

Dates

Dates, the manna of nomads and merchants who cross the desert, are rich in vita-mins A, B, and C, sugar, cellulose, fats, and minerals.

Highly nourishing, they can be eaten fresh or sun-dried.

Because of its sweet taste and expectorant properties, a date decoction (two ounces per quart of water) can be used to treat colds, sore throat, and all chest ailments.

Figs

Figs contain vitamins A, B, and C, nitrogenous substances, iron, mineral salts, lime, manganese, and an amount of sugar that varies according to the place they are grown. They are recommended for everyone and are a valuable therapeutic agent.

Because of their seeds, figs have a stimulating and laxative effect on the intestines. For constipation, wash five or six dried figs, put them in a bowl of warm water, and let them soak overnight; in the morning before breakfast, eat the figs and drink the water.

Figs have emolient properties and can be used for treating throat irritations, colds, lingering bronchitis, inflammations of the mouth, angina, and lung ailments. Make a hot decoction by boiling five or six figs in a quart of water or milk. You can also use this as a gargle and a mouthwash.

A mixture of figs, dates, and raisins is made into a decoction (two ounces per quart of water) for treating lung ailments.

To soothe the pain of burns, abscesses, boils, and skin disease, apply hot poultices of fresh or dried figs. Apply half a fig to a gum abscess.

A decoction of young twigs of the fig tree is a gentle laxative for children. Sweetened with honey, it relieves throat irritations. By eliminating water from body tissue, it treats dropsy.

An infusion of fig leaves (one ounce per quart of water) is an emollient and a good cough medicine. It eases menstrual difficulties if it is drunk a few days before the beginning of a period. For warts and corns, gather the milky juice that flows from the stem when a fig is picked from the tree and apply it morning and evening.

Figs are a tonic for the stomach and intestines, and are recommended even for children. Stewed or made into jam, they soothe delicate stomachs and relieve constipation. Dried figs can also be used to make a healthful drink. Put two pounds of figs into a small barrel. Add a few juniper seeds and two and a half gallons of water. Let the liquid stand for a week, then bottle it. Tie down the corks or use bottles with a mechanical closure. Wait another week before drinking.

Grapes

When thoroughly ripe, grapes are the richest of all fruits in vitamins A, B, and C. They contain sugar (about two ounces per pound), fats, albumin, tannin, iron, lime, phosphorus, magnesium, potassium, sodium, iodine, manganese, and arsenic.

In autumn, a diet of two to four pounds of grapes a day for one to two weeks will invigorate your liver, cleanse your kidneys, and put you in condition to confront winter. It will also help you to reduce if you are overweight. But wash your grapes carefully before eating them. When the vines are treated with copper sulfate, which is a violent poison, traces of it may remain on the grapes.

Rich in natural sugar, grapes are nourishing and digestible. Their food value is equal to, or greater than, that of human milk. The large amounts of iron and natural sugar they contain increase the body's energy. They are excellent for pregnant women.

Dried grapes (raisins) are also a good source of energy and can be used for treating chest disorders. Give them to your children.

Used as a lotion, grape juice invigorates the skin and clears the complexion. (Rinse thoroughly with warm water.)

Grape wine has great nutritive value. A tonic but also a stimulant, it should be drunk only in moderate amounts. Choose wine that does not contain chemicals and, if possible, buy it directly from the winegrower. You can tell if a red wine is pure by pouring a few drops of it onto a piece of chalk: If the wine is pure, the chalk will turn brown. Red wine is tonic and astringent; white wine is a diuretic and an appetizer. To remove a spot of red wine from a tablecloth, wet it immediately with white wine.

Grapevine leaves, a good green vegetable rich in vitamins, may be eaten cooked like spinach or rolled like cabbage leaves, in the Greek fashion. The sap has healing powers and reduces inebriation. It is used in lotions for treating eye inflammations and in compresses for healing cuts.

Lemons

Lemons contain vitamins A, B, and especially C, iron, lime, phosphorus, potassium, provitamin A (in the skin), citric acid, and ascorbic acid, which prevents and cures scurvy.

Lemons have many therapeutic virtues: They are an alkalizer, an antiseptic, an antiscorbutic, a diuretic, an astringent, a vermifuge, and a hepatic, and they combat rheumatism and neuralgia. Choose lemons that have not been treated with pesticides or preserved with biphenyl, a poison that seeps into the fruit.

Since lemon juice kills the bacilli of cholera, typhoid fever, and dysentery, add a few drops of it to water that seems suspicious to you, put it on meat and fish of dubious freshness, and on oysters and other shellfish. Because of its taste and digestive properties, lemon juice should replace commercial vinegar in your salads and on raw vegetables.

To quench the thirst of a sick person who has fever, make lemonade (lemon juice, water, honey) and serve it at room temperature. For liver ailments, pour a quart of boiling water onto three lemons cut into slices, add honey, let stand overnight, and drink the next morning before breakfast.

For intestinal worms, crush the skin, pulp, and seeds of a lemon, soak two hours in water with a little honey added, strain, and drink at bedtime. If a child has pinworms, give him crushed lemon seeds with honey every morning before breakfast. For sore throat, angina, and aphthae, gargle several times a day with lemon juice and honey in warm water.

For diseases resulting from infection of the alimentary canal, it is good to use milk curdled with lemon juice; the lactic ferments it contains act on the digestive system as a powerful disinfectant. Put the juice of a ripe lemon into whole milk, adding it a drop at a time. Stir with a spoon until the milk takes on a lumpy consistency. If it is consumed immediately, this curdled milk keeps its own vitamins and is enriched by those of the lemon juice, which also contributes the antiseptic action of its citric acid. (Milk can be curdled instantly by pouring it into a container that inside has been rubbed with thyme and mother-of-thyme.)

To relieve a bad head cold, pour a few crops of lemon juice into the palm of your hand and suck it up through your nose, after completely coating your nostrils with fresh butter or oil. Frequent and prolonged use of nose drops is dangerous; when they are put into the nose, minute drops of oil slip into the windpipe, then into lung tissue, and may cause pneumonia. To stop nosebleed, apply a cotton pad soaked with lemon juice.

For obesity, pour a cup of boiling water onto two camomile flowers and a lemon cut into slices, let soak overnight, strain in the morning, and drink before breakfast. You can also give yourself a course of treatment with lemon juice that will enable you to lose weight and strengthen your body. Start with ten lemons a day and gradually go down to one, over a period of three to four weeks.

Lemons are also used in beauty care and housework.

To keep your hands soft and beautiful, coat them with a mixture of equal parts of lemon juice, glycerin, and eau de cologne. Applied several times a day, lemon-juice lotion eliminates the sebum of oily skin; used occasionally, it clears the skin, restores freshness to it, and retards the appearance of wrinkles.

To relieve a headache, apply compresses of lightly salted lemon juice to each temple and the forehead. For the pain of neuralgia and rheumatism, rub with half a lemon.

For brittle nails, apply lemon juice morning and evening for a week.

Lemon juice is an excellent astringent and antiseptic for treating inflamed mucous membranes and all sorts of sores and cuts.

Extract of lemon, taken in the amount of five to ten drops on a lump of sugar, has important bactericidal properties.

To whiten teeth, brush them every day with lemon juice. To aid teething in a baby, rub his gums with your finger after dipping it in a mixture of equal parts of boiled water and lemon juice. Ink spots on the fingers can be removed with lemon juice.

To get rid of moths, hang little bags of dried lemon peel in your closets. To take out a rust stain on white cloth, cover it with a slice of lemon between two pieces of cloth. Apply a hot iron and repeat until the stain disappears.

To clean blackened copper, rub it with half a lemon sprinkled with coarse salt. Rub your jewelry and silverware with a slice of lemon, then rinse in hot water and dry with a chamois skin.

To clean a stained wash basin, scour it with half a cup of lemon juice with a large pinch of salt in it.

If lemons are soaked in hot water for five minutes just before being squeezed, they yield much more juice.

Olives

Black olives, picked ripe, sprinkled with salt, dried in sunlight, and preserved in oil, are preferable to green olives soaked in a caustic solution.

Rich in fats, and vitamins A and C, olives are very nourishing. Olive oil from the first pressing is the best of all table oils. For long life and good health, spread it on your bread.

A spoonful of olive oil taken before breakfast is good for people with liver ailments. By cleaning the walls of the intestines, it helps waste matter follow its course.

For colic during a difficult childbirth, take a spoonful of olive oil in a cup of warm milk.

To prevent drunkenness, take a tablespoonful of olive oil before meals or parties.

To prevent loss of hair, rub your scalp with olive oil every night at bedtime and wash your hair the next morning with warm water and a good shampoo containing clay.*

To lower blood pressure, boil twenty olive leaves in ten ounces of water until the volume is reduced by a third, and drink a cup of this decoction every day for a week.

Olive leaves are a vasodilator and lower the amount of sugar in the blood. They are recommended for treating high blood pressure and angina pectoris. Soak them in water.

Oranges

Rich in vitamins B and C, oranges contain iron, lime, phosphorus, magnesium, potassium, copper, carotene, and various acids.

---

*See the chapter on "Healing by Minerals."

Eat oranges to maintain resistance to microbic infections, especially in winter, when green vegetables, the usual source of vitamin C, are scarce and expensive, and stored potatoes have lost a large part of it. But make sure they are sun-ripened and have not been treated with biphenyl.

Oranges liquefy the blood and combat pimples, eczema, and other skin diseases.

Orange juice, recommended for invalids, old people, and babies, relieves influenza and colds. At bedtime, drink a glass of it mixed with two lumps of sugar, a jigger of rum, and hot water.

Oranges can help you to lose weight. Drink three glasses a day of the following preparation: cut an orange and three lemons into small pieces, boil them for ten minutes in a pint of water, add two spoonfuls of honey, and simmer for five minutes. Drink it cold.

Orange pulp applied to the skin provides it with vitamins, rests the face, retards the appearance of wrinkles, and improves the complexion.

Orange peel has therapeutic properties. To speed recovery from influenza, drink an infusion of half an ounce of bay leaves and an ounce and a half of dried orange peel.

Fresh orange peel contains an antiseptic substance that favors bile secretion and is valuable in treating infectious diseases, particularly those of the intestines. For constipation, boil a fresh orange for half an hour in the evening; peel it and boil the peel in new water for twenty minutes; eat it the next morning before breakfast.

Burning a piece of orange peel will dissipate the smell of tobacco smoke.

You can make a good orange apéritif for yourself: Soak six orange peels in a pint of brandy for two weeks, then add two quarts of white wine and a pound of melted sugar; let stand at least a week before drinking.

To calm the nerves, ease palpitations, and combat insomnia, drink several cups a day, including one at bedtime, of an infusion made with three or four orange blossoms per cup. An orange-blossom decoction (a handful in a pint of water boiled until its volume is reduced by half), taken before breakfast, is sedative and antispasmodic.

Hanging in a clothes closet, an orange with cloves stuck into it is aromatic and gives good protection against moths.

Peaches

Like all our orchard fruits, peaches are rich in vitamins A, B, and C, and are good for health and beauty. Easily tolerated by the stomach, they are a diuretic and a laxative.

An infusion of peach pits regularizes menstruation. Buzzing in the ears may be stopped by putting a few drops of peach juice into each ear.

The almondlike kernels inside peach pits can be ground to make poultices for treating headaches, burns, and skin diseases.

Crushed peach pulp applied to the face invigorates and clears the skin.

An infusion of peach leaves (two ounces per quart of water, steeped five minutes) can be used for treating diseases of the urinary passages.

For pinworms in children, apply poultices of peach leaves, blossoms, and ground almonds to the abdomen.

Pears

Rich in vitamins A, B, and C, sugar, fats, and tannin, pears also contain iron, lime, phosphorus, magnesium, potassium, and manganese. They are recommended for quenching thirst. They purify the blood, provide significant amounts of minerals, and are recommended for arthritic diathesis, gout, rheumatism, and high blood pressure. They are also a good diuretic; eat a fresh pear in the evening.

Plums

Plums, rich in vitamins B and C, sugar, and carbohydrates, contain iron, lime, phosphorus, magnesium, potassium, sodium, and manganese. They are an energizing fruit and a nerve stimulant recommended for rheumatics, overworked people, athletes, and everyone who has been poisoned by his food.

They relieve chronic constipation. Eat a few very ripe plums with rye bread before breakfast, or eat plum marmalade.

By drying your own plums, you can make prunes, a highly energizing food rich in vitamin A and iron. For constipation, soak eight prunes half a day, then boil for ten minutes in water to which you have added the juice of one lemon. Eat these prunes every morning before breakfast. Eat two ripe apples at bedtime and drink two glasses of water and lemon juice in the morning and afternoon. Plum leaves make a good infusion, and a decoction of them (one ounce per quart of water) is a diuretic, a laxative, a febrifuge, and a vermifuge.

Strawberries and Raspberries

Strawberries are the fruit of an easily cultivated plant, all of whose parts are beneficial. They contain vitamins B and C, sugar, cellulose, fats, albuminoid substances, potassium, sodium, silica, iodine, and bromine.

They should be eaten at the beginning of a meal, since they stimulate the appetite. Nourishing, refreshing, diuretic, and purifying, they are suitable for everyone, even diabetics, for whom a tablespoonful of wild strawberries in fresh cream is a good dessert. It is better not to wash strawberries from your own garden. If you do wash them, however, do it half an hour before eating them, so that they can regain their fragrance.

Being rich in iron, strawberries are particularly good for anemic and tubercular people. Their salicylic acid is favorable to the liver, kidneys, joints, and gall bladder. They are also an excellent laxative.

For facial care, apply a few crushed strawberries directly to your skin: They will invigorate it, combat wrinkles, and clear your complexion. Make a face pack as follows: juice of five large, ripe strawberries mixed with the white of an egg beaten stiff; add three quarters of an ounce of rose water and ten drops of tincture of benzoin; stir. Apply it to your face and keep it on for about an hour, then rinse with water in which chervil has been steeped.

Dried strawberry leaves and roots are rich in tannin, astringent, diuretic, and tonic, and they whet the appetite. They can be used to replace tea. Gather them in summer.

A decoction of an ounce of mixed leaves and roots per quart of water can be used for treating arteriosclerosis, arthritis, high blood pressure, kidney and bladder ailments, gonorrhea, and deterioration of the skin.

A stronger decoction (an ounce and a half per quart) of the whole plant is a good drink for people with liver ailments. Do not worry if your urine and stool are colored red after you drink this decoction: it is a harmless property of the root.

Raspberries have the same tonic and diuretic virtues as strawberries. They can be eaten by diabetics and are recommended for rheumatics. Dried raspberry leaves make good laxative infusions.

Mix strawberries and raspberries in your jams.

Walnuts and Hazelnuts

Walnuts contain vitamins A and B, fats, nitrogenous substances, iron, lime, phosphorus, zinc, and copper. Highly nourishing (half their weight is oil), restorative, purifying, and disinfecting, they are recommended for people with tuberculosis and diabetes.

Walnut leaves and husks have long been used in home medicine, and for centuries they were taken as a remedy for smallpox. An infusion of an ounce per quart of water is rich in tannin and is a valuable tonic recommended for tuberculosis. A decoction of two ounces per quart is good for chilblains and sweaty feet, and in compresses it can be used for treating inflammation of the eyelids and blisters.

To make a good apéritif, tonic, purifier, and aid to digestion, soak half a pound of chopped fresh walnut leaves in a quart of good wine for four or five days, sweeten, and strain; or soak a pound of chopped green walnut husks in a quart of brandy for three months, then strain, mix with three quarts of wine, and sweeten. Drink a small glassful before meals.

Boiled in a very small amount of water, walnut leaves can be used to make poultices for treating scabies, ringworm, and parasitic diseases.

A decoction of half a pound of walnut leaves mixed in a bath with two pounds of salt is good for skin diseases and nervous fatigue.

Hazelnuts have essentially the same virtues as walnuts, but to a lesser degree.

Today, noncommercial growing of vegetables, fruits, and herbs is dying out. Everyone who lives in the country or has a weekend house there should devote some space in his garden to growing good remedy foods.

If you use natural fertilizers (manure, sea-weed), potash, lime, and a little sulfur, the quality of your crops will reward you for your efforts. In gardening, you should harmonize yourself with the earth, the phases of the moon, the climate, and the cosmos. Respect the life of your vegetables; enrich your garden with fruit trees, strawberry plants, currant bushes, aromatic herbs, and a beehive.

Plant foods have always played a large part in human nutrition. Now that our modern errors in diet are becoming more threatening every day, it is good to stress foods capable of preventing destruction of tissue and maintaining energy reserves with a minimum of toxic wastes. Rich in vitamins and minerals, plants have a nutritional value which often surpasses that of many animal products, such as meat, milk, and eggs. Furthermore, they all have medicinal virtues that deserve to be rediscovered.

Whoever knows nature is sick less often.

And the fruit will surpass the promise of the blossoms.

Malherbe

Man has always had a special communicative relationship with plants. In the symbolic system of the *I Ching,* the sign for wood also designates wind, and there is a single sign for a plant and breath. Plants breathe. The wind makes tree leaves move. The song of a breeze in pines is not the harsh grating of a winter wind in an oak grove.

From one viewpoint, it can be said that there have been no radical changes in the human brain since the time when man lived in the primeval forest; but in our time the deep layers corresponding to patterns of life in primitive times have been placed in a kind of enforced inactivity, while the use of the cerebral cortex, corresponding to mental work, has been greatly accelerated.

In the primeval forest, man freely hunted and gathered food. He was an element of the ecosystem into which he was harmoniously integrated. When we go out to pick mushrooms or blackberries, or look for firewood, we often lapse unconsciously into primordial behavior. There is in man a deep, instinctive knowledge that enables him to recognize a fruit and tell whether or not it is ripe. From seed to flower, something is at work, whether it be in the spontaneity of natural space or within the restraints of agriculture. "The earth works." In the solar space that then leads from the flower to the seed, "each atom of silence," says Valéry, "is the chance of a ripe fruit." Human beings pick, gather, and harvest. They are in a festive mood; nature has revived and the days are long; they leap over flames, sing praises of the earth, thank the heavens, celebrate water and fire.

HOMEOPATHY

Homeopathy is a form of medicine that can be called different because, unlike official medicine known as allopathy, it is based on neither quantitative treatment nor the law of opposites. Homeopathy regards each human being as a special case and refuses to divide his body into distinct parts, considering it instead as a synthesis of interdependent elements. It is a mistake to treat a stubborn boil or sore throat without taking into account the general conditions under which the infection has developed. Intermittent relief may be achieved, but the root causes of the ailment remain unknown. The external symptoms of a disease are signs of an inner disorder that may have multiple causes; principal causes are often overeating, overwork, and emotional disturbance.

Discovered by Samuel Hahnemann, modern homeopathy is not much more than a century old. Its method has not become at all outmoded because it is primarily a state of mind, and secondarily a technique.

Dr. Jacques Michaud, a modern homeopath, describes homeopathy as a practice linked to the universal flow and movements of cosmic energy.

Are we dealing with a total medicine?

CONVERSATION WITH DR. MICHAUD

You attack official medicine and speak of a "polluting medicine." Why?

Because it pollutes. I don't systematically attack everything official. I freely acknowledge that there are some remarkable things in that medicine. But the state of mind in homeopathy is different, and that's what matters. We make a synthesis. Basically we regard man as a unity, from birth to death, an indivisible unity. All through life, pathological manifestations occur in that unity. They must be considered in relation to the individual's interior and not as sudden phenomena that we observe without any clear knowledge of how or why they appear. The individual should be viewed as a unique, irreplaceable particle of the cosmos. Homeopathic doctors can have that state of mind because they synthesize, and those syntheses are irreplaceable. I'll go so far as to say, however paradoxical it may seem, that in homeopathy, therapy is almost secondary.

I don't know how things are being taught in medical school nowadays, but I doubt that there's been much improvement since I was a student. You learn to know "diseases" but you never learn what a person is; you never learn to distinguish people from each other, to recognize in them the particle that makes each of them different from the others. In homeopathy we try to do that, which is why we have to put more stress on individual differences, and that leads to an interest in such things as astrology and acupuncture.

But the fact remains that I have nothing at all against certain allopathic medicines. I use them selectively, though of course I avoid antibiotics, cortisone, and tranquilizers because they're harmful medicines, as everyone knows, including official doctors. They cause physiological deterioration in the person who uses them. I'm very demanding about the quality of the homeopathic medicines I prescribe, but I don't feel that I'm being inconsistent if I also prescribe a few allopathic medicines, because I do it in the homeopathic spirit. I don't criticize all official therapy; my objection is that the way it's used is too systematic, too rapid, and too impersonal.

What is a homeopathic remedy?

It's a substance of animal, plant, or mineral origin which acquires therapeutic properties through dilution and succussion. If those two operations haven't been performed, the therapeutic properties of the substance, if it has any, can't be regarded as homeopathic. The classic example is lycopodium powder, a completely neutral substance that has no pharmacological properties. With homeopathic dilution and succussion, it acquires important powers; in particular, it's one of the main remedies for faulty liver functioning.

Dilution means diminishing the quantity of the substance, according to a geometric progression, to the point where there are no more detectable molecules, and even beyond. But although there's less and less matter as dilution increases, there's more and more energy.

As for succussion, it consists in energizing the bottle between two successive dilutions, which facilitates disintegration of molecules. Complex physical phenomena are involved here, but clinical experiments have shown the importance of this process.

In homeopathy, the wealth of therapeutic resources is infinite. There are no foreseeable limits because anything can be a remedy and can be used with all possible and imaginable dilutions. For example, a woman came to consult me because she had an allergy. I found that she was allergic to a product used for cleansing soil. I put some of it into a bottle and sent it to a laboratory. It's become a useful homeopathic remedy in other cases.

So we have an infinite range available to us. A homeopathic doctor usually knows and uses only a few hundred remedies. That's nothing compared to the possibilities that could be exploited if there were medical research in homeopathy. But even now the wealth of homeopathic therapy goes far beyond what's offered by allopathy, which seems to us a meager, narrow form of therapy.

Can it be said that your therapy is based on the principle of opposites?

No, not at all. It's allopathy that's based on the principle of opposites. Homeopathy is based on the principle of likes: We give a sick person a substance which, if it were given to a healthy person, would cause the disease we want to cure.

The two therapies share a large common area that includes, for example, glandular extracts, vitamins, and hormones. Those substances are used by both forms of medicine, but much more positively by homeopaths, in my opinion, because they can use them in a wide variety of ways, depending on their dilution. If, in homeopathy, you give an extract from the cortex of the suprarenal gland, you can give it in a dilution to the first, second, or third decimal, and its effects will then be very close to those produced by the form of it used in allopathy. But a high dilution, to the seventh or ninth centesimal, for example, has opposite effects. That gives us an extraordinary range of possibilities. It's the same with vitamins. Vitamin C in a 4C dilution has almost the same effect as allopathic vitamin C, but in 9C it has exactly the opposite effect. Again we see the amazingly wide variety of therapeutic action available to us.

How do you decide which dilutions to give each patient?

That's the important point. When we see a patient, the first thing we must do is to determine which remedy or remedies are suitable for him. The goal of a truly homeopathic consultation is to determine the *minimum* numbers of remedies covering the *maximum* number of the patient's symptoms.

The ideal would be to prescribe only one. There's a school of homeopathic doctors who do that. But today, considering the conditions under which our patients live, their environment, and the harm that's inflicted on them from every point of view, I no longer try to find a single remedy. That's true of most homeopaths, because the search for a single remedy is long, tedious, uncertain, and disappointing. And even if you think you've found one, how can you be sure?

So in each patient we look for symptoms that will direct us to the remedies we can best put to use. The higher the number of the patient's symptoms combined by a remedy, the higher the dilution in which it's given. When a patient has all the signs of a remedy, it's given in a high dilution, but if he has only a few signs of it, it's given for those signs, in a low dilution. We make a kind of hierarchy in remedies: those that correspond to the patient's mentality, temperament, and constitution are always given in higher dilution than others. In other words, when a remedy has the value of a basic remedy for a patient, it's given in a high dilution, and when it's limited to symptoms, it's given in a medium or low dilution.

Practicing that difficult but fascinating medicine really gives you the feeling that what you're doing is right, and you can't understand why a doctor should do anything else. It requires contact with the patient, an exchange. . . . It's an investigation, a game of patience, and a confession, all at the same time. It's very human.

During your consultations I was struck by the number of questions you ask.

Yes, and still I never ask enough. Everything is written down, spelled out, but you have to know how to look. My main objection to modern medicine is its depersonalization. Doctors no longer even look at their patients or listen to them, either. As a result, when patients come to see us, they feel lost. A patient will say, "I have three grams of cholesterol," or "I have spondylitis ankylopoietica." To us that means nothing or very little. But we're very demanding about finding out what the patient feels. It's not enough for us to know that he's suffering; we try to learn what personalizes his pain:

Is it soothed by cold or by heat, in what period of the day or night does it increase? There are patients who, when they're in pain, turn inward and isolate themselves, others are agitated and anxious, others take it out on the people around them, and so on. All those different kinds of behavior are important to us.

You ask questions about dreams and childhood. . . .

Yes. Dreams are a mysterious but important aspect of the personality. Although they haven't yet been thoroughly studied, the information we draw from them is sometimes precise enough to indicate a remedy. As for childhood, it lets us reconstruct the first links of the chain that leads to the present and explains it, because, under various masks, the disease is the same through time, and above all the patient is the same. All that is as important to us as an X ray, a quantity determination of urea, or an electrocardiogram.

We try to discover the patient's personality. When a patient comes to a homeopathic doctor's office, the doctor observes him all through the consultation, without seeming to. He notes not only his height and build, but also the color of his eyes and hair (the hair is very important), his teeth, his nails, his hands, the way he sits. The way a patient sits is revealing. It often tells me which remedy to give him. If a woman always sits with her legs crossed, you can sometimes conclude that something is wrong in the area of her uterus, that she has to use a muscular support because she has a connective tissue in bad condition. The movement of the body corresponds to the attitude of the mind.

Attentive observation of the patient lets you form a pattern for your questioning. That's why, in some cases, the doctor may tell the patient what his problem is even before the patient has said anything.

The doctor's questioning will establish the patient's case history. I put great stress on case histories because nowadays people's bodies are fouled by all sorts of things, especially their food, that have to be taken into account when you treat them. You never question enough. But you often run into an obstacle when you question a patient: He feels a little bewildered and doesn't give you good answers. You have to proceed slowly and ask the same question several times in different ways, then come back to it later.

Vaccination is part of medicine based on the principle of likes, but in your book, Towards a New Medicine,* *you attack it. . . .*

I don't attack it automatically. Giving the germ of an infectious disease to an organism that you want to protect from that disease is actually a caricature of medicine based on the principle of likes. Vaccination rests on the idea of the specificity of germs, and that's my main point of disagreement. Germs change into each other; they're not specific. Furthermore, if you try to protect yourself by attacking germs, you'll never be finished, because new ones are always being born. Microbes, toxins, and viruses have been successively combated, and the sickness has always reappeared in another form.

Actually, the only way to immunize the body against whatever may threaten it is not to concern ourselves with germs, but to strengthen the body itself. It then acquires a general immunity to everything. That's what homeopathic treatment does.

It's obvious that if prenatal homeopathic treatment were given to pregnant women from the beginning, and if children were given periodic homeopathic examinations, the problem of preventing infectious diseases would be practically solved. The results of prenatal homeopathic treatment are truly extraordinary. In such cases the child's body is healthy from the start, so its own defenses prevent it from becoming diseased.

I sincerely believe that there are cases in which vaccination is defensible. But they're rare. It's a serious mistake to impose systematic vaccination on a whole population without concern for the individual bodies on which it's being practiced. Allopaths tend to think that people are all made on the same pattern, and that what's valid for one is valid for another. We're all similar but each of us is different. I admit that vaccination may not have harmful consequences for certain people, but there are others for whom it may have very serious consequences. Allopaths don't know in

advance whether or not vaccination will be harmful to a given individual. That's why systematic vaccination is reprehensible.

Even from the standpoint of official immunology, the state of a child's immunological defenses isn't known at the time when he's vaccinated. A vague urine examination before vaccination won't tell you what the state of his health is or how strong his defenses are. So he's vaccinated haphazardly, and afterward there's no attempt to find out the extent to which vaccination has changed his potential for immunological defense.

Vaccination would be more acceptable if each patient were told, "There's a vaccination for such-and-such a disease, but before giving it to you we're going to give you a complete clinical and immunological examination." It would then be known whether or not the patient could take vaccination without harmful effects. But as long as that isn't done, vaccination isn't defensible, even on an official level.

There are no invariable reactions in medicine.

To return to your method of practicing medicine, couldn't it be objected that in our time, when population is growing at an alarming rate, your method of treatment is almost impossible? It would require doctors to spend a great deal of time with each patient, and that would mean an increase in the number of doctors that's hard to imagine.

You're posing the problem in terms that aren't medical. Society should see to it that high-quality medicine *is* possible. It's better to take time to practice valid medicine than to give each patient only five minutes. It will be to society's advantage, even for the future, since its members will be sick much less often.

Today, most doctors practice a superficial form of medicine. I don't want to speak too badly of doctors, even allopaths, because they don't deserve it. They're harassed by the government and their patients, who are becoming more and more demanding. They do the best they can, but I think they're led to practice a kind of medicine that's increasingly superficial. The effort to achieve inexpensive medicine has produced demagogic medicine. The result is that people are always sick. If homeopathic medicine were generally adopted, I believe people would lose the habit of going to a

---

*Published in France by Editions Denoël, under the title *Pour Une Médecine Différente.*

doctor at the drop of a hat, because they wouldn't be sick so often.

In my practice, I see the patient once a month at first, then every other month, then every three months. With homeopathic treatment adapted to the individual, long periods of health can often be maintained. Consultations are longer, of course, but there aren't as many of them.

Above all, patients must change their frame of mind and realize that they have to transform themselves. They mustn't expect a doctor, either a homeopath or an allopath, to give them some miraculous medicine which will instantly cure ailments that are usually caused by mistakes made since birth. I believe that a reform of public health requires first of all that the public become aware of these problems. Everyone has within himself a portion of health and a portion of sickness. If he's wise, he develops his portion of health.

The doctor is there only to help. Each individual is responsible for himself. Nowadays, people impair their health with bad food and a harmful way of life; they're not entirely responsible for it, of course, but they've become thoroughly used to it.

We must realize the need for a healthy diet and a balanced life. When we do, we'll already be much less sick.

Reform of public health involves the development of a totally different health policy, and therefore a reform of all current ideas and the emergence of a new state of awareness. I'd like to tell everyone, "Your health depends essentially on you." The health of television viewers will never be improved by showing them heart transplants. Everyone's health depends on himself. There are nonpolluting therapies that should be used as much as possible.

As long as that hasn't been done, it's unlikely that homeopathic treatment will become general. I don't mean to imply that people who have their sicknesses treated by homeopathy are an élite, that's too strong a word; let's say they represent a selection.

There are efforts that should be made: by the public authorities to redefine health policy; by labor unions to demand something other than mass-production, impersonal, ineffective medicine; by doctors to avoid the temptations of technological medicine which, in spite of appearances, is superficial; and by the public,

who must become aware of their own responsibility and not expect their mistakes to be wiped away by the discovery of a miracle drug.

WHY NOT TRY IT!

Homeopathic medicines are inexpensive, and if you use them you will have to consult a doctor less often. If you have a fragile respiratory tract, for example, you may need only one thorough examination and a prescription whose effectiveness you will experience for yourself.

There are even many cases of benign ailments that are cured by correctly administered homeopathic treatment in the home or by means of telephone consultations, which are quite common with homeopathic doctors.

But certain things must be borne in mind. With our hectic life, we always want to be cured as quickly as possible. Thus antibiotics are regarded as a wonderful advance because of the speed with which they act. All sorts of excesses have resulted from their development, however. We all know people who have become almost addicted to antibiotics and quickly go from one relapse to another during certain periods of the year. Allopathic medicine often cuts off an ailment without uprooting it. It does not treat the individual in his entirety and does not strengthen or rebalance his body; often, in fact, it overloads it.

Homeopathic medicine tries to restore the value of time. If you have influenza, for example, it is better to stay home several days and become completely well, and give yourself better resistance to winter by means of supportive treatment.

The first time one of us used homeopathic treatment for a serious influenzal cold, he noted a strange phenomenon: Each time he took a remedy, whether it was pellets or a nasal spray, the disease seemed to become worse. His nose became runnier and his cough increased. Used to the effect of immediate relief given by allopathic remedies, he had a period of doubt. But as he continued the experiment he quickly became aware of an improvement in his general condition, and he soon felt as if he were being literally emptied of his sickness. Being subject to this kind of infection, he was surprised to learn in the months that followed that he could stay in good health simply by using homeopathic remedies for a day or two whenever he had warning symptoms, such as frequent shivering, a tingling sensation in his nose, and pains in his back.

The example given here does not apply to everyone. Each individual reacts differently to treatment, depending on his personal history. It has often been shown that homeopathic remedies can also act with amazing speed, particularly at the beginning of influenza: Oscillococcinum 200 followed six hours later by ingestion of its minerals, Ferrum phosphoricum 9C and Eupatorium 9C ("9C" indicates the degree of dilution, which in this case is very high).

When you take those little white pellets that all look alike—three at a time every two or three hours when they are prepared with a low dilution (3C, 4C, 5C), or ten at a time at much longer intervals when they are prepared with a high dilution (7C or 9C)—you should place them under your tongue and let them melt, slowly impregnating your whole palate with their taste. Why? It would seem that the energy charge of the remedy plays the part of a coded message and reaches the brain, in the region of the basal ganglions, by way of the mucous membranes and the cranial nerves. It would also seem that when this message has been decoded it is interpreted by the brain as a demand for regulation of biological balances.

The better the doctor succeeds in applying exactly the right formula to the patient's particular case, the faster and more effectively the mechanism functions. This reflects a classical medical theory which says that disease is an expression of the body's reaction to an alarm stimulus and that it can be prevented or cured by a similar stimulus.

The principle of transmitted information is related to the basis of cellular life, which is governed by information received from the sense organs. The whole life of the individual is conditioned by these exchanges and reactions which, as modern science tells us, hinge on the DNA molecule.*

So let the pellets melt slowly, to enable energy to be discharged better.

---

*See the chapter on "Man/Life/The Cosmos."

Here are a few examples of common remedies:

Colds are treated with Coryzalia and sprays of Pulviplasmine. A beginning cold can be stopped with Camphora 4C and Nux Vomica 4C, three pellets of each every two hours.

The threat of otitis, laryngitis, and bronchitis can be quickly warded off with Oscillococcinum 200 and Ferrum 9C taken at intervals of two or three hours. Bryonia 4C and Sambucus 4C (three pellets every two hours) continue the treatment. Coccus Cacti 4C treats fits of congested coughing. The product L52 is useful in feverish conditions of the respiratory tract. But be careful. It is good to have doctor's advice because a sore throat, for example, requires different treatments depending on its form: redness, or redness with white spots, and so on.

It is surprising to note the great variety of remedies that apply to all sorts of ailments: black eyes, seasickness, sunstroke, nosebleed, boils, burns, infarct, indigestion, neuralgia. . . . Each remedy is based on specific symptoms. You can quickly acquire enough understanding of this system to use it yourself when necessary. If you feel nervous, take a dose of Ignati 9C. For fatigue, several doses of Arnica 7C, a product which, in a 9C dilution, is good for shock caused by physical injury. If a wound becomes infected, take one or two doses of Pyrogenium 9C. Calendula, a salve, gives quick relief when applied to wounds, contusions, and burns. The list could go on indefinitely.

Homeopathy is perfectly compatible with eating a healthy diet, drinking the right herb teas, and all natural healing methods. This should be understood before using homeopathy, so that the mind will help the work of the body. Understanding sickness and its real causes, seeing the body as a synthesis, and trusting its ability to rebalance itself—that is the basis of all homeopathic action.

NOURISHING YOURSELF, HEALING YOURSELF

If we eat naturally, in harmony with the environment, we not only eliminate the threat of most common diseases, but we are also unconsciously prepared to have the right reaction in case of trouble. If you learn to eat well and be healthy, you will have gone a long distance on the path to self-knowledge. If you have already done so, you have noticed how closely your states of consciousness are related to the kind of food you eat and the way you take care of your body.

As we have seen in the course of these chapters, it is impossible to separate plants that nourish from plants that heal. The products of the earth are a whole which influences another whole: the human body.

Health is not simply absence of disease. It is a state that can be defined as a person's normal condition. A person in good health is recognized by a certain strength, beauty, and purity that emanate from him. He is strong because he is perfectly relaxed; he has found the balance of his body and does not waste his energy in useless acts and words. He is beautiful because his face, body, clothes, and movements reflect the harmony of his life. He is pure because in his everyday living, concentrated here and now, he unconsciously receives vibrations from his environment, transmutes them into energy, and redistributes them according to circumstances and people.

being in the world

SEX

Masculine-Feminine

"Since my imagination took strength from contact with my sensuality, and my sensuality spread into all the realms of my imagination, my desire was boundless."*

Three poles: the imaginary, the perceived, and desire. The motive forces of all action, indissolubly connected in life, dreaming, feeling, desiring, feeling, dreaming. . . .

We have stopped listening to our body; we have veiled our nature and replaced it with morality and its barriers. If rules are necessary for leading our lives, each of us must find them for himself. We are all different and our underlying similarity only accentuates our differences. A man is a man in relation to women and other men, and a woman is a woman in the same way. In the network of contradictory yet complementary relations that bind us to others, play is an essential factor. This word applies both to the freedom of children at play and to a musician's concentration on his instrument. There is play in life and in love—but is not living an act of love?

A person uses his own self for playing. He plays with his energies and those of others, in order to play with his body and those of others. He plays at creating something indivisible but real: harmony in himself and around him. Money, love, honors, friendships, sadness, various successes and failures—everything passes, everything becomes tiresome, everything is a game.

There remains that time which is always present and past, but can be fully experienced and understood: the moment. Each moment can bring information about oneself and the countless facets of the cosmos. Each bit of information is a broadening of experience and therefore of oneself.

———

*Marcel Proust: *Swann's Way*.

We are never finished being created. This creation goes on ceaselessly. There are no final results. Until his last breath, each of us can learn, develop, fulfill his nature. Live. Love from birth to death.

Many people in our society complain, often without knowing it, of their *lack of being*. "Awake, they sleep; and asleep, they are dead," as Heraclitus said. Everyone has a long distance to travel within himself, without expecting too much of others, without dreaming. Love is a game, the supreme dance, a mutual awakening. If each wants it so, the dance is beautiful; otherwise it sinks into boredom. And "freedom" does not yet exist: It is a treasure hidden within oneself.

Sexual Liberation*

Sexual liberation? We're working on it. We're not happy. Maybe it's because we have bad orgasms or none at all. And how is it that something so natural has become so complicated? Sooner or later, we all question ourselves. Am I normal, am I abnormal, what's normal? It feels good to me, is it right? It feels bad to me, is it wrong? It feels good to him or her, but not to me. It feels good to me, but not to him or her. What does he want, what does she want, what do we want?

I need you, I want you, I desire you, so much that I don't know what I'm saying!

You don't know what you're saying, but it doesn't matter. I need you too, I want you, I desire you. What happens to us feels good, it feels good where it happens. It makes the blood circulate better, doesn't it? It warms you. So let's get together and enjoy it.

Ah, but it's not so easy! His erection arrives and he puts it to use (a little, a lot, passably). Let's say his orgasm is easy. It should be, at least, in "normal" cases. He may be a little thickheaded, she thinks, but anyway he's lucky it's automatic for him, or almost.

For him, it would be better to go fast, to reach his goal without lingering on the way. For her, there's a before and an after that matter as much as the during. She lives with a kind of repressed discourse. It's not so simple, it's not simple at all, in fact. What was I looking for, what were you looking for?

HOW IT WORKS

Sex information, sex education. My child will find out about it at school or from the parents of other children. Then, when he's grown up, he'll have a better sex life than mine and the world will be happier.

The new system is already past the break-in stage. People go to the movies to see genitals at work in closeups. There are sex shops for sexcentrics, sex publications, sex advertising. Sex is now displayed in store windows and described with real words. It's not dirty, it's the anatomy, the physiology of the thing. Its real face.

A crusade. The crusaders go off with their banners flying in the wind. They sing. I'm old enough, I want to see for myself, from one end to the other. I'll get my share of orgasms or know the reason why.

But oddly enough, now that women have the pill, now that their parents don't care if they start sleeping with men at fifteen, now that everyone knows how to go about it, how to begin so it will end well, sitting, standing, kneeling, lying, missionary position or not, Swedish style or yoga style, how can it be that they're not happy? Not often, anyway.

Sexually speaking, as soon as two people form a couple they do a rather bad job of it in relation to the model image.

It might be said that even if she's well made for enjoying life, she always keeps one eye on the ceiling while he obligingly labors to give her an orgasm simultaneous with his. As if she didn't know there's no such thing. Foreplay, my mouth, your mouth, my hand, your hand, my legs, your legs, my breasts, your

---

*Written in collaboration with a psychoanalyst.

breasts—ah, how good it is with you! For the moment, while I'm wondering how it would be with someone else.

Are you going to have that orgasm or not? Clitoral, vaginal, abdominal, or general. If you start when I finish, or if you finish when I start. Together, not together, what matters is having your little spasm. And with another person it's more fun, warmer than with the do-it-yourself method. In any case, it's something that means a lot to people. Because that little death gives you a rest from living. But the fact is that in a little death, as in the big one, you're alone.

Everything we've prepared together fizzles out at the last moment. Your orgasm and mine send us millions of miles away from each other, from everything. Because ultimately sexual pleasure is solitary. All pleasure is solitary. Who says that pleasure can be shared? I don't see how, because who feels my pleasure, who feels my pain? At least it can be perceived, and so my pleasure is enriched by the pleasure I see you take with me. I like to give you pleasure, you like to give me pleasure. We please each other. I like to be with you, you like to be with me, what pleasure! The finest orgasm in the world can give only what it is: a good discharge, a good recharge that unites us, each for himself, from head to foot. At that moment I don't even think of who brought me to the fireworks. Incredible! And yet maybe we'll want to go there again together.

SO GOES THE QUEST

Where does it come from? Can it be, as far as sex is concerned, that the human race has to continue, and that if it weren't for sexual pleasure, even when it's not very intense, there wouldn't be any more children? That's something that people have been saying for a long time.

The trouble is that where there's reproduction there's not necessarily orgasm, and vice versa. Freud began noticing that three quarters of a century ago. And, more important, he dared to say it. He didn't have an easy time of it: People thought they were normal in 1900. There's surely such a thing as a normal sex life; what is it? It must exist, since so much effort goes into explaining how to achieve it. But anyone who takes a close look at what actually happens will see that people's sexual behavior is highly varied, and sometimes very strange, and that in any case it's quite distinctive for each individual. Or would be, at least, if he could do what he wanted. Or if he could succeed in knowing what he wanted. Or if he could even succeed in really wanting to do it!

On the whole, good sexual appetite, release, and understanding don't "normally" happen spontaneously.

It seems, instead, that there's a "normal-but" sexuality. If so, in what direction does normality lie? In the direction of making children? That would mean raising *the* sexual question: After all, does the human race really have to reproduce itself? Is it a duty? If so, a duty to what? To Mankind?

Since Mankind with a capital *M* doesn't exist, no one has a duty to it. There are men and women trying to find themselves and each other. Must there be people on earth? It's a useless question, as long as new people keep being made all the time. From that viewpoint, "genital" sex is doing very well for itself, even if it's not our colors that triumph, even if the new people produced die prematurely in droves.

Sex acts like a lunatic, ignoring its frenzied waste. Male sex, that is. In a wild race for survival, one spermatozoon pulls ahead of the pack, leaving an astronomical number of losers behind, and goes looking for an ovum to fertilize. The splendor of motherhood. Her fertile womb will be her glory. Unless she's on the pill. Leave my sperm alone, he says, don't cut off my inspiration.

Sex—what a bag of knots it is! It has its good sides, of course, but you must know how to handle it.

ADULT SEX, SEX FOR TWO?

And those who are alone have no sex lives? Being alone doesn't mean one has no sex life. Nor is masturbation the whole sex life of an isolated person. The vital force of the sex drive doesn't waste its time. It must work, otherwise we die. It reappears somewhere else. Anyway, it's everywhere. For the worst, sometimes: One suffers foolishly and makes others suffer. For the better, too: It's the impetus behind all creation. Will you make children or sonatas? You can even do both, following Bach's example.

I like being with him, with her. It's precious, it's rare. But I spend my life looking for my way: a desire for whom or for what? I can't find my way or myself. Desire wandering in a maze. Tangled thread, broken thread, lost thread, cut thread.

ARE WE BORN DESIRING?

Now we're led to the navel, the belly button. It's supposed to be healed. After being made by two sexes, we come out of our mother's. That's our first sexual relation, the one we begin with. It leaves us with a certain "homesickness." Nothing will ever be like it again. It's not this nostalgia that awakens us to desire. It brings us back to fetal positions, turns us in on ourselves. Desire comes from something else.

We're born "in need," breathing, sleeping, eating. We're predisposed to desire by the desire of all our "antecedents," the closest generations in particular, our grandparents and especially our parents. We're "foretold"; long before we speak, we've been spoken of. Our family name precedes us, our first name is said before we've seen daylight.

We've been desired as a girl or a boy. We're like a book already full of words, ready for the rest of our story, unable to avoid it.

The newborn baby knows nothing about it. We don't know much more. The beginning of human life: our baby, sucking his mother or his bottle. Fists clenched, or an open hand on his mother's breast, or clutching her thumb. Toes spread out. His whole body taut. But what's happening? Panic. From the bottom, he feels an urgent need to free his little belly, but at the top he can't let go. It all hangs together, that bottom, that top, each as demanding as the other. The pleasure-giving digestive tract. His whole body is concentrated on what he's doing. Finally his mouth lets go of the breast a little and elimination takes place. The strongest push has won out. He cries, putting his whole being into it. He'll never do better.

Not one particle of his body that isn't ready to receive pleasure or displeasure.

The whole body is "sexual," animated by the force that keeps it alive. Every part of it makes its contribution. When it's nearly time for a feeding, the baby, rocked in his mother's arms and hearing her singing to him, stops his vehement demands. He's satisfied elsewhere, distracted, as they say. Gradually coming out of his initial confusion, he becomes aware of differences like presence and absence, and the world of sensations pressing in on him begins to take on a certain organization. Then comes a smile! My baby isn't a little animal! But is he already alive to desire?

Some children and adults called mentally ill seem to be "sick from desire." That has made their therapists try to go as far as possible into the "depth psychology" known as psychoanalysis. What it discovers about the origin of desire is invariably based on a kind of rupture, an intolerable laceration that occurred in the young child's beginning organization. Something caused that rupture, that laceration. It remains totally, irremediably lost to memory, but the effects of its occurrence are there; it's a hole, an abyss, an opening into a void, producing a kind of suction. It gives desire its breath. That lost "something" functions as the cause of desire.

The adventure of the lost "something" is different, unique, for each of us, and it induces a certain singularity into our body, that is, our "being in the world." Our life of desire, caused by a loss, will take place against the background of a "lost cause." We'll always have something to desire. A common expression: "It leaves something to be desired." That "leaves-something-to-be-desired" is the very movement of desire. Gradually attaining desire will mean facing that lack, not turning away from it. The search for a complement, for completeness, for fullness, turns us away from the lack and fills in the hollow: We aspire toward the peaks, with our head in the clouds. We speak of "elsewhere," but that elsewhere is in us.

The young child who has become alive to desire goes on seeking satisfaction of his needs above all else. But that will no longer be enough. Something more remains to be asked for.

There was once a little girl a year and a half old. She was often given something to drink, as is often the case with little children. But she had vague yearnings. In her mother's belly was a baby. It was called "the baby" and people talked to her about it. *The* place was taken. She no longer felt that she belonged anywhere. From then on, whenever anything went wrong—a lost ball, a stubborn doll, the approach of darkness—she always asked for the same thing: "a drink of water."

There is always "a drink of water" lacking.

WE ARE ILL-BRED

At first the young child's sex life, or love life, is turned only toward himself. It's an apprenticeship. Knowing his body, so he can later imagine other bodies as sensitive. Knowing his pleasure, so he can later give others pleasure.

That feels good here and here, but not here. Do some parts of our body "love," and not others? In early childhood, as everyone knows, we go through different phases. The oral phase, the anal phase; those areas—doors of the body, points of access and expulsion, openings to the world—are then privileged: Our pleasure in them, at those times, is great. Later, something of it remains. In adulthood, oral or anal erotic pleasure isn't called a "perversion" unless it's exclusive. There may well be a little perversion or aberration in every so-called normal sex life. Nothing could be more common. No use getting upset over it.

After all, isn't the "normal" sex life for me the one that suits me? Is that scandalous? Where are the limits? This and not that, here and not there. Because that and there are nasty, and this and here aren't? If I'm alone, it's my business. If I have a partner, then we can say that my best sex life is the one that suits us both.

Conventional souls will be glad to know that it's not so simple, not so easy. It involves training and self-discipline, if you don't mind those words. There's no model sex life. There are no model couples. There are no recipes. No ideal success. If you can manage to make yourself and your partner a little happier, it's worth doing.

And if a genital and generative sex life pleases me and my partner, we make children. Is it because we like it that way, and hope they'll like being born, and being born of us rather than someone else? That's not certain. It's an attempt, a trial.

Needing a child doesn't necessarily involve a kind of surplus value of a couple. It depends on their personal relations with life and death. To give life is, at the same time, to condemn to death. Is it a way of living on after death? Maybe it's not the only way to do it, assuming it's necessary.

Is there any need to point out that this ideal—making three from two in one, making a family from the parental couple—doesn't exist? Because two don't make one. Two coupled sexes never make one. He and she, whether one is in the other or not, remain distinct. The male sex and the female sex are capable of joining, but not of "uniting." Their difference unites them and separates them. Sex is *the* difference. And the child that comes from the couple is another person, radically other. Different.

LIVING ONE'S SEX

Living one's difference. Our internal chemistry destines us more or less to be a man or a woman. Our anatomy, in general, and thank God, is more precise. Strangely enough, though, our psyche isn't always satisfied with our chemistry or anatomy. We do our best because it's convenient, useful, and proper to conform to our apparent sex. He makes himself virile and she makes herself feminine because that's what they're expected (by whom?) to do.

Homosexuality asks indiscreet questions of femininity, virility, and the sexual ideal of a union between a male sex and a female sex. When a man desires a man, one of them is thought to be "feminine." When a woman desires a woman, one of them is thought to be "masculine." Not necessarily.

Feminine, masculine—we're all feminine-masculine, or masculine-feminine, in various proportions. Why deny it? That mixture, to one degree or another, is what makes our charm. We have other things to do than imitating the picture in the catalogue. I do whatever makes me feel at ease with myself and others, the way I want to be.

And, after all, what's the sex of that sexual fulfillment we hear so much about?

Childhood—which adults like to think of as so happy, those same adults who want it to be "pure"—is convulsed by violent sexual conflicts, all the more violent because the child's impulses haven't yet been assaulted from all sides. We have no memory of them, as sometimes happens after an overwhelming shock.

The victims of those struggles are penned up in the unconscious, behind strong barriers. All sorts of compromises have had to be made. We have to bargain for love. The result is successful and happy in widely varying degrees. We have everything and nothing to do with it. That's how it is, how can we change it? We all remain more or less attached, fixed, fixated, at some point, some crux, of our childhood. It's more visible in some of us than in others, that's all. On the whole, the practice of forming man-woman couples seems to have stood the test of experience, that is, it seems to be more or less satisfactory for both men and women. In any case, it seems to reassure everyone. We must still leave each person the freedom to be different.

In general, the barriers of our upbringing and the weight of schooling and social life dry us up rather effectively. We eventually begin living on only a trickle of water. We have to go back as close to the spring as we can. To achieve our desire is to achieve our destiny. Learning to know ourselves in order to achieve our desire is living.

Sex Life and Cosmic Life

LOVE AND THE WEST

Inner experience passes by way of communication with the elements. Modern, urban, civilized man often forgets that. He has repressed the "paradisiac" potentialities contained in his body like seeds in fertile soil. He has paved over the living earth and built cities. He has set up a system of defense and protection against his unconscious and constructed his thought on it.

Culture, as we have known more clearly since Freud, functions as a dam, building up a formidable pressure of energy partially converted into forms acceptable to society. Around us, morality no longer has the support of faith and eroticism no longer has the alibi of the sacred. Times are changing. More and more people are becoming aware of what does not change. The family is falling apart. Young people are forming communities among themselves and openly proclaiming the right to sexual pleasure. There are many indications that we are now witnessing the beginning of a combination of circumstances which will lead a growing number of individuals to a practical consideration of sex in its deepest, vastest, and most secret dimension.

Sexual ecstasy, like divine ecstasy, makes Westerners either stammer or lapse into lyricism or aestheticism; they do not have the tools (concepts) to convey their experience, which is that of the body and of the void. Ecstasy is not a goal, of course, since there can be no goal in the practice of the Way. Moreover, the word "ecstasy," which we use for lack of anything better, comes from the Greek *ekstasis* ("standing outside"). Its original meaning concerns a specific phenomenon known to all shamans: My body remains here, inert, and I travel. The Greeks, thinking themselves clever, said with Plato that the soul leaves the body. Christianity, with Paul, had only to give a privileged status to one of the two factors, the soul, in order to try to expel the body with the aid of the notion of sin. We are now living amid the fossils and debris of that little miscalculation.

Antimorality, the sexual revolution programmed by the media, and group sex, as practiced by young executives, are something like a disturbance in a classroom by high school students who have forgotten even the idea of playing hooky. Let us be more specific: Anyone who goes on thinking while making love, and

especially thinking about something other than making love, is as far removed as possible from the root of experience. Lovemaking is the prime occasion for concentration. Concentration means being present here and now, totally involved in what one is doing, becoming, being what one is doing.

Perhaps it will be useful to dwell a little on the basic technique of concentration (other authors would say "on the magic recipe for sexual ecstasy"). Mental activity can be controlled by breathing. The essence of correct breathing is slow, deep, powerful exhalation directed toward the area of the lower abdomen, with inhalation coming naturally. When you are conscious of something during sexual relations, you may as well be conscious of your breathing and your partner's and synchronize them, that is, exhale together. If you exhale properly you will be able to make love for several hours. If you can already do that, bravo! But that is not the goal. There is no goal; the idea is to remain spontaneous.

Communication between two (or more) people in the dimension opened up by erotic pleasure—in which the relation changes from sexed to sexual—is an experience so basic to human consciousness that mankind has always obscurely, spontaneously regarded union as first and separation as second. Let us try to elucidate the aspects of this formulation that may seem enigmatic. On the genetic level, the embryo has masculine and femine potentialities. On the symbolic and metaphysical level, what tends to be come rejoined was originally united. In amorous rapture, the mortal couple revives the ancient figure of the androgyne: less a half-male, half-female creature than a radiant being possessing the attributes of both sexes and radiating the power of their harmonious pairing.

From the Age of Chivalry, the Western tradition of courtly love (the West here includes the whole Indo-European world) sends a message radiant with the same secret light. School children who like stories of chivalry have no one to give them the keys to such stories. In his relationship with his lady, the knight is not only like a vassal before his suzerain: He is a saint before his God, filled with wonder by the inexpressible.

The theme of the soulmate, celebrated by the Romantics has its origin in the most ancient intuitions of the loving person. Its most recent embodiment is the *amour-fou* of the French surrealists, placed under the sign of the Star, the seventeenth arcanum of the tarot. We must recognize that in becoming intellectualized through the centuries, the feeling of the complementarity and cosmic play of the sexes has been surrounded with barriers.

In prehistoric but still living cultures (their days are numbered), such as certain Indian cultures in Mexico and the Amazonian jungle, communion with natural forces is explicitly felt as a sexual relation with the Great Mother. It is a highly sacred relation. The object is to retrace the path of birth in the opposite direction; the initiatory experience, accompanied by the taking of natural psychedelic substances like peyote and yajé, is surrounded with a whole set of ritual rules and precautions designed to maintain the subject's psychosomatic balance and the organic unity of the community. The sex we are speaking of is thus not only that surplus or lack that we carry between our legs. It is the enigma of separation and the wonder of reunion. It is also the offspring, the link between the individual and the species. It is what the Taoists call *yin-yang che Tao*, the game of yin and yang.

THE PATH OF PLEASURE, THE WAY OF KNOWLEDGE

In truth, each body is the universe.
Nirvana Tantra

Modern men and women have not only lost the means of formulating an experience, they have also forgotten the ancient knowledge that makes possible the experience itself in its entirety. The reason is that in a type of civilization based on production and rationality, erotic experience, if it is at all authentic, radically departs from the norm and is placed by the uninitiated in the category of pure expenditure: play, revelry, excitement, and waste of energy—abandon and oblivion.

In our time, there are frequent expressions of the idea that the body is a machine, though we realize, of course, that that is only a comparison. The ancients, however, often saw the body as a tree. At the foot of the tree is a coiled serpent. This is the tree of knowledge, and it is

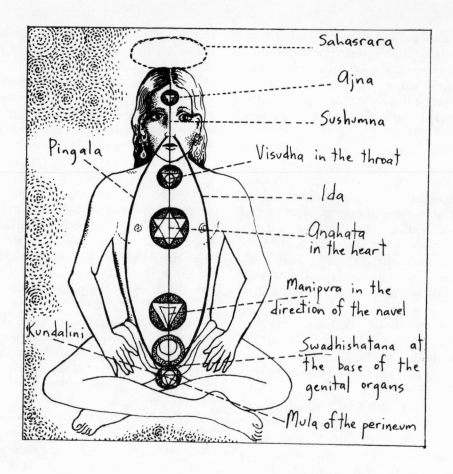

Sahasrara

Ajna

Sushumna

Visudha in the throat

Ida

Anahata in the heart

Manipura in the direction of the navel

Swadhishatana at the base of the genital organs

Mula of the perineum

Pingala

Kundalini

therefore also the tree of good and evil. We are here giving only one vision of the tree, for there are several, the tree being man's friend and indispensable complement. Here the sap that rises in the trunk represents sexual energy which, according to traditions,* rises along the spine to the brain, manifesting itself in a specific way at each stage of its ascent.

The serpent, guardian of the tree, is also a figure of energy. Like energy, it is an emanation of the earth and, when it awakens, its power is formidable. And just as the rise of sap corresponds to the descent of sunlight, so, according to tradition, energy is charged with influences from the heavens when it descends along the axis of the body.

In other words, sexual energy is also psychic energy.

---

*See *The Indian Ecstasy,* by P. Rawson, and *The Chinese Philosophy of Time and Change,* by P. Rawson and L. Legaza, both published by Thames and Hudson Ltd., London.

THE CHAKRAS

According to Indian tradition, there are seven focal points on the path followed by energy. We will not go into the highly complex details of the functioning of the "subtle body," as it is called by the authors of ancient treatises. It is enough to know here that our body, that tree of life, functions according to seven degrees. Those doors through which energy passes appear in the background of many legendary stories that seem absurd or confusing. It is good to know how to recognize those radiation points of cosmic energy (for that is what is involved), so that they can be controlled if necessary.

Muladhara: vital instinct, animal power.

Swadhishatana: sexual energy.

Manipura, or "stronghold of the jewel," or "red region of the flame"; corresponds to the Zen *hara.**

---

*See the chapter on "Zazen."

Anahata: the heart, emotion; perhaps the only chakra still well known in the West.

Visudha: the chakra of sound, received and emitted.

Ajna: between the eyebrows is an "infinite space, resplendent with the splendor of the infinite suns"; this is the region of the intuitive flash, the light of wisdom.

Sahasrara: the place where the vital breath penetrates, and where cosmic forces on the psychic level are fully deployed.

> *Unless man is like*
> *him who is dead,*
> *in his limbs and in his breath,*
> *he cannot love.*
> *That is why I cover my body with these ashes,*
> *ashes that remain from that consumed world.*
> *I have consumed it with my third eye.*
> *And when man discovers his sakti,*
> *His feminine counterpart,*
> *he returns to his origin, where he finds only his self.*

Words of Shiva, in the *Tantra Shastra*

The lower chakras are all interdependent and lead to knowledge of natural elementary forces. These centers of latent energy can be awakened by certain yogic practices, particularly breath control, and by sexual exercise. When they are stimulated they release energies which, if controlled and channeled, make it possible to attain levels of broadened consciousness.

The yogi and yogini awaken the power of the *kundalini* ("the serpent of energy"): By disciplining and directing the vital breath, they enable energy to expand and rise from chakra to chakra along the path that starts at the muladhara and ends at the sahasrara.

Tantrism is the form taken in India by this current of knowledge and access to illumination by the way of sexual union. Unlike other traditions, it has remained vigorously alive down to our time. The way of the tantras is explicitly conceived as a method of liberation adapted to makind's darkest age (the age of the "obscuration of light"), in which man's forces of disinterested psychic radiation have been repressed and imprisoned by his own material achievements.

For an adept of the tantras, any means of attaining liberation is permissible. He rejects nothing that makes life sweet. He is not afraid of evil. He is beyond the pleasure principle, beyond good and evil. With his partner (or partners), he decides to devote himself to an enterprise which is a return to the original promised land. He goes upstream to the source. He goes from the dark age to the golden age. His path through the fields of the psychic and physical worlds leads him from darkness and dispersion to light and concentration. This itinerary corresponds to a progressive transformation of his body, a metamorphosis invisible to the uninitiated. He reaches the state of his conception, and even beyond.

"Woman's sex is the cosmic liquid, and fire when it is united with man's sex, the *vajra,* the diamond. It is the representation of darkness, night, the moon and stars, as well as *sunyata* (*ku,* emptiness). Sexual union is a symbol of the unification of all opposites, the annihilation of all thought formation, the transcendence of space and time by diamondlike bliss, the attainment of unity."*

THE RITE OF SEXUAL UNION

As in courtly love, certain rituals require the man to live with the woman he has chosen, to sleep where she sleeps, without touching her.

---

*Daniel Odier: *Le rêveil de la Kundalini* (*Kundalini Reawakes*) (Planète).

Then, when the new Adam approaches his divine mate to worship her, each gesture is as laden with signs as the movements of a tree agitated by the wind or the curve of a bird's flight in the sky. He possesses the virtue of the Word, and by mantras he makes the cosmos and the woman's body vibrate in unison with his mind. The rite is performed in a predominantly purple half-light, purple representing male energy, while red is the feminine color. The ritual union may take place beside a fire, or even beside a pyre on which corpses are burned.

Sound and colors supply the chakras with energy, by means of breathing. Breath control and emptiness of mind are accompanied by control of ejaculation, which occurs (when it occurs at all) only after long exercises. The couple is radiant with a single light. Two make one, one equals zero, zero becomes infinity, and individual consciousness merges into cosmic consciousness.

NATURE

Flowers

When winter loses its force in February, nature's activity resumes. Seeds buried in the ground revive, the pollen of trees is scattered by the wind. With the coming of warmer days, each week of March brings its surprise: the first birds in the woods, catkins on willows, blossoms in orchards. From the buds of chestnut trees come compact little clusters that stretch, rise above the leaves, and expand into white or pink corollas. At first sight, all the flowers of a cluster look alike, with their wavy corollas from which curved stamens emerge. But many flowers (male ones) have only stamens, while others (female ones) have stamens and pistils. The flowers wither. A few fecundated pistils remain and will be transformed into fruit. The flower is the plant's genitals.

As soon as man has a little patch of land, he sows or plants flowers. He makes bouquets to decorate his house and please his friends. He gives flowers as gifts, he adorns his environment in relation to the particular feeling or atmosphere that he consciously or unconsciously wants to create.

SAY IT WITH FLOWERS

Because of its calyx, the flower is a receptacle of celestial activity, a symbol of love and harmony. Each flower has its own particular symbolism.

The lotus grows on the surface of marshy water without being sullied by it. Its blooming is like the hatching of the egg of the world.

By its radiant, spherical appearance, the chrysanthemum is a solar symbol. Taoism regards it as a plant of immortality. Being especially hardy, it is considered to have properties favorable to longevity. The flower of the dead is also the plant of the immortals.

By its whiteness, the lily symbolizes innocence. "Consider the lilies of the field," said Jesus. The French kings chose the lily as an image of prosperity, glory, and fecundity. It is also the flower of love. "Its scent is absolutely the opposite of a chaste fragrance; it is a mixture of honey and pepper, something pungent and sweetish, pale and strong; it is reminiscent of the aphrodisiac preserves of the Levant and the erotic jam of India."*

The orchid represents spiritual beauty, perfection, and purity. In ancient China, orchids were used in springtime festivals to drive away bad influences and ward off sterility. The orchid is also a symbol of fecundation.

The rose is to the West what the lotus is to

---

*Joris-Karl Huysmans: *La Cathédrale.*

the East. It is a symbol of love, the gift of love. Its shape, fragrance, and fragility have been the themes of countless poems. It is also the image of a mystic rebirth. White, red, pink, or yellow, with innumerable delicate shadings, it was always one of the favorite flowers of alchemists, whose treatises sometimes bore such titles as *The Philosopher's Rosebush.* A rose at the center of a cross, at the location of Christ's heart, is the emblem of the Rosicrucians. In the *Divine Comedy,* the poet's inspiration reveals the cosmic rosette to him: "At the golden center of the eternal rose, which expands and goes from stage to stage, and gives off a fragrance of praise in the always vernal sunlight, Beatrice attracted me. . . ."

Each flower gives off a particular vibration, according to its shape, color, texture, and smell. Everywhere the presence of flowers ennobles and vivifies the atmosphere. Flowers brought to a sick person help him to regain his smile. Flowers place their sovereign imprint wherever they are. There are close links among man, plants, and the universe. Recent studies have shown that flowers are sensitive to the joy, pain, and intentions of living beings around them.*

Today, modern civilization represses the intuition of the harmony of nature, which is obscurely present in the hearts of all human beings, and tends to replace the grace of traditional gestures with the stereotypes of mechanized movements. This leads to picking flowers without caring where and how it is done. Picking a flower is a sacrifice, a sacred act. If we have established an intimate dialogue with it, a communication "from my heart to your heart," the chosen flower will be truly radiant. The Indians humbly ask the flower to offer itself. As we walk in fields, forests, or mountains, herbs, flowers, berries, and mushrooms give us a chance to regain the spirit in which our ancestors gathered plants.

If you cut branches, do it very carefully. The wounds produced by cutting often cause a danger of infection and death to the tree or shrub. Use good pruning shears and make a slanting cut three or four inches above the base of the stem, to allow the plant to give birth to a vigorous new shoot. Unless you intend to replant, avoid pulling up roots.

You can make wonderful bouquets with branches, leaves, moss, berries, or flowers, using them in such a way that each bouquet respects and reconstructs nature. Learn to know, love, and feel intimate with nature in order to find the essence of the art of arranging flowers. Your bouquets will become brighter, simpler, and more eloquent.

THE WAY OF FLOWERS

In Japan, the Way of Flowers is regarded as a true Way of development and coming alive to oneself. Although the help of a teacher in this Way is indispensable, it is still good to know its basic points so that you can give your bouquets another dimension.

Ikebana, "placing living flowers in vases of water to keep them alive," was at first practiced by monks and warriors in Japan. Beginning about a hundred years ago, women have been initiated into that Way. Besides its methods and essentially spiritual attitude, this art involves a particularly profound symbolism, since the flower is a perfect archetype of the development of life. It is a microcosm, a stage in the plant cycle, a synopsis of the whole universe.

What is the origin of Ikebana, which has passed into everyday Japanese life? It comes from *kuge,* a Buddhist custom which consisted in making offerings of flower arrangements in temples and was linked to the tea ceremony practiced by emperors, noblemen, and priests. A monk named Shuko was the first to have the idea of a small, almost unfurnished room where that ceremony could take place in an atmosphere of peace and calm meditation. In that room, a very simple flower arrangement was composed. It later became more complex, even going so far as to resemble a landscape.

A beautiful, mossy stone is placed in a wooden container filled with water, for example. The principle consists in watering the stone often and placing tree seeds in some of its recesses. By a particular natural phenomenon, the trees that grow are dwarfs, sized to fit the stone, and can form amazing miniature landscapes. This art, which came to Japan from

---

*See *The Secret Life of Plants,* by Peter Tompkins and Christopher Bird (New York: Avon Books), 1974.

Taoist China, is a powerful support for meditation.

The principles of Ikebana have not deteriorated. The object is to create beauty by the use of lines, color, and space, to make an interpretation (not a copy) of nature. In Buddhist temples, plants of all species, along with branches, were placed in heavy bronze vases or boxes filled with sand. The central branch was vertical. On each side of it, lower branches were placed in an asymmetric arrangement. A third group of plants "supported" the whole and gave it cohesion. When Buddhism spread over Japan, the temples became centers where monastic life was associated with artistic activity. Painting, calligraphy, and poetry were taught in them. Students learned simplicity and regained naturalness.

By subjecting himself to cosmic laws in this art, man enters directly into the linkage of universal relations and his hand acts of its own accord, spontaneously, naturally, and unconsciously. There are few writings on Ikebana; the students must find and experience by himself the teachings of his master and the spirit of his art.

Arranging flowers is not a diversion. It requires a special mental attitude; anxiety, haste, and impatience cause the forces of life to be wasted. To compose a bouquet, one must first have great receptivity that makes it possible to be in harmony with the forces of the universe. "Man and plants," writes Gusty Herrigel, "are changing and perishable; only the meaning and essence of the flower arrangements are eternal. As you work, you must seek the outer form within yourself. Remain in a calm, pure frame of mind. You can find the solution without thinking." This intuitive approach leads to the essence of things and reveals their heart.

In flower arrangements the spaces left between the plants are as much a part of the composition as the plants themselves. They represent formlessness, silence, emptiness. The disciple must try to treat each plant in such a way that he respects its natural shapes and tendencies. He intuitively finds the right attitude, for his teacher influences him by his presence and example. Seeking harmonies of colors and shapes is pleasant, but the reference line of the composition is the primary consideration in the Way of Flowers. The principle of the threefold structure is always fundamental.

Man is a link between the heavens and the earth.

In the early stages of practicing Ikebana, attention is focused only on placing the three main branches—high, intermediate, low—so that their ends form a triangle. If they are as-

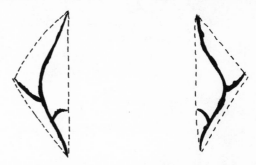

sembled according to the rules, they give the impression of a single branch with twigs extending in various directions.

The earth may be on either the right or the left.

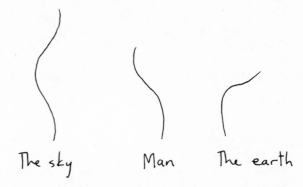

The sky   Man   The earth

The principle of the threefold structure is based on the cornerstone of the edifice, its reference line, and the foundation of experience and inner vision. The three natural forces of man, the earth, and the heavens must be in harmony to form the universe; the branches must be balanced naturally in space. The procedure is therefore not to learn the traditional forms of flower arrangement by heart or to copy them superficially. Progress in this traditional art requires a slow evolution, an inner maturation. One must practice as long as necessary to reach perfection in nonthought right action. Man is made for living in communion with plants as well as the whole universe. The threefold principle enables him to explore, by a subtle game, the interaction of natural cycles. In building his floral edifice, the pupil produces a new arrangement of the heavens-man-earth totality.

It is therefore not enough to acquire a technique. The Way of Flowers goes byond all rational understanding, all utilitarianism. It stems from a spiritual attitude which is acquired through years of practice and concentration and enables the disciple to attain the secret of the act.

Ikebana is an ancient, extremely rigorous discipline that requires the presence of a teacher. Few Westerners can claim to be fully initiated into it. Yet anyone can find the essence of it within himself. Ikebana is life, the upsurge of spontaneity in the perfection of immobility. An immobility that is only apparent and a spontaneity that means abandoning ourselves to an order which surpasses us. If treated in the right frame of mind, a bouquet of wildflowers or an armful of branches gathered in an autumn forest can be perfect. In Greek, "cosmos" means "arrangement." The arrangement of natural elements by man is a reflection of the condition of his body and his mind.

The Garden*

THREE GARDENS

Three gardens, three worlds. Each is the expression of an exchange and an essential work, and each illustrates, in its own way, the relations between man and nature. They concretely display man's maturity, love, and strength in the bosom of the universe. A great deal of sweat, attention, and reflection: a peaceful, boundless joy. The weekend gardener is not so far from perfection: He lacks only awareness of his work.

The Food Garden

Garden of the body, the food garden. Tilling the soil in order to live, to nourish oneself. A long, patient, agrarian alchemy unfolds through the seasons, to the rhythm of the heavenly bodies, winds, and rains. Germination of the seed, growth of the plant. Waiting for the natural offering. A daily concentration in multiple areas: preliminary study of the soil and subsoil, enrichment of the earth with potash and quicklime as well as natural fertilizers, respect for climatic conditions and light. The gardener protects his plants, makes a proper irrigation system, prunes and grafts his fruit trees. Direct contact with nature, an exchange indispensable to life.

Learning to deserve the fruits and vegetables sown by your hand and nurtured through their gestation in the natural womb. This work can give us a better grasp of cosmic energy and order, and help us to see ecological balance as a whole. Each plant is bound to the earth, sunlight, the phases of the moon, the slightest breath of wind. In the midst of his tomatoes or strawberries, the apprentice gardener learns to see himself as an integral part of the universe and to realize that, like a plant, he lives in unison with the world of energy.

The Pleasure Garden

Garden of sensitivity, the pleasure garden. Beauty, harmony, pleasure of the senses. A place vibrant with flowers and lush shrubbery where the gardener's whole personality, and his love and respect for the plant and mineral worlds can blossom and create. From the Loire region of France to the gardens of Kyoto in Japan, man has created those marvelous domains in which he can daydream, stroll, and contemplate the eternal transformation of things and the world. In them he composes a special setting: He plants trees and makes basins in which fountains flow beneath foliage with colors that he has chosen. The food garden gives the satisfaction of eating; the pleasure garden gives joys of the eye and the soul.

But this type of gardening must also take into account the seasons and the surrounding landscape, so that personal creation will not be out of keepiing with the natural environment. The gardener must respect the demands of life and harmonize each detail with the whole. Although it seems to be gratuitous work, only for peasure, it is actually a subtle apprenticeship in a unique contact between the soul and nature. The pleasure garden is a magic mirror that

---

*Written in collaboration with Jean-Michel Varenne.

reflects the wedding of man and the world. And its composition, its choice and arrangement of shapes and colors, reflects the gardener's inner world. This garden is a vibrant, loving communication with nature and other people.

The Rock Garden

Garden of the mind, the rock garden. It does not exist in the West. The Chinese and Japanese have cultivated it in relation to their religions. It is closely, perhaps even indissolubly, linked to Taoism and Zen. Yet the Westerner can learn to *see* these places as pure reflections of the boundless. A closed space, open to the gaze on one side. It presents an apparently frozen arrangement of rocks in a symmetrical radiation on a carpet of gravel or sand that is carefully raked each day.

In this composition the uninitiated see no meaning, no beauty, nothing. Is it the creation of an overly complicated intellect? An embodiment of an abstract, if not absurd geometry? A mental puzzle of a stylized riddle? It is a world of stones and silence, inaccessible to "ordinary" understanding. A representation of emptiness, formlessness depicted in form. A world of inner, underground work. Slowness and difficulty. Its rocks and concentric circles exist. All that can be said about them is that they are *there*. This garden is what we are. Only a concentrated mind can embrace it all at once, see it without aesthetic references or formal criteria. Yet it is no more inaccessible than the sky or the ocean, and each of us can cultivate one like it, his own.

GARDENING

The Vegetable Garden
Cultivating beans or cabbages . . .
it ultimately rests on very simple rules:
loving what one does, loving nature,
respecting the natural order.
Jean Boucher

Gardening is a perfect exercise of concentration. It imparts peace, inner riches, and love of life in all its forms. A real gardener does not exploit his land, he does not seek the largest yield; his goal is different. He cultivates, that is, he maintains the soil and the myriads of microorganisms that live in it. Chemical farming kills, destroys the natural balance with a wild abundance of synthetic fertilizers, some of them intended to make up for lack produced by others. Love of the earth and knowledge of the plant, animal, and microbic cycles that constitute it begin by abandoning forever all the unnatural substances commonly used today. The goal is to maintain a viable exchange with nature, not an absurd, destructive relation of forces.

Nourishing the soil, making it live. This means eliminating the deadly nourishment of chemicals. As opposed to a cultivation of death, gardening is life.

Maintaining and fertilizing the soil. Intense cultivation, like that practiced in a vegetable garden, tires the soil and exhausts its capacity for self-maintenance. You must contribute to the full development of the plants growing in it by adding a supplementary humus: compost. And adding natural fertilizers such as derivatives of ground seaweed, or sowing green fertilizers such as the different varieties of clover, will help fermentation and formation of a stronger, more nourishing humus. The gardener should also loosen the soil to facilitate circulation of air and water, which are necessary to the life of microorganisms.

Keeping the soil fertile. Growing the same plant on the same piece of land for two consecutive years will exhaust the soil; too much is demanded of it. Crop rotation must be practiced.

Aeration of the soil. Hoeing and watering the soil, when done properly and at the right intervals, are always advisable.

Humus and compost. A layer of organic residues of varying thickness is naturally formed on the surface of the ground. In this mixture of rotting leaves, roots, moss, and algae, an intense life circulates: earthworms and countless microorganisms. There are about six thousand pounds of living matter per acre of land. Such is humus; an active, devouring life exists in it, maintaining a cyclical, regenerative process. It is essential to the growth of plants.

We now know that all artificial procedures, all unhealthy chemical operations intended to make up for the inadequacies of a soil that has been compressed and mistreated, make it sick and may even kill it. A gardener who knows the resources and needs of the soil will be able to help it by maintaining its natural functioning. He can enrich it with compost, which is a kind of humus produced by the transformation of various organic wastes. It is a natural medium for the growth of microorganisms.

We will not go into the details of making compost here, but is is important to point out the dangers of manure, particularly stable litter, which is often considered equivalent to compost. Stable litter, a mixture of straw and animal waste products, gives off harmful gases when it ferments: ammonia nitrogen and potash. The arrival of a large number of harmful insects, as well as many plant and soil diseases, can be attributed to its use. Fertilizing a meadow with manure that is too thick or moist will often make animals refuse to graze there. The excessive use of manure should therefore be avoided. Good compost can be recognized by its friability and lack of unpleasant smell. The gardener's intuition is important in evaluating the quality of his compost by touch and sight.

Compost.

1. Composition. Animal wastes, organic residues, sawdust, straw.

2. Technique. The ground should be sloping to facilitate runoff of liquid waste. Water the compost heap regularly to keep it relatively moist. Pack it down without crushing it too much. Do not expose it directly to sunlight; maintaining continuous warmth can be facilitated by covering with bundles of straw. Ripe compost is recognized by its black color, similar to that of the *materia nigra* of alchemy.

Green fertilizers. The use of green fertilizers between rows of vegetables fixes nitrogen and feeds microorganisms. White clover is the best kind for a garden. It contributes appreciably to the growth of vegetables and fruits, and it reduces the risk of parasites by harboring many small beetles which feed on plant lice, red spiders, and the larvae of Colorado beetles.

Clover adds a considerable amount of humus to complement your compost. Green fertilizers are an aid to growth and harmony that no gardener should fail to use.

Crop rotation. For the first plant to be grown in a plot of earth, it is important to choose a species with a strong ability to fix nitrogen. It can be a variety of green fertilizer if the soil is very tired; it must then be followed by a leguminous plant that has the same ability: broad beans, soybeans, lentils, peas. Only after this first crop can the gardener grow plants that need large amounts of nitrogen. (Having first been fixed by the leguminous plants, nitrogen shoould continue to be fixed, if possible, by green fertilizer growing in the immediate vicinity.) These plants with a large need for nitrogen are vegetables with roots or tubers: carrots, cabbages, radishes, turnips, salsify, celery, beets, potatoes.

Combining such vegetables as radishes, carrots, and lettuce in the same plot of ground can sometimes be very beneficial.

A small table of crop rotation

Onions	Beets	Tomatoes
Peas	Carrots	White onions
Carrots	Peas	Yellow onions
Radishes	Cabbages	Scallions
Tomatoes	Spinach	Carrots
Peas	Tomatoes	Spinach

The Orchard

Before planting fruit trees, you must first examine the soil. Its nature is very important and should determine your choice of trees. The preliminary clearing of the land should be done without turning over the soil, so that the humus will remain intact; its presence and the life it contains are essential to the very existence of trees. For each tree, dig a hole about three feet across and three feet deep and add ninety pounds of compost mixed with the arable earth removed in digging the hole. This should be one a few weeks before planting.

It is worth noting that the good quality of a tree is shown by the number and size of its roots, chiefly the smaller ones, which should grow almost as densely as human hair.

Ideal soils for trees:

Almond: dry, chalky soil.
Apple and pear: deep, clayey soil.
Apricot: light, deep, permeable soil.
Peach: light, deep soil.
Plum: clayey, siliceous soil.

Autumn is a good season for planting. Winter is inadvisable because its harsh weather hinders healing.

Growing green fertilizers around trees increases the richness of the humus and brings a proliferation of small beetles and predatory insects that are very useful in combating parasites.

Combating parasites. With the use of a wide assortment of chemicals, the struggle against parasites has been stepped up almost to the point of paranoia. It is a ludicrous escalation in which both useful and harmful insects are destroyed, leaving the field open to others for which a new chemical antidote must be found.

In our opinion, man should not meddle in the unending natural struggles among living things. He should limit himself to maintaining the best conditions for such cycles, nurturing as well as possible the natural environment in which vital ecological processes take place. Because varied flora and fauna are maintained by the substances and incessant work of the soil and humus, and because of the protection provided by vegetation, hedges, and ditches, the marvelous saga of microorganisms, insects, and birds can unfold naturally without interference by man.

Natural harmony and the biological environment. A garden is a privileged place, a private domain where man can still play an essential part. His work must be creative. The gardener is the touchstone of the system.

Protecting and helping ecological balance is the primary task of any gardener. If its real knowledge of the natural order by which gardening becomes truly spiritual work that puts man in his right place in the universe.

Making a Pleasure Garden

Composition. In the past, Japanese master gardeners spent days and nights at the site of their future creation. They constantly and attentively watched and studied every feature of the ground, each movement of the wind, sun, and water. They set branches adorned with paper into the ground to represent trees so that they could properly choose the locations of hedges and clumps of shrubbery. In short, the garden was given life on the spot. Such work expresses a real love of nature, an exchange, and not a disruption brought about by whim or fashion.

Some people will say they do not have time, but it is much more a matter of attention and intuitive reflection than of time.

Once you have chosen the place, look.

Light. Its natural movements (sun and moon) will decide many things by themselves. Will shade be necessary? If so, should there be a small, medium, or large amount of it? Choice of colors (flowers and trees) in relation to the color of the sky. Marking off shady areas. Planting trees or shrubs in relation to the sun's motion in the course of the day.

If you dream of moonlight reflected on water, you can choose a place that will let you have it (being careful not to plant trees that are too high or thick).

Water. On either flat or sloping land, rainwater traces a line that should be followed if you create a stream or a basin (and should be avoided in planting certain trees and clumps of flowers). Remember that water flows downhill. Never put a pool in a place higher than the ground around it; it should always be in a natural situation.

Winds. Study them carefully, since drafts are very disagreeable in a pleasure garden. Determine the direction of the prevailing winds and consider putting in hedges or other windbreaks if necessary. Remember to locate resting places where they will be sheltered from the wind.

Attentive examination of light, water, and wind will already delimit certain centers and lines. Creation of the garden itself should be based on these natural forms.

Nature of the soil. It is advisable to probe the soil in many different places. Your choice of trees, shrubs, and flowers will obviously depend on its quality (along with climatic conditions).

This contemplation followed by thorough study of the site will enable you to decide which trees and other plants you will use, their approximate locations, the positions of pools or streams and where you will have resting places and clear areas.

The character and personality of a garden depend a great deal on its paths. They should blend in with the landscape. In our opinion, one should be able to walk in a garden "flowingly," without abrupt turns.

Avoid straight lines on slopes and too many curves on flat land.

It is better to make a sketchy, tenative layout before the plants have reached their full growth. When the lines appear clearly, they can be altered or even eliminated wherever necessary. The layout will then be in harmony with the site.

Avoid changing the landscape too much; adapt your creation to it without transforming it with such things as enbankments or ramps.

Save the rocks, plant debris, roots, and branches that you have moved; they all may be useful.

A garden forms a whole. The object is not to center it around this or that part of it (pools, flower beds, trees), but to establish relations with proper and hormonius proportions.

Avoid cement and concrete!

Before buying a tree, find out its dimensions and consider its shape in relation to those of other trees.

A garden should be beautiful to look at from anywhere.

A lawn, three rocks, two trees, and a flower bed may be enough. Avoid "overloading" your garden by putting in too many things for its size.

Study colors, blend shades and shapes.

The pleasure garden reveals our sense of natural beauty and harmony. Beyond gardening, with the inner peace imparted by work well done, begins the exchange between man and nature.

MAN, LIFE, THE COSMOS

Man cannot be completely seen separate from mankind, nor mankind separate from all life, nor life separate from the universe.

Pierre Teilhard de Chardin

Who are we? Where do we come from? Where are we going? These questions are not raised only by children, geniuses, and the last of the first men who, for a little longer, are still lost in the primordial forest. In the shadow of his machines, buffeted by the upheavals of history, torn by the anguish of being in the world, anesthetized by comfort, and poisoned by the ideology of the productivity race, civilized man nevertheless continues to wonder what heights feed the spring that vivifies him, the spring whose secret song he still hears now and then, and what original light is the source of the spark that animates him, the spark whose brief flash he sometimes sees.

In performing such basic acts as eating, lying down to relax, sitting down to concentrate, walking, making fire, making love, giving life, and receiving death, he is given a chance to have a sudden realization that his existence is not only the programmed behavior of a numbered unit in a hyperbureacratized society, the ludricrous agitation of a puppet deprived of its own being by the Megamachine, but that he is also a person within the human race, a living being on the planet Earth, a composite of matter endowed with consciousness, a particle of the cosmos radiant with psychic energy.

Thinking with the Body

Such a realization, necessarily intuitive, is in itself a transformation of the person. Each of us bears within himself the germ of his knowledge of reality. The person who understands himself for the first time must overcome fear, for he confronts the void. Thought stops, the personality is eroded, he has the feeling of going back into his body. For experience passes by way of the body, it is the body.

We have already seen the extent to which, in order to be correct, the acts of everyday life must be connected to the universal rhythms of life, in communication with the elements, bound to the infinitely variable flow of energy. And now we see that the body is the cosmos. The flows and pulsations of the body machine participate in the rhythms of the universe, and we live as "golden sparks of nature light." The question of origin, of birth and death, of beginning and end, is now sustained by contemplation of nature in a renewed light, upheld by the sound of a brook and the murmur of pines, hurled like a challenge or a prayer to the remote constellations.

We gradually come to realize that the answer to the question is in the question itself. Or rather that there is neither question nor answer, since the posing of the question is human posture itself: Humanization is the story of a slow process of placing the spinal column upright, from nonhuman primates to the first hominids. The answer lies in that nervous system erected between the earth and the sky, like an upside-down tree, rooted in the human brain, the most highly developed brain yet produced by the planet Earth.

The Roots of Consciousness

Man all at once stops being fooled by space and time. This advance of consciousness is the course of an experience. It cannot be reduced to language, but that does not mean it eludes formulation. Formulation of knowledge of the universe passes through the crucible of accepted signs, or symbols. The traditions of all peoples convey such symbols.

It is generally accepted that modern man has the same cerebral aptitudes as the earliest human beings, even though the movement of evolution, accelerated by the process of civilization, has repressed his "paradisiac" potentialities into the subcortical region of his deep brain. But the history of the last ten thousand years is that of a being who forsakes the predisposition toward play, laughter, and hunting possessed by "children of the sun" and enters a movement in which action is preceded and followed by the detour of thought. Discourse makes up for the lack of reality, and unobtrusive, harmonious integration into the natural environment gives way to the practice of transforming nature. The thinking being sees himself as master of the universe. Having reached one of the peaks of knowledge, he discovers that he has a boundless power and an immense responsibility. It depends on him, for example, whether the energy he has awakened—nuclear energy, the basic energy of the universe—will serve life or death.

The Eye Exists in the Wild State

In their natural condition, human beings go to sleep beside the fire and awaken at the first light of dawn, which announces the coming of the heavenly body that dispenses energy: the sun. Morning celebrates the victory of the forces of life over those of darkness. The sun awakens sleeping bodies and opens man to vision. The children of the sun receive the essence of light and discern the inner nature of things. They have an intuition of the whole, they understand the circulation of energies.

But with the development of the world of thought, which surges up in the breach of the separation from nature, the sun comes to be taken not only for itself, but also for the image of a purely spiritual Being who governs "superior" mental life. The development of civilization, with the invention of agriculture and writing, gives rise to the formation of the first empires and thus concentrates the power of radiation in a sovereign, a paternal figure invested with solar authority. The monarch is the living image of the celestial god.

Not only does the moon refract the sun's rays and send them to men plunged in darkness, but men in return project to it the intimate aspirations of their hearts, the unreasoned impulses of their imagination, the flow of their secret yearnings. It is the confidante of lovers, the poet's inspiration, the sage's companion. In traditional rural societies, people fraternally united by the full moon are placed outside of time and diurnal norms. They do not work, they dance. Young shepherdesses whirl around the fire like the planets around the sun. In India, worshipers of Shiva, heirs to a prehistoric fire cult, often wear a representation of the crescent moon in their hair. For them, a secret bond unites the sun, the moon, and fire. By the practice of yoga they train themselves to bring forth and control, in the cosmos of their body, the energy whose most vivid image, to our physical eyes, is the luminous heavenly bodies.

A short circuit between the sky and the earth, an intervention of fire from above accompanied by a deafening noise, lightning reveals the world in an instantaneous light more powerful than that of the sun. Heraclitus said, "Lightning is the pilot of the universe." Shamans have always had a tool that both represents and conveys the forces of thunder and lightning. That metallic instrument, lightning, is an attribute of the old Aryan divinity Indra. In Buddhist Tantrism, lightning (*vajra*) becomes a diamond and a phallus, and finds its female complement in the bell. Similarly, in a society that has become religious with the transition from hunting to agriculture, Zeus, associated with his totemic animal, the eagle, is the celestial avatar of the European shaman who knew how to speak to the elements.

After the violence of the coupling between the sky and the earth, the rainbow is for human beings the sign of a new alliance with the powers above. The radiant semicircle of seven colors is a good image of the relativity of the phenomenal world: I see it, but if I move, it disappears. Let us not try to know if phenomena that have always been regarded as omens bring happiness or unhappiness, announce salvation or disaster, or indicate the satisfaction or wrath of the powers beyond our world. Man has always projected the most intimate part of his desires into events that are nothing but remarkable manifestations of the interplay of cosmic energies.

So goes the world of symbols. Everything is a sign of those who know how to see. "The eye exists in the wild state," writes André Breton. The mountains of Judea sing the glory of the heavens, and all of nature is God's writing. The ancient combination of earth, air, fire, and water was perfectly suited to the existence of peoples living between the sky and the earth, on intimate terms with the plant and animals worlds.

In the original cloud, a mixture of air, water, and fire, the earth is formed by condensation. The primordial waters on its surface are fecundated by breath. The heat and light of the solar fire (not counting the subtler influences of distant stars and galaxies) bring forth life from the primeval mud.

Fables, myths, sacred texts, and old legends handed down to us by tradition express man's natural wonder as he opens himself to knowledge of the universe. Such stories are initiatory; that is, they lead back to the experience that nurtured them, if we know how to understand them. The sage is like a pebble or a log, and he rides the wind. The clear light of the Tibetans or the ascent to the zenith of the Siberian and American Indian shamans, for example, shows forcefully that, by the way of communication with the elements, man can identify himself with formations of matter that he cannot conceptualize with his limited reason, much less contemplate with his physical eyes.

The Stag

Civilized man, used to the mysteries of modern technology and subjected to the imperatives of industry, has ten thousand years of rural, pastoral life behind him. Still more deeply, in the subcortical layers of his "primitive" brain, he bears the memory of hundreds of thousands of years of hunting and food gathering in the primordial forest. Prehistoric cave paintings, as well as survivals of shamanism, show how thoroughly the act of giving death to assure life involved the whole human being in close combat with an animal which he had entreated to come and expose itself to his arrow, and before which he experienced the feeling of the sacred.

As soon as man began raping the earth to draw his sustenance from it, hunting became a diversion for the powerful of this world and, no longer being an essential activity of the body in search of its food, it remained a representation of the soul watching for its god. In the image, old as mankind, of the hunter lying in wait, invisible, ready for the sudden appearance of the quarry that gives life, it pleases us to see an image of man watching for a manifestation of a hidden dimension of himself, ready for a sudden appearance of the inexpressible. And, as we know, it sometimes happens that animals speak to man and, if he renounces killing, give him the keys to a more secret kingdom.

If you seek the stag, you must turn inward,
Huddled in the warmth of oneness,
secretly, on your knees, before dawn,
breathless in the thickness of the mountains.
                                    P. J. Jouve

The Life and Death of a Star

Matter is composed of assemblies of molecules, which are in turn composed of *atoms.* * The number of atomic types is known to be finite. They vary with the number of protons in the *nucleus,* going from the hydrogen atom, the simplest (atomic number 1), to the uranium atom, the most comlex (atomic number 92). Assembled on the loom of evolution, the ninety-two *elements* are the threads that compose the fabric of the universe. If we consider both the infinitely small and the infinitely great, we realize that "we owe our corporeal existence to events which took place billions of years ago, in stars that lived and died long before the solar system came into being."**

Scientific explanations of the genesis of the universe involve the action of three forces: the nuclear force, the most powerful, which binds protons and neutrons together to form the atomic nucleus; the electromagnetic force, which binds electrons to the nucleus to form the atom, and binds atoms to each other; and the force of *gravity,* which keeps Earth and the other planets in orbit around the sun and holds together the vast group of stars composing our spiral galaxy.

In the beginning, then, is space, filled with thin *hydrogen clouds* swirling in the dark sky. As time passes, isolated atoms "fall" together by the effect of gravity and coalesce at the center of the cloud. This accumulation of gas, which contracts and thereby becomes heated, is an embryonic star. It goes on contracting until its diameter has shrunk from ten trillion

miles to a hundred million; when its temperature reaches a hundred thousand degrees Fahrenheit, the hydrogen atoms come apart, and protons and electrons float separately from each other. It continues contracting for millions of years until it has shrunk to the size of our sun and its temperature has reached twenty million degrees. At that temperature, protons begin colliding with each other, overcoming the electrical repulsion between two positive poles. "In the final moment of the collision the force of nuclear attraction is so strong that it fuses the protons together into a single nucleus. At the same time the energy of their collision is released in the form of heat and light. This release of energy marks the birth of a star."*

Continuing reactions transform protons, or hydrogen nuclei, into helium. This gigantic thermonuclear combustion of hydrogen being converted into helium lasts 99 per cent of a star's lifetime. In the case of the sun, the process began five billion years ago and another five billion years will pass before its reserves of hydrogen are exhausted. At that time, the sun will show signs of aging; it will have expanded to a hundred times its present size and its color will change from yellow-white to red. Astronomers call such aging stars *red giants.* Betelgeuse, in the constellation of Orion, is one.

When its hydrogen reserves are completely exhausted, the red giant collapses into itself and helium atoms are concentrated at its center. If its temperature reaches the critical point of two hundred million degrees, helium nuclei begin fusing in groups of three to form carbon nuclei, releasing more nuclear energy and giv-

---

*Words in italics are explained in the Glossary at the end of the chapter.
**Robert Jastrow: *Red Giants and White Dwarfs* (Harper & Row, 1967).

---

*Ibid.

ing new vigor to the fire at the heart of the star. Eventually the star's helium is exhausted and it again begins collapsing under the effect of gravity. If it is small, it will end its existence as a body about the size of the earth. Incandescent because of its great heat, it is what astronomers call a *white dwarf,* slowly cooling and being transformed into a dark body.

A large star has a different fate. It reaches the temperature of six hundred million degrees required for fusion of carbon nuclei. Through alternating collapses, reheatings, and nuclear reactions, the star makes heavier elements, from oxygen to sodium, then the whole range of elements up to iron. Iron has a nucleus so dense that it absorbs all the energy produced by combustion. The star is compressed like a spring, then explodes violently. Its temperature rises into the billions of degrees and all elements heavier than iron are formed during the several minutes of the explosion. This cosmic fireworks display is called a *supernova.*

"The supernova explosion sprays the material of the star out into space, where it mingles with fresh hydrogen to form a mixture containing all 92 elements. Later in the history of the galaxy, other stars are formed out of clouds of hydrogen which have been enriched by the products of these explosions. The sun, the earth, and the beings on its surface—all were formed out of such clouds containing the debris of supernova explosions dating back billions of years to the beginning of the Galaxy."[*]

What becomes of the nucleus of a supernova after the explosion? In 1967, radio telescopes picked up signals that revealed the presence of a sphere of superdense matter at the center of the Crab Nebula, projecting particles and radiation into space. Its mass of billions of billions of tons is compressed into an incredibly small volume: its diameter is something like twenty miles. It is in the region where a supernova exploded in A.D. 1054. It has been named a *pulsar.*

Under certain conditions, a star may continue collapsing beyond the stage of the pulsar. When it shrinks to a diameter of about two miles, its gravitational force is so strong that it prevents light rays from leaving its surface. It is then a *black hole* in space. According to the present laws of theoretical physics, the star goes on collapsing, reaching microscopic size. An object that began with a diameter of ten trillion miles becomes unimaginably small. But intuition says that such a process must necessarily end. From the effect of what superpowerful energy? We here reach the limits of knowledge.

The Origin of the Universe

The world is one, and was created by no god or man. It was, is, and always will be a living flame that flares up and dies down according to definite laws.

Heraclitus

Like all the ancient sages, Heraclitus intuitively grasped the universality of the cycle of death and rebirth in which the death of a star, for example, as modern science tells us, releases elements that nurture the birth of a new star. But we have good reason to believe that this cycle is not eternal. On the one hand, reserves of pure hydrogen, the basic material of the universe, are slowly but surely being exhausted.

There are fewer and fewer stars in the cosmos. On the other hand, the galaxies seem to be moving away from each other at amazing speeds. The universe is expanding, as if it were itself the result of a gigantic explosion. Its density is contantly decreasing.

It is now possible to posė in scientific terms the question that lies in everyone's heart: What is the origin of the universe? In 1931 a Jesuit priest, Father Lemaître, put forward the idea that the universe began as a drop of dense, hot matter, a fireball emitting extremely intense radiation. Support for this theory came in 1965 when two physicists at the Bell Laboratory happened to discover sources of extremely intense radiation several billion light-years from our planet. They called these sources quasars

*Ibid.

(quasi-stellar objects). Quasars are explicable if they are regarded as "fossil" remains of the original fireball.

In the depths of his heart, man asks this question: Where do we come from? Intuition suggests an answer; tradition and then science give theirs, each in its own way, according to its symbolism, like a man moving forward by advancing first one foot and then the other. But the child in each of us keeps asking, And then? And before? What about that famous fireball? Is it not also a "living flame that flares up and dies down according to definite laws?"

Having reached this point, we are again plunged into the dense darkness of nonknowledge. When we open our eyes we again find our ordinary world, everyday nature, calm and radiant as always. We now now that we know nothing. As the patriarch Ch'an Wei-neng said, "From the viewpoint of ordinary men, enlightenment and ignorance are two different things. The wise man who thoroughly fulfills his own nature knows that they are both of the same nature."

The Origin of Life

We now know that the earth was formed by condensation at the same time as the sun, about five billion years ago. Thanks to the discovery of fossil remains of the oldest living organisms—bacteria and simple plants—we can trace back the appearance of life on our planet to about three and a half billion years ago. Until recent times, no one was able to explain how life might have appeared on that globe composed of cosmic dust and particles of rock and metal (hydrogen and helium had escaped into space in massive quantities). What happened during the first billion years? What is the origin of life?

The discoveries of molecular biology now enable us to state some basic certainties. During the fusion of substances that constituted the earth, volatile compounds floated around it, held by the force of gravity. These gases were compounds of hydrogen, oxygen, carbon, and nitrogen: carbon dioxide, water vapor, methane (CH_4), ammonia gas (NH_3). The gas molecules were directly exposed to solar radiation capable of breaking the bonds among atoms and giving rise to new combinations which were the ancestors of the first organic compounds. At this point, "two characteristics of life were forever fixed: the bases of its chemical composition: carbon, hydrogen, oxygen, and nitrogen; and its permanent source: the sun."[*]

After the action of fire, that of water caused a continuation and acceleration of the chemical transformation of organic matter. Water assembled on the surface of the planet the proto-organic molecules that had "fallen from the sky." It dissolved many organic and mineral compounds. In the primordial "hot soup," as Haldane calls it, encounters between individual molecules were favored and the chances of chemical reactions were considerably increased. Life originated in "shallow lagoons where evaporation concentrated the solution of organic substances, the mouths of rivers uncovered by the tide, or fissures in the ground that were alternately dry and moist. Layers of clay, sand, or lava may have played the part of activating surfaces."[**]

The stage was now set, and we know the play that was about to begin unfolding, although we do not know its ending. But how were the actors to make their entrances? We know where life began, but how did it appear?

A brief theoretical detour is necessary here. It will enable us to integrate the main points established by molecular biology in the last ten years.

All living organisms are composed of two kinds of molecules: *amino acids* and nucleotides. There are twenty kinds of amino acids and five kinds of nucleotides. And each amino acid is itself a rather complex molecule com-

---

[*]J. de Rosnay: *Les origines de la vie (The Origins of Life)* (Seuil).

[**]Ibid.

posed of about thirty hydrogen, nitrogen, and carbon atoms. Amino acids combine to form very large molecules: *proteins,* each of which contains several hundred amino acids. Some, known as structural proteins, are the basic elements of which living organisms are composed. Others, known as enzymes, of which there are many kinds, control the multiple chemical reactions required for maintaining the life of the organism. The nucleotides are the second group of fundamental substances. They combine in long chains called *nucleic acids.* Nucleic acids assemble the proteins that form the living organism. The most important one is deoxyribonucleic acid, or *DNA.*

DNA is the largest known molecule. In the human body, it contains billions of atoms. It is the programmer of *biogenesis,* the molecular reservoir of genetic information, the governing structure of the organism. The order in which its nucleotides are arranged along its macromolecular chain determines the assembly of amino acids, and therefore the formation of the different kinds of proteins.

"The segments of the DNA molecule are 'read' like the words of a book. Each DNA segment, controlling the assembly of one protein, is a word; each nucleotide within a segment is a letter; the order of the letters provides the meaning of the word—that is, the protein to be assembled. The full set of DNA molecules contained within a cell is the library of genetic information for the organism."*

Amino acids and nucleotides are the same in all forms of life on the planet; it is DNA and, through it, proteins, that differentiate one organism from another. In 1952 Stanley Miller circulated a mixture of ammonia gas, methane, water vapor, and hydrogen through an electric discharge for a week and succeeded in "manufacturing" several types of amino acids in that way. In 1962 nucleotides were produced in a laboratory from mixtures of gases. Today, laboratory "synthesis" of a rudimentary living organism seems quite possible.

We have thus returned to the primordial mud bombarded by alpha particles, subjected to electrical discharges from thunderstorms, exposed to ultraviolet radiation from the sun, and heated by volcanoes—energy at work in matter, breath on the waters. . . . Ever since the cloud of fire, the original hydrogen cloud, a continuous, accelerating movement has drawn on enormous amounts of energy to make matter pass from simple to more complex forms: heavier atoms, larger molecules in the original assemblies of molecules, cells that reproduce themselves (for DNA molecules split in two) and maintain an exchange of energy with the environment by *photosynthesis* and respiration.

The appearance of life? Let us speak, rather, of a continuous evolution of preliving, then living matter, produced by the constant action of energy, a progressive illumination of matter. Irradiated by the flow of energy, matter becomes organized.

The Chain of Mutations

The rest of the story is better known; dramatic developments occur at an increasingly rapid rate. The first fossils, of one-celled plants, algae, and bacteria, are three billion years old. Six hundred million years ago, sea animals began proliferating; two hundred million years later, the first vertebrates (fish) appeared. Reptiles soon left the mother water and inaugurated the reign of animal life on dry land.

The origin of species? We have known since Darwin that it lies in the process of natural selection. "Natural selection," he wrote, "is

———

*Robert Jastrow, op. cit.

daily and hourly scrutinizing, throughout the world, the slightest variations, rejecting those that are bad, preserving and adding up all that are good; silently and insensibly working at the improvement of each organic being in relation to its . . . conditions of life."

Natural selection operates by means of mutations. A mutation is an alteration in the order of the nucleotides in the DNA of a germ cell. It may be caused by an error of reproduction (the process of reproduction is never perfect) or the action of *cosmic rays.* If it favors better adaptation to the environment, it will be propagated throughout the species.

The Origin of Man

The disappearance of dinosaurs seventy million years ago enabled mammals to proliferate all over the surface of the planet. For a time, however, one group of mammals remained in trees: the *primates*. Initially they were small, insect-eating animals the size of a squirrel, with valuable assets in the struggle for life. They had hands and opposable thumbs with which to grasp branches, and keen eyesight that helped them in leaping from tree to tree. Gradually, through tens of millions of years, by the effect of successive mutations, these little forest creatures were transformed into animals close to the monkey. The most gifted of them began engaging in rudimentary manual work.

Certain primates evolved, formed groups, and, by means of favorable mutations, gave birth to the *anthropoids,* with a more complex brain. A few million years ago the most highly evolved anthropoids (the first *hominids*) were hunting, fishing, constructing shelters, and making stone tools, and they already had a rudimentary social organization. "It is highly probable that not only tools, but also hunting, language, and culture were developed during the process of *humanization,* before *Homo sapiens* appeared."*

Technology, language, and society (culture) combined to produce Homo sapiens in the space of five million years. The development of social complexity gave rise to a corresponding increase in the complexity of the brain, whose size has doubled in the last million years. Not only was the activity of the cortex developed, but new connections and centers were made possible by an increase in the number of neurons. Culture, in both the history of each individual (ontogeny) and that of the species (phylogeny), programs regression of instinct and growth of the brain.

When Homo sapiens appeared in the Neanderthal period a few hundred thousand years ago, he was a particularly fragile and helpless creature at birth. A naked ape. Somatically, he is one species among others, belonging to the family of hominids and the order of primates. Psychically, he has inaugurated a new reign, that of reflective thought. Thought, his thought, has now spread throughout the earth.

The Origin of the Future

For tens of thousands of years small groups of Homo sapiens wandered over the planet, surviving by gathering plants and killing animals. A decisive step seems to have been taken about ten thousand years ago in the Fertile Crescent of Mesopotamia. Agriculture was developed, writing was invented, empires were formed, war replaced hunting, and history began. Agriculture, writing, war, empires, and cities finally spread over the planet like wildfire. Early hominid societies were made up of only a few dozen individuals; the hunting-gathering societies of Homo sapiens brought together several hundred individuals; societies in historical times have included at least several thousand individuals and often several million.

"History began a few thousand years ago. If we consider the time that has elapsed since the date presently assigned to the appearance of hominids on earth, 2 per cent to 5 per cent of that time is occupied by the existence of Homo sapiens, and 0.2 per cent to 0.5 per cent by historical evolution. It is amazing to realize the creativity and destructiveness that have emerged during that very short period."**

In the last few decades, man has shown that he is capable of systematically killing his fellow men on a large scale by using industrial procedures; he has mastered the basic energy of the universe, nuclear energy, which constantly bursts forth from the billions of stars that compose our galaxy and in the millions of galaxies scattered throughout the cosmos (let it be said in passing that the Hiroshima bomb was only a toy compared to what we are now threatened with if we do not behave ourselves);

-----

*Edgar Morin: *La nature humaine: le paradigme perdu (Human Nature: The Lost Paradigm)* (Seuil).
**Ibid.

he will soon synthesize living organisms in a laboratory; he has already walked on the moon.

We are man, he is you and I. Is it not urgent for us to learn what life depends on? Is it not imperative that we learn to live? The time has come for us to contemplate our original face, so that we can go forth in space-time while respecting the laws of the universe, in harmony with the breath of energy that fecundates matter and produces life, and with the irresistible movement from which mind arises. Man's mind, my mind, your mind, Our brains. You and I know where we come from. Particles of the cosmos endowed with psychic energy, "golden sparks of nature light." Where are we going? In the only possible direction, Ivan Illich tells us: toward an ultraconsciousness expressible in ultrahuman terms.

The Energy Crisis

The present energy crisis in the industrialized nations is one of the first signs of a worldwide crisis that is rapidly approaching. "The crisis is rooted in the failure of the modern enterprise, that is, substitution of the machine for man. The great project of transforming nature has changed into an implacable process of subjugating the producer and poisoning the consumer."*

Man's destiny is not necessarily bound to history. The pressure of an impetus toward a necessary mutation is making historical societies break apart. It seems that the time is ripe for what Edgar Morin calls a fourth birth of mankind.

The concept of conviviality, introduced by Ivan Illich to characterize a possible model of society, essentially involves a series of radical reversals: reversing our relation to technology (it should be controllable, rather than mobilizing us as servants of the Megamachine from birth to death); reversing our relation to energy (finding energy in ourselves, rather than constantly pumping it out of the environment until either our resources are exhausted or the environment is smothered); reversing our relation to the environment (trying to fit harmoniously into our cosmic niche); and finally, we will add, reversing our relation to ourselves (dropping our little ego and connecting ourselves to the flow of cosmic life). Then "the monster will be consumed from within by ferments of light, and from its ashes, with all chains broken, will rise the bird of freedom and kindness that we incubate in our fragile hands."*

How will the human race cross the threshold of its fourth mutation? Perhaps its necessary plunge toward an ultrahuman mentality depends on the way in which each of its members, you and I, lives his everyday life. If we make a void within ourselves, concentrating here and now, we will be receptive to all influences, unconsciously harmonize ourselves, and find the right act. We must plunge into the stream of life. Together. And reach the other bank.

---

*Pierre Teilhard de Chardin, *Oeuvres*, Vol. III (Seuil).

*V. Bardet: *Canyon/Californie* (Seuil).

A Little Glossary for
Modern Homo Sapiens

Amino Acids. Small molecules which link together to form proteins.

Anthropogenesis. The appearance of the human zoological group.

Anthropoids. Higher apes which resemble man and live in societies. In our time, there are four main groups of them: gibbons, organgutans, gorillas, and chimpanzees.

Atom. A nucleus and its shell of electrons.

Biogenesis. The process of increasing complexity and organization that leads to the appearance of living organisms.

Black Hole. A pulsar that has contracted to a diameter of a few miles. Its matter is so concentrated that the force of gravity prevents light from leaving its surface; it thus becomes a black (lightless) hole in space.

C. The velocity of electromagnetic radiation (without mass) and the limiting velocity of particles endowed with mass. It is often called the speed of light, which is only a particular case. C = 186,000 miles per second.

Cosmic Rays. Natural nuclear radiation that comes from particles endowed with enormous energy, circulating in interstellar space. There are primary and secondary cosmic rays. Primary particles are nuclei traveling through space at very high speed; secondary particles come from nuclear reactions caused by primary particles when they penetrate the earth's atmosphere. On the average, the earth is bombarded by these particles at the rate of about a hundred and thirty per square inch per minute.

DNA. Deoxyribonucleic acid, the genetic determinant present in the nucleus of human cells.

Electromagnetic Radiation. Radio waves, heat waves, infrared radiation, visible light, ultraviolet radiation, X rays, and the gamma radiation of atomic nuclei are increasing frequencies of a single phenomenon: electromagnetic radiation.

Element. A chemical type of atom, characterized by the number of protons in the nucleus. There are ninety-two natural elements.

Elementary Particles. Elementary units of matter, which at present seem to be indivisible. They are characterized by a mass and an electric charge. The three basic elementary particles are the proton, the neutron, and the electron. Within the framework of high-energy nuclear physics, physicists have discovered about thirty other particles that have very short lives (on the order of a billionth of a second) and are often endowed with amazingly high energy.

Gravity. An attraction created in space by matter. According to Newton's law of universal gravitation, the force of attraction between two bodies is proportional to the product of their masses and inversely proportional to the square of the distance between them.

Hominids. A group of primates including modern man and his extinct precursors, such as Pithecanthropus erectus.

Homo Sapiens. Modern man, constituting the most recent phase of humanization.

Humanization. The progressive transition from animal life to reflective human life.

Hydrogen Cloud. A concentration of hydrogen atoms within a galaxy. It is usually a relatively short-lived phenomenon, but in some cases, by successive contractions and heatings, it produces an embryonic star. If it reaches a temperature of twenty million degrees, nuclear fusion transforms hydrogen nuclei into helium nuclei, releasing energy in the form of heat and light. A star is born.

Light. Light is propagated as waves in a continuous medium. The waves are characterized notably by their amplitude and frequency. The intensity of light varies with its amplitude, and its energy varies with its frequency. Matter receives light in a discontinuous, corpuscular form.

Messenger RNA. Ribonucleic acid that conveys the information contained in DNA from the nucleus to the cytoplasm.

Metabolism. The aggregate of chemical processes that take place in the cell.

Nucleic Acids. Giant molecules that are the basis of genetic information.

Nucleus. The basic assembly of matter. Extraordinarily dense, nuclei compose 99.9 per cent of the matter in the universe. They are made up of protons and neutrons bound together by an enormously strong force of attraction, the nuclear force. When they are surrounded by a shell of electrons, they become atoms.

Photon. The elementary "grain" of light or heat.

Photosynthesis. The process by which green plants exposed to light absorb carbon dioxide from the air, give off oxygen, and fix carbon. It depends on the presence of a green pigment, chlorophyll, which uses light as a source of energy.

Primates. An order of plantigrade mammals which are social except for its most primitive members, lemurs. Besides the latter, it now includes tarsiers, apes, monkeys, and man.

Protein. A giant molecule formed by a chain of amino acids attached to each other. It is the basic constituent element of living organisms.

Pulsar. A sphere of superdense, incredibly compressed matter formed by the collapse of a massive star at the end of its life. Pulsars project particles and radiation into space.

Quantum Theory. The theory formulated by Max Planck in 1901, according to which energy appears discontinuously in whole multiples of a certain quantum. In particular, the energy of electromagnetic radiation is proportional to its frequency.

Radioactivity. The spontaneous emission of elementary particles (such as protons, neutrons, electrons, helium nuclei) by certain atomic nuclei. It is accompanied by the emission of high-energy electromagnetic radiation or gamma radiation.

Red Giant. An aging, reddish star, distended to about a hundred times its original diameter, which is consuming its last reserves of hydrogen. Example: Betelgeuse, in the constellation of Orion.

Supernova. The explosion of a massive star at the end of its life. By alternating contractions and heatings, the star produces a chain reaction of nuclear fusions and, in a spectacular cosmic fireworks display (temperatures rise to billions of degrees), gives birth to all ninety-two elements. The explosion lasts several minutes. The Crab Nebula is a large cloud of gas containing what remains of a supernova explosion observed by Chinese astronomers in A.D. 1054.

Transmutation. Alteration of the structure of an atomic nucleus. It can be either spontaneous (disintegration) or provoked (nuclear reaction).

White Dwarf. A small star at the end of its life which has exhausted its reserves of hydrogen and helium. Its center is filled with a residue of carbon nuclei. White hot at its surface, it slowly radiates the rest of its heat before being transformed into a dark body.

THREE MEDITATIONS

Seeing

"Seeing. It might be said that all life is there—if not finally, at least essentially. To be more is to unite more, and unity grows only if it is supported by a growth of consciousness, that is, of vision. That is no doubt why the history of the living world is based on the development of steadily improving eyes within a cosmos where it is always possible to discern more. The perfection of an animal or the supremacy of the thinking being is measured by the penetration and synthesizing power of their gaze. Trying to see more and better is therefore not a whim, a curiosity, a luxury. See or perish. Such is the situation imposed by the mysterious gift of existence on everything that is an element of the universe. And such is, consequently, on a higher level, the human condition."*

If to see is to be more, let us look at ourselves, into ourselves, and we will live more. We will contemplate our original face.

Walking**

When the baby stood up for the first time, his whole family applauded. Now he is an adult, seated, with his shoulders sagging. Comfort means not having to get off his backside: from his bed to his car, from his easy chair in front of the television set to his relaxing vacation, it is always the same sluggishness, the same apathy. Modernistic streamlined furniture is made for rubber spines and spongy vertebrae.

As in the good old crying days of babyhood, the first steps count most. Learning to walk, walking. . . . This does not concern city strollers or avid shoppers, but those who want to make a final break with the whole sitting life of the machine-oriented world.

In fairy tales and initiatory stories, the approach to the sanctuary is made on foot. Valiant knights and seekers of the Grail dismount from their fiery steeds.

Reality is vertical.

We should be able to slam the door and leave, and walk alone, in pairs, or in groups.

---

*Pierre Teilhard de Chardin, Prologue to *Le Phénomène Humaine.*

**Written in collaboration with J. M. Varenne .

Walking is natural; the body spontaneously finds its ideal postures as it strides along. Breathing slows or quickens without conscious effort. We have only to walk and let things take their course. The stroller's casual gait, the hunter's lithe tread, and the scout's wary steps across a grassy plain all lead to the same goal: inhabiting one's body, being at ease, enjoying one's natural functioning. Walking creates a contact, an understanding with nature. It participates in the flow of energy and the swirl of particles. The tiresome, hypnotic torrent of ideas, revealed by all yogis as a fetter, as the source of all suffering, is cut off. Walking rests and calms. I walk in the heart of the void, smoothly, without exertion, with no demands on my attention from anything but the earth beneath my feet and the sky above my head.

First steps: almost a race; the stunted, sedentary victim of compartmentalized work is quickly exhausted. Then something else is born and takes on human, divine form in the course of continued walks and strolls. Here is man!

> The sun's course
> feet striking the earth
> all senses alert
> slow penetration of the world into the self
> lighting the inner fire.
> Seeing is walking at last walking
> walking and seeing

Making Fire

Man traces his appearance on earth back to the first signs of fire that he left there, along with the first chipped flint. Fire was already there, unforeseeable and devastating. He discovered it and never parted with it. But in our time, after the industrial mutation, he makes use of natural energies to assure his comfort through highly technical processes.

Urbanized man pays for the light that illuminates his home and the heat that cooks his food, with a control of his environment that gradually exhausts its resources. By counting on the machine to draw energy from the environment and transform it for his benefit, he cuts himself off from the power of simple communication with the nurturing elements, and especially with the very sign of the human condition: fire.

Like fire, man consumes oxygen and gives off carbon dioxide. Like so many other symbols, the comparison of the human heart to fire has scientific support. In Indian tradition (the Sumyuttavi Kaya), we find this: "I stoke the flame within me . . . my heart is the hearth, the flame is the tamed self."

Making fire is not an expedient or merely a technique; it is an art, a sacred act.

A fire can be started with only a twig. Try it little by little, feed the growing flame. Harmonize yourself with it. Give to it according to its needs. Know the power of wind (a little stimulates fire, too much extinguishes it) and the breath from your lungs. Attentive to fire, you are concentrated, you find the right act. Your body is vivified by its heat, your mind is illuminated. Which is better for man (and his children): watching television every night or making a fire and sitting beside it?

The unconcern of shepherds and farmers who extended plains at the expense of the original forest, and the unbridled exploitation of forest resources for the needs of industry (with newsprint in first place) have destroyed the balance between man and forest on most of the earth's surface. The last spaces where man was still integrated harmoniously into his ecosystem—the great Amazonian forest, for example—have now been "penetrated" for the needs of industry and the glory of civilization. In our time more than ever, a wood fire is a sacrifice. Not only because wood has become a luxury item in urban centers, but because wood links us to the activity of the universe and gives us a glimpse of its primordial face.

DEATH

Life flows into death as rivers
flow into the sea.

G. Bataille

For us, death is the Unknown, the Impossible.
Nothing can be said about it. It is the limit of
knowledge, the blind spot of language. "The
greatest problem that man has ever posed for
himself surely remains that of death. To him,
death represents the unknown abyss, the void,
but also the disappearance of his own image,
the annihilation of his personality. This idea
and this attitude are still the supreme anxiety,
onto which are grafted all the fears of the fragility and solitude contained in consciousness.
Man shudders before death because, no matter
what he says or does, he is afraid of being alone
forever."*

Death Always and Everywhere

Experience of the human condition expresses
itself through us and, especially with the development of depth psychology in the West,
we know that the deep impulses which govern
us in relation to life and death adjust to an un-
bearable reality by forging vast symbolic systems that extend into society in the form, for
example, of religious movements.

Lived as a personal experience, anxiety in
the face of death often evokes a collective re-
sponse. The appearance of man is traced back
not only to the first signs of fire, but also to the
first vestiges of graves. The living gather
around a dying man to help him die well. Then
his body is committed to the elements: his
mother the earth, in which he is placed in the
fetal position, or the water of human origin, or
fire. The operations performed around the dead
have always and everywhere been surrounded
by ritual. Behind these ways of behaving toward death when it intervenes in the course of
everyday life, there is always a refusal of it as
an end, no matter what form that refusal takes.

We know that categories do not encompass
reality; they congeal experience within limits.
Yet they can be useful. It seems to us that the
living, whether they accept or reject death,
have always approached it by four dif-

---

*Marc de Smedt and Daniel Odier: *Les mystiques orien-
tales* (Denoël).

ferent ways, which do not exclude each other: the way of salvation, the way of reincarnation, the way in which death is annihilation, and the way that leads to merging with the great Whole.

In the first way, life is regarded as a preparation for an afterlife that is more or less consciously placed outside of space and time. The Sioux Indians, for example, believe that death is a great journey to the hunting grounds of the ancestors. Similarly, African forest tribes believe that after death they will rejoin their ancestors on a distant mountain or shore, which they often visit during initiation ceremonies.

With the emergence of organized societies that left hunting, fishing, and food gathering behind them and devoted themselves to farming, the projection of an ideal afterlife took on an institutionalized form. Priests codified the conditions for admission to paradise: If you do good you will go to heaven, if you do evil you will go to hell. Childish though it may be, that attitude often makes possible the sacrifice of innocent lives ("holy" wars still occur). Behind the imagery of popular religions there is always a more secret truth: Heaven and hell exist on this earth as constituent dimensions of the human psyche, which they polarize in the manner of light and darkness, pleasure and pain, ecstasy and torment.

There is a second way of approaching death. Attentive observation of the environment reveals to man that natural phenomena are cyclical. He also has the intuition, with varying degress of clarity, that energy never ceases to exist. The quantum of energy, the immaterial soul or particle of breath, the spark contained in a human being, therefore does not disappear at death. It is capable of other combinations of elements. This vision has perhaps found its most perfect expression in India. In the Bhagavadgita, cosmic energy is called Atman—and the individual particle is called the atman. "The atman is not born and never dies; it does not become and will never become; nonengendered and eternal, it does not die when the heart dies." The metamorphoses in our fairy tales are a reminiscence of the old belief in reincarnation.

In the two preceding ways, whether death leads to an afterlife or rebirth, the doctrine was taken over by a religion that centered everyday life around the conquest of a Sovereign Goodness—after death. Man had to lead a moral life in order either to deserve a place in heaven or have a reincarnation closer to the divine being. When, in the conquering movement that began in the West, man set out to transform nature according to his desires, doing violence to it if necessary, religious beliefs soon came to be regarded as old myths. Thus, a few years ago, an idea went through civilized brains and shook up public opinion: God was dead, sacrified to Progress. But life must have a meaning, otherwise it is not worth living. Confronted with the anxiety of death, modern man, with the most refined means of scientific analysis at his disposal, finds no escape from the implacable logic of matter. Death is a passage from being to nothingness. It is what gives meaning to life. As André Malraux says, "Death changes our life into a destiny." Life, the experience of existence, is the only reality there is. The universe is absurd. If one lives one's life well, death—accepted, approved, decided upon—is not only an example for future generations, but a sacrifice for the good of the human race.

The three ways we have considered may lead one to the gates of wisdom. Whether it is motivated by a religious or an existentialist doctrine, a lucid approach to death leaves man naked before something frightening.

"Civilizations are mortal," writes Edgar Morin. "The earth will die. And the stars. And the universe itself, that slow, gigantic explosion. Human death, already an infinite emptiness, dilates on all levels of the cosmos, more and more empty and infinite. It is like the universe: expanding."

Fear before the prospect of the dissolution into the great Whole of everything that makes our individuality is precisely the means by which our little self protects itself against the irruption of the unfamiliar. In traditional forms of wisdom the master often transmits the essence of the attitude toward life and death by telling his disciple that he must behave as a warrior. Don Juan, the old Yaqui sorcerer,* for example, distinguishes four perils to be overcome, four stages that one must pass through in

---

*See Carlos Castaneda: *The Teachings of Don Juan, A Separate Reality,* and *Journey to Ixtlan* (New York: Simon and Schuster, Inc.).

order to become a man of knowledge: fear, clarity, power, old age. Death is constantly beside the disciple on the path of his apprenticeship. The man of knowledge knows that, at the edge of the abyss, even clarity is illusory. And once terror has been transcended, no one can rest on the feeling of having overcome death. One finally mistrusts age, which produces habit.

What is the way of the warrior? He has let go, and his whole being is now nothing but an emanation of the energies of the universe. The natural world appears to him as a reservoir of energy laden with signs. By all sorts of means—including the ritual taking of natural psychedelic substances and the practice of disciplines that enable him to know and transform his body—he attains knowledge of the Great Mother of all living beings. The sage is like a pebble or a log and he travels on the wings of the wind. In that initiatory way he meets on his path hell and heaven, torment and ecstasy. But he does not stop at any experience or vision because he knows they are products of his own mind. The universe is his body and his mind is the universe. He is alive, nothing distinguishes him from the ordinary man, and yet he can rightly be regarded as liberated from imprisonment in the duality of life and death.

Death Here and Now

One of the basic features that distinguish the Eastern and Western attitudes toward life and death is the place assigned to the notion of the self and the way in which that idea is considered. Briefly, the Westerner has always tended to place high value on the self, insofar as it is the basis of the personality (and the concept of the person), while the Oriental sees the self (in this case more commonly called the ego) as an ultimately illusory construction.

We do not underestimate the importance of the personality; constituting the self seems to us a necessary stage, but one that must be transcended. Our efforts to cut ourselves off from what is outside us, says Chogyam Trungpa Rinpoche, have the effect of creating in us a kind of big bubble made of nothing but air and water, which represents fear and reflection of external things and lets no fresh air penetrate inside; such is the self, the ego. The goal is to avoid being smothered by one's own self. We are not meant to live and die inside a shell, having understood nothing of the world and being. To live well, in the right middle way, is to die awake.

What a Zen Master, Taisen Deshimaru, Says about Death

Abandoning the ego (the little self) is very difficult. A person may believe in his consciousness or his mind that he is abandoning his ego, but his body does not always follow. It is very easy to abandon the ego in thought, but abandoning it *here and now*, immediately, is very hard.

How can the ego be abandoned at the last moment of life? In Buddhism, the notion of sacrifice is not very important. When we must die, we must die. Death is the end. When one must die, one dies. It is not at the moment of death that one should ask oneself, "How am I do die? Why must I die?" In a saber tournament, one does not say to oneself, "I don't want to die, what am I to do?" In combat, it is the body and the mind together that act and accept death.

When we must die, we die, without moving, without anything. But when it is not time to die, there is no use dying. One can accept the idea of death, of course, but the body must also make the decision. That decision has no special meaning, nor any meaning at all. One must die, that is all. It is impossible to die by thought. Even if a great master says, "I want to die now," in the depths of his being he does not really want to die. There always remains a little thought of refusal in the brain.

Traditional religions always speak of a paradise or another life after death. It is a way of preparing people. They think of death with the hope of a future life, in the Beyond; or, if they do not believe in that, they live in fear of the grave. But if, here and now, I must die, and if my body accepts death, my consciousness remains peaceful. If, before dying, one thinks of one's body, death is difficult, for the body does not decide to die either. The body is matter, it is not the true self. Neither is consciousness the true self; it is always changing.

Nothing is important. If we understand that, there is no use even trying to abandon the ego. What is the ego which understands that? It exists, it is Buddha, it is God, it is the highest truth.

At the last moment, the attitude of the body and the mind is very important. What should it be? Accepting death, unconsciously. Anyone who achieves that finds the serenity which precedes death.

How can others be helped to live that moment of death? What does helping them mean? What is helping? Helping to do what? Helping whom? Is it making love? Giving money? Zen says, "We must beg from beggars and give money to the rich." The highest help is to bring people inner freedom and individual peace.

We can help at each moment, but we must first achieve that inner freedom in ourselves. There are no precise instructions that tell us how to do it: Each of us must find his own way.

THE JOURNEY

Modern civilization tries to solve the problem of death and birth by thinking in terms of having (progress, happiness) rather than living in terms of being (harmony, wisdom). People no longer know how to nourish or heal themselves. They lack energy. They no longer know themselves. They are not in the world. In societies that have not yet broken the harmony with nature—or in states of consciousness corresponding to that mode of existence—birth and death, along with sexual experience, are regarded quite practically as movements over the bridge that connects being with nonbeing, through the door that leads from the visible world to the invisible world, or across the border between ordinary reality and "the other reality."

When we say that death and birth can be regarded quite practically, it means that, within the community, the question of origin finds an answer not at the level of thought (the way pursued unsuccessfully in the West), but at the level of the act, of the sacred, of initiatory experience. But it would be too simple to believe that the question of origin no longer arises in our world of concrete and steel. Like the child and the Amazonian Indian—but through endless misconceptions and anguish (the weight of history)—civilized man, in the shadow of his machines, continues to ask himself, "Who are we? Where do we come from? Where are we going?"

The practice of psychoanalysis, psychedelic experience, and exploration of Oriental disciplines of meditation and concentration, to take three examples, enable him to break out of his shell of illusions. He again gives himself the possibility of contemplating his original face. It is not by chance that Indians of the New World (for example, the Huicholes with peyote and the Indians of Amazonia with yage) program their psychedelic experiences in terms of a return to the Womb. Similarly, when a Tantrist couple unite, something burns and reduces to ashes all conscious notions of attachment to life and death.

The Oriental practice of meditation, whether it be in the framework of yoga, Taoism, or Zen, always refers explicitly (to give an idea of the content of the experience) to such images as entering one's coffin, becoming a log or a pebble, and returning to the womb of the universe. Having reached this point, language fails; but the experience is there, possible here and now for everyone. Silence is the booming of ten thousand thunderbolts, the brightest light is a dark night. Each of us must find his own way. In absolute solitude he will discover that it is transmitted to him by someone else. For the journey is an encounter.

For readers of

LIFEARTS

—books from St. Martin's Press
to improve your
sense of well-being…

Inspiring techniques of freeing the body through
controlled movement and dance—
and a sensitive psychological approach
to emotional difficulty in children

Body Alive!

Towards an Education in Movement

By Yvonne Berge

"Deprived of movement, the body is in danger," is the credo of
Yvonne Berge, author of BODY ALIVE! Both a teacher of dance
and an authority on physical education, Mme. Berge has developed a system of movement and dance techniques by which
children can be brought in touch with their bodies, and provided
with a way to find or restore their mental and physical balance by
learning how to move and dance while maintaining coordination and control of themselves. Mme. Berge feels that children
raised in cities, restricted to narrow confines of apartments or rigid
classrooms, are prevented from reacting naturally to a variety of
mental and emotional stimulation—therefore becoming inhi-
bited when it comes to physical activities. The result is often
tension, nervousness and "anti-social" attitudes, which could
possibly lead to emotional disorders.

BODY ALIVE!, which is illustrated by dozens of striking photo-
graphs, is ultimately not just a plea for early dance and movement instruction for children, but an appeal to everybody and a
call for greater awareness of the body in terms of rhythm and
movement as well as in terms of everyday life—coordination,
action and true relaxation.

Yvonne Berge, a student of the International School of Dance in
Salzburg, formerly directed the Isadora Duncan Memorial School
in Paris, then her own school. She also studied psychology and
educational theory.

The paperback edition of this popular gourmet guide

The Book Of Coffee And Tea

A Guide to the Appreciation of Fine Coffees, Teas and Herbal Beverages

By Joel, David and Karl Schapira
Illustrations by Meri Shardin

"This delightful guide to coffee, tea and herbs for infusion is a wonderful addition to the growing list of books concerning food lore."—Publishers Weekly

The Schapira family has been roasting beans daily for the epicureans of New York City since 1903, at the Schapira Coffee Company on West 10th Street in Greenwich Village. By writing this book, three members of the family decided to share their knowledge about what makes a delicious cup of coffee, a perfect cup of tea, an exhilarating herbal brew. With authority and wit, the authors cover the history and mythology of coffee and tea, their cultivation and manufacture, the varieties and methods of preparation, and the characteristics and virtues of herbal teas. They reveal the delights and pitfalls behind exotic names like Jamaica Blue Mountain, Maracaibo, Assam, Darjeeling, and Yerba Maté. Approaching their subject matter from many angles at once, the authors have produced a virtual bible: a definitive consumer's guide to selecting coffees and teas, a discriminating connoisseur's guide to tasting, a comprehensive gourmet's guide to preparation and serving.

The Schapira brothers live in New York City and upstate New York.

A readable and eatable guide to the best in grains, nuts and beans

The Book of Whole Grains

The Grain-by-Grain Guide to Cooking, Growing, and Grinding Whole Cereals, Nuts and Beans

By Marlene Anne Bumgarner
Illustrations by Maryanna Kingman

THE BOOK OF WHOLE GRAINS is a uniquely practical handbook about the earth's favorite staples. The author offers a comprehensive survey of whole grains, nuts, and legumes, a framework for building them into your household diet, practical advice about preparing your own cracked cereals and flours, and over 250 specific recipes for breads, cakes, cookies, casseroles, vegetarian and meat main dishes, appetizers, desserts, salads, soups, stews and porridges.

For maximum utility THE BOOK OF WHOLE GRAINS is broken down grain by grain, each chapter covering the history and mythology of the cereal, how to shop for it or grow and harvest it yourself, tips about milling and preparation, and an exhaustive recipe collection. Chapters include: wheat, oats, rye, buckwheat, triticale, barley, corn, rice, millet, nuts and seeds, dried peas and beans. Special sections at the end of the book give detailed suggestions about milling and grinding equipment for your kitchen, availability of foods, nutritional values, and further recommended reading.

Marlene Anne Bumgarner is a freelance writer and teacher who lives in the country near Morgan Hill, California, with her husband and two children. She grinds all her own grain and makes do with neither electricity nor running water.

The oldest—and newest—way to cook,
utilizing the simplicity of basic necessity to create
delicious, healthful recipes that form
the staple diet of most of the world's peoples

The Peoples' Cookbook

Staples, Delicacies and Curiosities from the Earth's Humble Kitchens

By Huguette Couffignal
Translated and Adapted By James Kardon
Additional recipes by Marlene Anne Bumgarner

At a time when economic concern is becoming the most essential ingredient in all our daily menus, there is a wealth of information to be learned from people who throughout the ages have used the meagerest of resources to produce basic and appetizing dishes for both survival and delight. THE POOR PEOPLES' COOKBOOK pays homage not to poverty, but to the talent, ingenuity and good spirits of poor people around the world who can adapt to what's available. From the nearly nothing at their disposal, these people create sturdy simple dishes and elemental feasts that respect food's natural taste better than the complex, over-wrought recipes of haute cuisine or the adulterated concoctions of mass producers.

An introductory essay dedicated to simplicity, freedom and the 'art of living,' takes the reader on a fascinating pilgrimage through third world cultures and traditions and explains the conditions of poverty in relation to both the world's distribution of resources and the often illogical demands of human desires. An extensive section on "Resources" offers insight into the multitude of plants and animals—from palms to reptiles to seaweed to insects—used as staple foodstuffs by the world's peoples. The "Recipes" section, arranged by categories such as Breads and Pancakes, Porridges, Grain Dishes, Soups, Vegetables, Meat and Fish, Desserts and Drinks, contains over 300 recipes ranging from Tamales to Chapatis to Borscht to Manioc to Chickpeas to Peruvian Fish Ceviche. This cookbook offers everything a 'new simplicity' cook's heart and stomach could desire.

Huguette Couffignal is the author of more than ten cookbooks, among them Cuisine of the American Pioneer and Rustic Cuisine.